Whatever the mind can see
the mind can achieve.

Believe in your dreams.

Blair & Jill

Cashing in on

GOD

WHAT THE CHURCHES DON'T WANT YOU TO KNOW ABOUT GOD, JESUS CHRIST AND THE HOLY BIBLE

The Truth from God

Glenn Harrison

Glenn Harrison was born in the world famous steel and high quality cutlery producing city of Sheffield, England, UK, in 1954. He was brought up in some of the roughest parts of Sheffield and quickly learnt the meaning of 'survival of the fittest'. His family upbringing was a hard lesson, with little or no family loving interaction. He quickly became a 'hard' unloving man, who was afraid of giving love in case he was 'taken advantage of'. Although baptised as a Church of England Christian, his family never followed the faith and Glenn quickly became an atheist.

He went through an extraordinary amount of pain in his life; both physical and emotional; to the extent that it would have buried most people. A series of significant emotional events in 1993 transformed Glenn into a more caring, emotionally intelligent person. In 1996 he established a training company, which developed into teaching people emotional intelligence and better communication skills.

In 2005 he was contacted by angels; which for an atheist, freaked him out. Laughing it off at first, Glenn had to sit up and take notice, as over months, the angels persisted in contacting him.

Glenn was given a mission: "Ease their pain."

This book is the first of many; dedicated to...

- All the people who want to know the truth behind religion.
- All the people who want to connect to God; light; the creative energy.
- All the lost children's souls who didn't get the love and affection a child so dearly wants and needs.
- All the people who were abused as children.
- All those parents today that simply don't understand that they have children who are craving their love and attention; but fail to see it, leaving their children with the belief that they don't deserve love, and opening them to the emotional trauma of not feeling loved.
- All the people who are in emotional pain and feel they have no-one to turn to or believe in.
- All the people who have no religion; yet are still searching for a new belief.
- All the people that have forgone, or doubt their spiritual beliefs or their religion.
- All the people who feel there is no hope and have no spiritual beliefs, one way or the other, regarding spiritual matters.

Acknowledgements

These people either knowingly or unknowingly have helped contribute to the writing of this book:

My father and mother: Bill and Rita Harrison. My brother Mark Harrison. My children: Jodi, Bianca, Brett, Max and Cooper Harrison. Janine. Jean and Derek Cartwright. John and Tracey Emsley. Chris Woodruffe. Dave Thomson. Anne Reeves. Robert Marshall. Florence and Marilyn, Jimmy, John and Rosemary Dent, Della Watts, Lyndsey Cooper, Glyn Booth, Karen Jones, Fred Davies, Keith Davies, Malcolm Roper, Terry Layton, Ian Hall, Roger Stone, Dougie Upton, Brett Steele, Mark Feltham, Ross Feltham, Roy Payne, Pep, Caroline Roper, Doctor Sharrard, Doctor George Kinghorn, Martin Bennett, Linda Gill, Andy Cooke, John Fenton, Brian Tracy, Napoleon Hill, W. Clement Stone, Don Hutson, Metatron, Azrael, Chamuel, John Mettam, John Armitage, Steve Smith, Patrick O'Brien, Susan Blanchflower, Steven Maskrey, Jack Glossop, Ken Bagshaw, Anne Lord.

Above all, my unconditional love and great appreciation to my wife Jill Harrison, who was the inspiration for starting and finishing this book.

Elwood: *"It's 86 miles to Chicago. We've got a full tank of gas; half a pack of cigarettes; it's dark; and we're wearing sunglasses."*

Jake: *"Hit it!"*

Elwood: *"The Lord works in mysterious ways."*

Blues Brothers
1984

Book Glenn Harrison for your next conference / event speaker.

Glenn is available to speak for associations, ministries, churches and societies.
Glenn is an international motivational speaker, who will travel anywhere in the world.
He speaks on spiritual subjects such as:
How to connect to God.
To change your life; you have to change yourself.
From atheist to believer.
The leader within.
Just who do you think you are anyway?
Moving from 'being' to 'doing'.
Living from the heart, not the head.
Bridging the gap from here to there.

Contact: **glenn@anewbelief.com**

Published by: Harrison Publishers

ISBN-13: 978-1-905923-00-7
ISBN-10: 1-905923-00-7

CONTENTS

i

CONTENTS

Preface

9th October 2005

Jill: Metatron wants to speak to you.

Glenn: That's OK. Let him come through.

Jill: It's not a case of 'let him'. This angel has such a powerful presence. I've no choice. I've put him off enough times recently and he's not happy with me for that.

Jill went quiet. I could see her drifting off into the stars. It took ages for her to channel. Much longer than before. I rushed to get the Dictaphone to attempt to record her.

This is what we got:

Metatron: At last we have the ability to speak. You have many questions and we will do our best to answer them, but only if it is in the realm of God's will. I feel it is important at this time, that we look towards what fears you so.

You have pre-ordained the path that you must take. So why do you fear it so now? Why mistrust us, when the feeling within you is so strong?

Glenn: Who am I talking to?

Metatron: My name is Metatron. I have guided you since birth. I have watched over you. I have presided over you. You have chosen a hard task in this lifetime. You have chosen many, many hardships; and through those hardships you have become strong, which is what 'we' agreed.

It is important now that you follow your destiny.

Glenn: 'What' is my destiny?

Metatron: To be a teacher of the world. As you well know, but yet you deny. Do not look to the past, but look to the future. Look to what you can become. Look to where you have achieved. Your standing in this life. It has been through your own pre-determined world that you have become a reckoning; and yet, you do not believe so.

Glenn: What is it you want me to teach?

Metatron: The truth! The truth of pain, and of the ability to change one's pain into triumph. For when one believes in one's self, one has the power to predestine their future. For so long now we have advised and tried to cajole human kind, into the forwardness of the future.

Glenn: Cajoled?

Metatron: Cajoled... We have tried to guide; to advise. Unfortunately, not in a detrimental way that free will is 'bad' for human kind, but we would say it has outlasted what we thought would be envisaged. It has outgrown and manifested itself into something far greater than we envisaged; and we need, for the sake of the universes that exist, for it to continue; but not develop at too fast a pace.

Glenn: Is it true that you; in a life you were Enoch?

Metatron: I was many names; including Yehwah.

Glenn: Yehwah?

Metatron: Yehwah!

Glenn: And we understand Yehwah in Hebrew to be God?

Metatron: God comes in many forms: The Creator, Allah, Buddha. They are all one.

Glenn: I understand that, but why would you be given the name Yehwah?

Metatron: It was ordained with the one thought, the one creation you cannot comprehend.

Glenn: I understand (laughing). There's an oxymoron: "I understand, I cannot comprehend." I understand, I cannot comprehend. So what is your relationship to The Creator; to God?

Metatron: I am the true connection. Without me there is no connection.

Glenn: Meaning?

Metatron: I am the vein; the capillary that connects you to The Creator.

Glenn: But that would be said of Michael, Azrael, Gabriel... (Metatron interrupts)

Metatron: No! They are intermediaries, and will remain as so, as they were created as such. The word of God has been misconstrued throughout time. For political and power usage. More so than you can imagine.

Glenn: Probably not!

Metatron: It has become a depth which has created your downfall. So much implication has been 'put on' this word; instead of feeling the God and The Creator, that we designed within. You are 'of God; internally. Your entire being is of God; and together collectively creates the one God thought; The Creator, the universe; the entire intelligence connection.

Introduction

What you're about to read would have got my wife and I burnt at the stake 200 years ago. My wife Jill would have been branded a witch; and I'd have been branded a heretic. Talking to God, angels and spirits was tantamount to signing your own death warrant.

I'm Glenn Harrison. I was born and raised in Sheffield in the County of Yorkshire in England, UK. My family were far removed from the spiritual and religious faiths, so I grew up to become a confirmed atheist. In fact, my logical, cynical mind grew to detest religion and detest hearing the words Jesus and God, used out of other people's closed doors.

I grew to detest singing hymns at school; and cringed as I got married at the age of 22 in a 'Church of England' Christian church, listening to the Vicar's speech. I was only doing it to appease my wife to be.

I had no belief in God, angels or spirits. As far as I was concerned, you were born; shit happened; and then you died. Circle of life. Candle's out. Worm fodder.

Ironically, the records will show that I'm a Christian, baptised in The Church of England. Back in the 1950's; and I guess even today to a certain extent; it was traditional to baptise a child if you were British; even if you weren't a practising Christian. It was programmed into the masses: Have a child and throw a party so that everyone in the family can see the child. Might as well make it happen in a church; it's free. Don't really have to be religious. But it's the done thing; isn't it? Plus we can all get dressed up in our 'Sunday best' and it's a good excuse for the blokes to get to the pub. You get your photo taken too. Yet no-one seemed to care whether or not the child would want to be baptised. Too late when they grow up and can make decisions for themselves; they're already baptised.

I'd scoff at spiritualists, church sermons, prayer, 'Born again Christians', grace at meal times; and anyone who was thankful to 'The Lord'.

I was bitter in my youth and walked around with a big chip on my shoulder, feeling that life owed me something.

In 1995 the God Channel appeared on satellite T.V. Talk about laugh when I saw it. I'd watch it from time-to-time because there were some good motivational speakers on the

www.anewbelief.com

channel. I was launching my speaking career; and although I wasn't happy with the content of their speeches, watching some of the speakers gave me some speaking tips. I'd no idea how this programme would come back to haunt me later, with a different agenda. Not for what the speakers were preaching; but for how passionate they could be about a subject which was misleading so many people.

You see; I was the typecast non-believer. I didn't believe in God, Jesus, the Bible or spiritualism in any way. We western male non-believers seem to have a collective word for it all: "Bollocks!" The number of times I've heard that response from men when you talk (in particular) about spiritualism. And that was me; for years.

That is; until I was with Jill in 1997 at the age of 43. We met in 1994. I was just about to hit 40 and Jill was 29. She waited three years before she dropped the bombshell on me that she was psychic. She told me she didn't want me to know at first in case it frightened me away from her.

Something freaky happened in 1997. We were driving on a motorway, from the South, back North to our home, when she drew breath sharply and sat up in the car, bracing herself with her hands on the sides of her seat; pushing her head back against the head restraint; as though we were about to hit something with the car, and have a serious accident.

I swerved at high speed with the shock, thinking that I'd not seen something ahead of us that we were about to crash into, or run over. We were doing about 85 mph at the time. But there was nothing there. I had a major adrenalin rush. "Why did you 'do' that?" I shouted, "What did you see?" "Nothing!" she said, with a dismissive, yet fearful voice. I asked her a number of times, but she repeatedly told me it was nothing.

One of my strengths and often a weakness, is that I don't let go. I persisted with her until she finally, sheepishly, blurted it out that she'd seen a spirit. A monk, stood in the middle of the motorway; and we ran straight through him. She admitted to me for the first time that she was psychic. She sees dead people! And that's when it all started. My life took on a paradigm shift of massive proportion over the next few years; and at that time, I'd no idea of my destiny. And if someone had told me; I'd have just laughed at them.

A smirk appeared on my face, but I was curious. Jill told me of her gift from birth; which she'd suppressed for many years, because of the ridicule and trouble that it brought. But then went on to tell me that at times she had no control over it. She described the monk, with no visible face. Then it happened on two more occasions over the next few miles.

The following morning, we looked at a road map. And guess what? The section of the motorway we were on at the time Jill saw the monks, had an ancient Monastery ruin at the side of the motorway. Now I wouldn't say that this freaked me out; but it was an eerie coincidence.

At the time, we were living in a house that had been built, only about 6 years earlier, on land purchased from a church. It was the far end of the church graveyard. The church was 15th century, standing 100 yards from our house. The nearest graves were only about 30 yards away.

As time went by, many spirits would appear in our home. Jill would describe them in the finest detail. The vast majority were friendly; but some were evil. Having a great thirst for knowledge, and having known Jill for 3 years, it was difficult to ignore this intelligent, rational, focussed woman, when she told me about the after-life. I guess at first I just played along with it, so as not to offend her; but she never rammed it down my throat, and as time went by, there was less and less that I could find fault with.

There was one particular spirit that we called 'Smokey Joe'. You knew he'd been around because of the smell of cigarette smoke; which 'I' could smell too. Jill explained that she was a little like a telephone. She couldn't ring out (YET), but they could ring in. And the more people she allowed to ring in, the more that spirits would queue up to talk to her; until finally she'd have to blank them out and tell them to go away. As time went by, she started to earn some extra income by doing psychic readings. Little did I know where this was going to lead. My world, that I thought I knew, was about to be shattered.

As time went by, she grew stronger with her gift. To the extent that I sensed there was more to what she'd admit to.

1: Cashing in on God

It was the beginning of November 2005 and I was flicking through the satellite T.V. channels. Because of the recent spiritual events in my life which 'rock the Casbah' about religion, had been escalating; I was flicking to the religious channel; and there to my surprise were now 11 channels, where only one was in place 10 years ago...
GOD Channel (USA)
GOD 2 (USA)
Wonderful (USA)
TBN Europe
DAYSTAR (USA)
revelation (UK)
UCB T.V.
INI (Inspirational network international) (UK)
LOVEWORLD T.V. (USA)
EWTN (USA)
Gospel Channel (UK)

I started to watch some of the channels and here are some of the things that I observed and heard:

There were many virtually 'all black' audiences; and many virtually 'all white' audiences. Then on closer inspection, there were some further significant differences in the audience. Being a behavioural analyst, I'm able to notice quite easily the behaviours of different people, from their expressions, movements, adornments, emotions and what they wear.

The mainly black audiences were what intrigued me first. Why were so many black African people being drawn to these religious meetings, listening to motivational speakers interpret the Bible to them?

I'd recently had a visit from a black spirit; through Jill, who'd asked me to write about the oppression of black people; in particular the children. Since the slave-trade days when black people were kidnapped from Africa and sold as slaves, black African people have suffered immense oppression, particularly in the USA. Whilst we'd like to think that it's behind us now; it's not.

In 2003 I was holidaying in Orlando; Florida. I approached a Policeman who was having a discussion with a Policewoman in a car park. I wanted some information about demographics of people in central Florida. I was thinking of emigrating to Florida at the time. This Police Officer had been in the force for 32 years. We got on well together and he started to tell me about his life in Florida. As he got comfortable with me, he 'opened up' and told me of the 'White Flight' in Florida. I'd laid a map of the Orlando and surrounding areas, on the hood (bonnet) of his car and he showed me where racial people had moved 'out' to get away from black and Hispanic people. Some of the areas, he told me, were really wealthy 'white' areas and others were suburban 'redneck' areas. I didn't understand.

He explained that some of his 'force' lived in these areas and if he was to tell me that some of their names were Billy-Bob, Bubba, Chuck and Cletus; would I get his drift? He then went on to tell me that KKK (Ku Klux Klan) was still active in these areas. He 'then' went on to tell me that his Grandfather used to be a very active member in the KKK.

I told him my understanding of KKK territory was that it had been around the Mississippi Delta; but he put me straight and explained it was anywhere deep South; and was still active.

I came away surprised. Reflecting on that, and seeing these black African people listening to the speakers on the religious channels, made me start to realise that that the oppression was still giving them a deep insecurity. They were looking for hope and salvation. Yet there was a difference between these audiences and the mainly white audiences.

The mainly white audiences had a different kind of oppression. As I waited for the cameras to pan the audience and give some close-ups; I started to see the difference. There were far more people in the audience who were passive, reserved and introverted. There were very few outgoing, extroverted people.

So what's the significance, you may be thinking? Well outgoing people tend to have a higher self-worth, or self-esteem than passive, reserved people. Outgoing people can also have high ego. They don't necessarily need other people to help them find salvation or self-esteem. They find it from within. They have inner confidence and assertiveness. The people in the audience lacked that confidence. They were searching. Searching for strength from others. They needed leadership. Outgoing people don't have such a great need for leadership. They have the self-esteem to go and do things on their own.

Here were two different types of audience, with very similar needs. They were both looking for salvation; and they hoped they'd find it in the leadership of God; Jesus; the Lord; and through the motivational (and some not) speakers.

Then it dawned on me. God is big business. These media people have latched on to a highly religious nation who will pay 'big time' for salvation. According to various 'gathered' statistics, around 67% of the American population are actively religious. That's 234 million religious people in the USA in 2005.

According to www.adherents.com there are around 225 million Christians in the USA, of which over 160 million are adults. That's 160 million potential Christians to prey on in the USA alone.

Around the world there are around 2 billion Christians. What a market place! Recent statistics show that there are around 300 Bibles a day being sold. God is big business. Can 2 Billion people all be wrong?

Ministries are preying (not praying) on the oppressed and passive, reserved, religious people; through their interpretation of the Bible; to feed hope for salvation.

In December 2005 I tuned in to a religious channel. They were selling atonements.

So what's atonement? I had to do some research on this. Most descriptions seemed to follow a similar definition, in that atonement is a way of making amends to repair a wrong-doing, or to seek forgiveness for a wrong-doing. To remove sin. Jesus Christ supposedly died as a final atonement for the sins of the whole world. Some say that man is a sinner, so cannot atone himself; and that atonement can only come from God; which of course is useful for the media, in that they can now sell you an atonement; presumably from God, since 'man' can't atone.

The channel was selling 7 atonements at £50.00 apiece. That's around $85.00 US. If you bought all 7 you got an additional bonus. The programme was about how everyone sins and was preying on the passive, reserved, compliant people. O.K., we're back into behaviour again here: Compliant people (14% of the US and UK nation.) are afraid to break rules. Let's take the 160 million adult Christians in the USA. That's 22,400,000 Christian adults who are compelled to follow rules. And if they don't, they feel a need to repent. So now we've got at least 22.4 million people to sell atonements to. God is big business.

300 Bibles a day at an average of only $15 a Bible is $1.6 million a year. God and Jesus is big business. Have you seen

the quality of the suits that most of the speakers wear on the religious channels? God is big business. More and more people are cashing in on God and Jesus.

Go to www.godnetwork.com and look at the size of their shop. This is the website for God T.V. Look at the section for partnering, where they're asking for donations. God is big business.

It was 5.45 pm; 28th December 2005 and I was flicking through the religious channels, when I came across a programme on Daystar Channel. It was about the 'Subject Bible'. It was yet another new Bible being sold. As if there weren't enough already. There's a constant moving panel on the bottom of the screen, advertising the price, Sorry! Forgive me! Not a price! They're asking for a 'gift' of $150.00 plus $5.95 shipping. That kinda inflates my $15 a Bible forecast a little, doesn't it? Oh; and would you look at that: you can buy it in two easy payments of $75.00. They're really selling it hard. Two people sat on a sofa, bring in a well-known, long-time Bible salesman; who started door-to-door as a teenager. He's giving testimony that this is the best Bible he's ever seen; and he should know; he's been selling Bibles all his life, and claims he's probably sold more Bibles than anybody else. I'll stab a guess that he's around 60 years old. The selling pitch is that you don't have to run any references; saving hours of research time. There's a bonus video of how to use it and a CD of the book. The CD probably costs them all of $1.00. Wow!

What I find so irritating is the way these people soften the $150.00 blow, by calling it a gift; as though the money was going to a needy cause. Got to hand it to them though. Great selling; and a great way of cashing in on God.

Can 2 billion people have been so misled? Think about it! No-one we're aware of has any proof of whom or what God is. We've got stories in a Bible; and we've got religious sects and organisations that have used the fear of the unknown to control the masses and develop powerful organisations.

There are so many people now cashing in on God and Jesus, knowing that there are billions of people out there looking for hope and salvation... and it's wrong. Salvation comes from within. We're being misled and God's had enough. God gave us free will; and we've abused it; and without some changes, the world will be hell for our children.

Now I sense some of you thinking, "Well hang on a minute. Aren't you just doing the same thing, only under a different guise? Aren't you just cashing in on God too?"

Well Lordy, Lordy! Hallelujah! Send round the collection box. Yes I am! And I make no claim that I'm not. But there is a significant difference. You see, 'I've' been asked to tell you the truth. Yes I want to continue with a good life-style. I'm not one for selling a Ferrari to become a monk. I don't want the life of solitude, quiet, simplicity, poverty and male-only company. Life's about choice. We have free will. We all have different opinions of what happiness is. What I 'will' do though, is I'll use some of the income to 'pay it forward'; to teach the world the truth about God; light; the creative energy. To bring God's update on the Bible to the masses. To teach people how to connect with God; light; the one creative energy. To teach people the meaning of life. Why we were put on this planet. How to make the most of it. What happens when we die? How the universal life force grid operates; and our place in it.

Do you know what a prophet is? A person who speaks by divine inspiration. One who through a divinity, expresses his or her will. A prophecy is a message of divine truth, revealing God's will. Divine; means Godlike; another name for God. Religious groups would have you believe that prophets only existed in the past.

Well I beg to differ, 'cos I'm married to a prophet. Prophets are channelled by angels with the word of God; yet according to the angels, there is only one angel which can speak directly for, and through God; and that is Archangel Metatron. The other angels are in a hierarchy below. They speak 'for' God, but don't have a 'direct phone line' from God, through them, to mankind. Only Metatron has this ability. Anyone in the Bible who thought they were talking to God; was talking to Archangel Metatron; the Angel of Presence; the Supreme Angel of Death; The One.

He's the only Archangel that, on behalf of The Creator, can use the name of God, The Father, Godhead, The Heavenly Father, Jesus, Christ, Allah, YHWH, YHVH, Yahveh, Buddha, Jehovah, Yehwah, Yahweh, Elijah, Yahushuah, Yehoshua, Yeshua, Lord, Elohim, Adonay, Adonai, Brahman, Vishnu, Shiva, Shalom, Shekinah, Divine, Zeus, Jupiter, Ra, Odin, Wakan Tanka... and thousands of other names that people give to The One Creator.

Jill, my wife and partner in our training business, channels angels: Archangel Metatron, The Council of Elders and many other entities which comprise the structure that God has created to evolve the universal life force energy.

Jill was to find out later, from The Council of Elders a confirmation she's been made aware of by the spirit world, for a long time. That in a past life, she was a 'Daughter of Isis'.

Many of us have past lives. Some of us have hundreds of past lives. Have you ever had a 'déjà vu' experience? You feel that you know that you've been there before? You feel that you can even tell what's around the corner; and you end up being right? You just may have experienced a past-life regression.

Daughters of Isis were spiritual guides and prophets for Isis.

Jill is incredibly gifted. We're told that she is one of the very few people that has witnessed the first human life on our planet; and will reincarnate to be one of the last people to leave.

"You don't have to see the wind to know it exists."
Glenn Harrison

2: Archangel Azrael; the Angel of Death

4th June 2005.

I was laid in bed reading. It was around 10.30 in the evening. Jill, my wife, was laid at the side of me. She'd not long stopped reading herself. She'd fallen asleep reading. I took the book gently from her hands. She resisted slightly and then realised it was me tucking her in. She smiled as I kissed her on the cheek and she snuggled down into the covers as she quietly said, "Night babes."

That day I'd arrived home after two weeks working in Dubai in the United Arab Emirates in the Middle East. I'd been teaching Emotional Intelligence and Leadership Skills to Muslim senior managers from companies such as Saudi Aramco. I only went out for a week; but I was asked to stay for another week. Prior to that, the longest Jill and I had ever been apart was for a week, on two other occasions. Jill and I are very close. We detest being away from each other.

The two weeks apart had been a strain on Jill. Apart from missing me, she had our house, office and our two young boys of 7 and 5 (Max and Cooper) to look after on her own; along with running our training business:-

www.motivationaltraining.com and Jill's own business: www.psychicwoman.com

Jill was worn out. We were so pleased to see each other. She'd admitted to not sleeping too well while I was away; and now she admitted to feeling secure and settled I was home. She had a big beam on her face as she started to drift to sleep. How do I know when she's drifting into a deep sleep? Because she snores terribly when she's drifting off. It usually stops after a few minutes, so I leave her be. It's that loud, you'd swear the walls were shaking.

This time though it was different. She started to take deep breaths and blow through her mouth. A little like a horse blows through its lips making a faint trumpeting noise. Her breaths got deeper and the blowing became stronger. She was laid on her back, with her head on a pillow, face facing up to the ceiling. I was concerned; to the extent of being frightened. I turned to her and asked her if she was OK. She opened her eyes and just gazed at the ceiling. Her eyes were bloodshot red; so bad she looked like she'd got a serious eye infection.

She started to breathe deeper and faster as I watched her face start to contort. At first I thought she was just pulling a disgruntled face, as though she was repulsed by something. Then I could see she was straining the muscles in her face and neck. She pulled her chin into her neck so that it appeared that she'd no chin. She flared her nostrils, breathing heavily out of them. Her nose seemed to elongate, get thinner, more pointed and hook over on the end, like a hawk's beak.

Her cheek bones seemed to raise and become more prolifically edged. It was disturbing.

When I asked her again if she was OK, she spoke to me, but not with her normal voice. I'd heard this voice before, and I knew it wasn't Jill. What I mean by that, is that Jill, when she's tired and relaxed, is susceptible to being taken over by spirit, and she goes into trance.

Being a logical male and previous non-believer in the spirit world; it took me a long time to accept Jill's gifts. When you've experienced what I've experienced over the last 9 years; you can't deny the spirit world. When she's in trance, she speaks with clarity. Gone is the Northern English accent. Gone are the verbal fillers like, 'you know', 'yeah but', 'errr', 'to be honest'. She speaks with a clear, precise, accurate, steady, fairly monotone English accent.

Here's my recollection of how the conversation went. I can't remember it all; we talked for over half an hour, so I'll give you what I remember:

Jill: Although we've asked of you many times now, to write; still you don't write.

Glenn: Jill, what are you talking about?

Jill: We keep asking you to write, yet still you concern yourself with lesser things.

Glenn: Jill, wake up; you're babbling and I want to get back to my book.

Jill: You said you would write. It is important that you ease their pain.

Glenn: Who's pain? What are you on about?

Jill: You must write to ease their pain.

Glenn: We've had this conversation before. No-one is going to want to read about a nobody, and I just don't know what to write about.

Jill: Just write!

Glenn: About what?

Jill: Your deepest fears.

 www.anewbelief.com

Glenn: Who 'are' you?

Jill: I am 'Athrielle'. (I spelt it the only way I could remember it.)

Glenn: Who?

Jill: Athrielle! I am the Angel of Death. I take away pain as well as pass people over to the other side. I'm not the angel of Satan. Do not fear me. It is not your time yet and it is not the time for your wife. You have much to do in your time here yet. You are very special people and you also have a very special son in Max; he's an Indigo Child.

Glenn: What's an Indigo Child?

Jill: He will be a great healer, just like you, and he will play a major role in healing the world.

Glenn: What's my part in this?

Jill: You are a great healer and you will also play an even greater role in healing the world, which is why you must write.

Glenn: But write about what?

Jill: Your deepest fears.

Glenn: Yes, but what do you mean by that?

Jill: Write about your pain.

Glenn; When you say pain, what exactly do you want me to write about. I don't know where to begin?

Jill: It's not just about your parents; it's all your other pain.

Glenn: Why would anyone want to read about my pain? I'm no-one special.

Jill: Yes you are. You're a great healer. There are millions of others like you, without hope, in pain, that don't know which way to turn.

Glenn: But how will me writing about my pain help them?

Jill: You have an immense depth of emotion. You can heal with your words. You must reach out to these people and ease their pain. I know you don't believe in God, even though God exists. It's not important, because you have your own faith and you must give others that faith too to ease their pain. You must believe and not try; then you will see the angels. They are constantly with you. And yes Glenn, I know you are laughing inside, thinking of Yoda, "Do or do not, there is no try!" Your humour is a good thing.

Glenn: You want me to write about my beliefs?

Jill: Yes; and your pain.

Glenn: When you say pain, what do you mean by that?

Jill: All the adversity in your life and how you've overcome it without a God to pray to. What you've discovered. How you've coped. So that other people can have the same hope and new religion. There are millions of people in the world without religion; looking for the truth; looking and hoping for someone or something to heal their pain.

Jill is a very special soul, but she's very lonely. She buys the material things for acceptance from others because she's so lonely. She'd live in a tent with you if you all could be happy. She's not much time in this life. She's destined for much greater things in our world. Raphael and Gabriel are always by her side; and with you too. Jill is very special.

(It was at this point that I realised that Jill's voice was changing. She was speaking with a Germanic accent. It was getting stronger as time went by. Not a Germanic accent I'd witnessed before. It seemed 'old world'.)

Glenn. What do you mean?

Jill: Her destiny was to find you and support you. She's your soul mate. Once she's supported you, she's destined for greater things and will pass on.

Glenn. What did you mean when you said she's not long of this world? How long will she be with me?

Jill: 10 years.

Glenn: 10 years? (And I start to cry because I know the reality of this.) Please don't take her away from me so soon. I love her. She's so very special to me too. It's not fair to cut her life so short and take her away from her family.

Jill: She's very special and destined for greater things in our world. It was never meant to be for her to be in your world for a great deal of time. She knows this and she is unafraid. She will be waiting for you on the other side, with open arms. It's not Jill's destiny to heal like you and Max. Her destiny is on the other side. She chose you, to introduce you to spirituality, so you can heal.

You have immense power to heal the world. You will live a very long time. Your destiny is to heal millions of people. We're extremely frustrated; you haven't written a word yet. Jill's destiny in this world was to get you to start writing.

Glenn: OK; what if I do write? What will you do for me? Will you allow Jill to stay with us longer?

(Long Silence)

Jill: The longer you write, the longer she can stay with you. Write about your pain. Write about meeting Jill. You're a great healer. Max is a great healer and will become special: famous. He needs your attention and guidance to become a great healer. Speak about your pain and suffering for the people who are searching for an answer. Write about self-esteem, your spirituality and love. I am always with you by your side.

Glenn. What do I do when I've written? Who will read it?

Jill: Don't worry about that. People will read it.

Glenn: But how will they read it. We don't have the resources to spend the time on this to publish a book.

Jill: I understand your values for material gain. I won't let you fail.

Glenn: But I don't understand. If we don't market the book, who's going to read it?

Jill: When you write, I will send the people. Jill is fading fast now and I must leave her. Remember, I will always be by your side.

At that moment, Jill's face quickly changed shape back to normal. Her eyes closed. She put a big grin on her face and snuggled up to the side of me. She sighed heavily. She was fast asleep.

I leaned over to the left to the vanity unit on my side of the bed to grab a notebook and pen. I quickly wrote down as many things as I could remember and then drifted off to sleep.

In the morning I asked Jill what she could remember.

Jill: Nothing! What are you talking about? Do you know, my face really hurts this morning? It feels like I've got a bad case of sinusitis. My cheek bones really hurt under my eyes.

Glenn: I'm not surprised the way your face changed last night. I'd have had face-ache too.

Jill: What do you mean?

Glenn: Who's Athrielle?

Jill: Who?

Glenn: Athrielle! Have you heard of the name before?

Jill: Doesn't sound familiar.

Glenn: Is it one of the characters in the spiritual world that you've read about in the past?

Jill: Not that I can remember.

Glenn: What's an Indigo Child?

Jill: A what?

Glenn: An Indigo Child.

Jill: Never heard of it.

That was my way of testing Jill, to evaluate whether or not it was just Jill talking from her sub-conscious mind. Scientifically, someone could still argue that it was, but knowing what I know about Jill, I had enough to believe.

3: The Indigo Child

5th June 2005

I began to tell Jill about the previous night's experience. Jill's often talked about Armageddon (Call it what you will.) in circa 2012 - 2014.

Note the coincidence with the ten years that Athrielle gave Jill for time in this life. Jill has told me many times about what will happen in 2012 - 2014, and that's when she'll be 'called away'.

Here's a synopsis:

It's prophesied that sometime before this, in around 2010, there will be a unification of the 'yellow' Asians and Arabs in a third world war. It will turn into biological warfare, which will destroy a third of the world's population.

In 2014 a comet will strike the Earth and tilt the Earth on its axis, back to its original position. Another third of the world's population will be destroyed as a result of the comet impact. The comet heat will melt the ice caps, create tidal waves and set off a chain of earthquakes and volcanic eruptions.

Many countries will disappear under the sea as a result: Florida, part of California, Japan and many others. This catastrophic calamity will cease the on-going third world war as countries reunite to save the planet. Think this is far fetched fantasy? This is written in every religious Bible. Any good psychic will be able to tell you about this too.

Jill, with her usual humour then told me I'd better write slowly, so that she could live longer. She went off to do some research. So did I. We found Athrielle under many different spellings, all saying the same sounding word; but what struck me the most was the Muslim spelling: AZRAEL, pronounced Ath-ray-ell.

I knew then that was how he'd been pronouncing his name. Then it clicked into place. I'd only just returned from Dubai, teaching Emotional Intelligence. It seemed ironic that he would use that phonetic way of saying his name, and refer to my 'immense depth of emotion' after I'd returned from the Middle East, teaching people how to deal with emotion in leadership.

It was as though Azrael had to wait for me to get home to be able to use Jill as a channel to be able to communicate with me. We looked up 'Indigo Child' on the internet. We now have three books on the subject. Indigo children have been around for about 100 years. They are a breed of mankind who are pro-active in searching for the 'truth' about God; and are more spiritual than most. Max, our son, is one of the last. These people are paving the way for the next wave; the Crystal Children. Cooper, our younger son, is a Crystal Child. Very spiritual, but more passive with the spiritualism. These children are said to be the next evolutionary step in the human race.

The reason for the Indigo Children coming to the earth plane is to break down the old systematic ways that no longer suit the human race; including man-made false gods and man's limiting self beliefs. These Indigo Children are the bridge from this world (known to the spiritual community as the third dimension), into the new world, which will be a world of love, peace and strength. These children are the light of hope and our future.

The Indigo Children have different character traits from other children, and their behaviour tends to be non-conformist. Although these children find it hard to follow rules and regulations, they also possess high intelligence. It's currently believed that many children diagnosed with Attention Deficit Disorder (ADD) and Attention Deficit with Hyperactivity Disorder (ADHD), are in fact Indigo children.

Some of these character traits are said to be:-

1. Is extremely energetic.
2. Has a short attention span and gets bored easily.
3. Sensitive to their surroundings and people's emotions.
4. Prefers to learn through exploration, and tends to resist auditory learning. Rebels against the way standard education is taught.
5. If interested in a subject, becomes totally absorbed.
6. Thinks outside the box, tending to have abstract thoughts and ideas that challenge normal conformist ways.
7. Has a lot of compassion for others.
8. Tends to get easily frustrated because they feel misunderstood.
9. Tends not to fit in with their peer's unless those peers are Indigo Children.
10. Will show great reasoning ability when challenged.

If you'd like to discover more about Indigo Children I'd recommend 'The Indigo Children' by Lee Carroll & Jan Tober - published by Hay House, ISBN 1-56170-608-6.

Prior to the trance, Jill had told me many times that spirit had been pushing her to tell me to write. It was draining her and she had to shut them out.

Today is 29th July 2005 as I write this. So you can see, I didn't get my finger out to start writing. Spirit (According to Jill.) has been getting anxious with me not writing. Each time that Jill relaxes, they beckon her to tell me to write. It drains her, so she keeps blocking them out.

4: The religious conspiracy

Until this year, I'd be described as a strongly viewed atheist. Perhaps I still am, in the traditional sense of thoughts on religion.

When Archangel Azrael started contacting me, it was refreshing to have my faith paralleled with a traditional faith; but at the same time have validation on my thoughts on religion; which to me is a conspiracy for power and control of people.

Many people put their faith in outdated, traditional organisations; probably because they have no-one else to turn to. Thousands of years of programming through schooling, and often violence and abuse.

But hey; the world is changing rapidly. The media is so strong that the youth of today are being programmed in a different way. In the past we were programmed to fear the wrath of God. Now kids are programmed to fear not having a mobile phone. Religion isn't on mainstream T.V. unless you really look for it.

Children are also programmed by the media about the homo-sexualism in the clergy and the paedophiles. Comedy sketches in the media ridicule the church. And let's face it; the vast majority of churches are boring places to be for kids.

Kids lose their belief in Santa at a very early age, and many don't believe in God; with more non-believers on the way.

Young kids are programmed with excitement by the media. What are they going to prefer to do? Go to church and listen to a sermon, sing some hymns, have a short Bible lesson and learn to pray; or play a 64 bit virtual computer game; or watch a visually stunning DVD with the latest FX?

I'm one of these children too; in that I never got on with religion; but I 'do' have a faith. That faith is in 'me'! Self-reliance; self-esteem; self-awareness and the universal energy of the one conscious mind, the one thought; and the journey of the soul beyond the third dimension.

Most people are programmed to think of God as a 'being', in a particular plane, in man's image. That's what I could never get my head around. What I can get my head around though, is a creator. A creator that we are linked to, with the one thought; the one super-conscious mind; linked together through energy fields.

We still can't get our head around just what The Creator is; and I guess we're not ready for that in human form; just as we can't get our head around 'how it all started'.

That's my belief! People need to have a belief. At some point in everyone's life, there comes a point when we all sit in a daze, with a glazed look over our eyes, or stare up at the stars in the night sky, and ask the same typical questions: "What am I doing here? How did it all start? What's my purpose in life? What happens when I die?"

Having angels channel through Jill to talk to me has added to that belief, in that I can not now dismiss the after-life; and the purpose of that after-life is unfolding and will continue to unfold on our website: www.anewbelief.com

I guess you've got to be there sometimes. Jill and I are (In our opinion.) intelligent, focussed people. We're also materialistic achievers.

We're not tree-huggers, bohemians, new-age-travellers, hippies, or spaced out on drugs. We're also not particularly socially conscious. Apart from a beer and a G&T or three in the evening, we're sober the vast majority of the time; but we 'do' like to party now and again.

In Christian religions, the Bible generally looks down on people 'raising the dead', speaking to spirit and even people who supposedly speak to angels. But is that the way that people have interpreted it? The Bible 'does' advocate talking to spirit; to angels; and there are many references. But what you get from Christian leaders, is that if the angel isn't specifically mentioned in the Bible, then it must be a demon; a fallen angel; Satan. And that Satan comes in many guises to trick you into a false sense of security. And of course, 'we' must be talking to Satan, mustn't we? Interesting that Archangel Metatron is mentioned many times in the Jewish scriptures, yet isn't accepted by the Christian Bible.

So, come on, let's get real. If I can be contacted by, and speak to angels, and there's thousands of clergy, priests and 'Holy People' out there, that have never had a 'sign' in their life; do they even 'want' to believe 'me'?

Maybe it's just easier to preach that it's wrong to contact spirit, just in case people start asking why religious ministers mostly can't.

Don't get the wrong end of the stick here. I can just sense some of your thoughts, "Who's this guy think he is, another Jesus Christ?" Well OK, I did have a medium once say to me that she sensed I had great healing power, and that I could walk on water if I so chose to; but I didn't let that go to my head. And this is another example of where communication breaks down. Can't you just see it now? Someone is going to read this book; speak to someone in the media about it, and before you know it; I'm quoted in the press as saying I can walk on water like Jesus. Then I'll be quoted as saying I'm bigger than Jesus; but then again they'll have to re-phrase that, because John Lennon got the patent on that.

5: Ease his pain

I broke my leg on 19th July 2005. At 51 I decided I needed some incentive to keep in shape. I struggle to get motivated to get to a gym.

My crippled left foot prevents me from road running and swimming seems a chore; so I bought an Enduro bike (Like a motocross bike.) so I could ride to green lanes and motocross tracks and keep fit. I love to ride motorbikes, so this was a great way for me to keep fit.

It was working too. This was around my tenth ride out. I'd met up with some other lads; about seven of us took off to trail-ride and 'chase' each other around.

Riding a motocross bike on rough terrain at speed is like riding a bucking bronco, with the added excitement of acceleration to 60mph in 2.5 seconds and breaking hard to stop just as quickly. If you're out of condition; ten minutes hard riding on bumpy terrain will leave you flat on your back, on the floor, gasping for breath. The following morning, nearly every muscle in your body will give you pain.

I overshot a corner and crashed the bike. Crashing is pretty normal in this sport, without injury; but on this occasion I tumbled down a bumpy grassy bank with the bike on top of me. The bike broke my leg over one of the bumps. I was so winded, that when I tried to sit up, I nearly fainted. It took a few seconds before I could take a deep breath. As I lay there winded, my friend came and helped me up.

As I stood, I got excruciating pain in my right foot as I felt the ligaments and bones realigning themselves. I could feel them all knitting back together into position. I could move my foot in all directions, but at certain points as I stood, I got searing pain at the base of my leg. My friend tried to kick-start the bike for me without success.

The bike is a 400cc single cylinder four stroke competition machine. They are of the most difficult bikes to kick start because of their high compression. You have to be pretty strong and pretty fit to get one started; and there's a knack to each different brand, to get them started.

I knew I had to get home to get checked out and we were in the middle of no-where. I seemed to be able to walk in a fashion, so I got on the bike and got my friend to support the bike as I tried to kick-start it. Little did I know that I was trying to kick start the bike with a broken leg.

www.anewbelief.com

That night, in casualty, my worst suspicion was confirmed: A broken tibia of the right leg at the joint above the ankle. Six weeks minimum in plaster. It was the beginning of the summer six-week holidays for our two young boys. We'd got all sorts of day-trips planned, and I'd let my family down. I felt a right Pratt.

Jill was furious. She'd made several comments about me taking it steady and not hurting myself, so that we could go walking and make trips to theme parks on day-trips with the boys. I'd shattered the chance of our recreation time together.

I managed to get the bike back home; took the bike to the garage door, left it on the stand and hobbled round to the front of the house, to get in the front door. By this time, my body temperature was dropping. My body was transferring heat to the damaged area of my foot, and leaving the rest of me cold. I 'played it down' with Jill at first. Jill and the boys were in the kitchen serving dinner. I hobbled in to be greeted with, "What have you done?" Jill was livid. I sat down and started taking my motocross boot off. My foot looked OK. I took my sock off and started moving my foot around to check for damage. The boot is a tight fit, which must have been containing the swelling. Before our eyes, we watched my foot start swelling, until it got to twice its normal size. So off we went to the hospital where I got it plastered.

Jill tells me that spirit have a way of making things happen, if you don't collaborate with them with something they're insistent upon. What better way to get me to write about my pain, than to 'give' me some; immobilise me and get me thinking about writing.

My biggest problem was where do I begin? I couldn't get my head around why anyone would want to listen to, or read about the ranting of a 'nobody'. I'm not a celebrity. I'm not a famous or upcoming novelist. I'm not a missionary or Saint. Hell; I don't even believe in God, or have belief in a recognised religion. I'm just an average bloke who's had his fair share of ups and downs; or so I thought.

I've never seen myself as too much different to Joe Average, other than I'm a self-starter, with more determination than most people; don't readily take 'No' for an answer and keep persevering to find happiness.

That is of course; until Azrael contacted me. What really gave me the paradigm shift was when Jill told me she didn't know who Azrael is, or was; or what an Indigo Child is.

ARCHANGEL AZRAEL

According to Sarah at www.sarahsarchangels.com In Muslim and Islam theology, Azrael is the Angel of Death who is forever writing in a large book and forever erasing what he writes: What he writes is the birth of man and woman. What he erases is the name of the man or woman at death.

Other faiths name the Angel of Death as a different angel: In Judeo-Christian lore, Michael, Gabriel, Sammael, and Sariel are all named as the Angel of Death. In Zoroastrianism, the Angel of Death is Mairya. In Babylon it's Mot. In Rabbinical lore there are 14 Angels of Death: Yetzerhara, Adriel, Yehudiam, Abaddon, Sammael, Azrael, Metatron, Gabriel, Mashhit, Hemah, Malach ha-Mavet, Kafziel, Kesef, and Leviathan. In Falasha lore it is Suriel. The Arabic angel is Azrael.

Jewish lore says this angel is Rahab, who, lore goes on to say, was destroyed by God for refusing to part the waters of the red sea. The new Angel of Death then became Yama (Malach ha-Mavet).

The Talmud says the Angel of Death was equated with Satan, and thus became the legend that the Angel of Death was evil, rather than the good angel he is.

Azrael, also known as Izra'il, one of the four Archangels of Islam (Mikhail, Djibril, and Israfil), is pictured as having gigantic proportions: one foot rests in either the forth or the seventh heaven, while the other is on the bridge between hell and paradise.

Supposedly Azrael brought God a handful of earth from which to create Adam and therefore earned his title as the Angel of Death. Izra'il keeps a roll of humanity, on which the names of the damned are circled in black and the names of the blessed, in light.

When a person's day of death approaches, a leaf with the person's name on it falls from the tree beneath God's throne. After forty days have passed, Izra'il must sever the individual's soul from his or her body.

Azrael will be the last to die, but will do so at the second trump of the Archangel. He is the angel who accompanies your soul to Heaven.

The phrase 'the Wings of Azrael' refers to the approach of death; the signs of death coming on the dying.

Call on this angel at those times of grief to comfort those loved ones left behind.

If you want to know a lot more about Azrael go to www.songofazrael.org

According to www.angelicartistry.com the Archangel Azrael is forever writing on a large scroll and forever erasing what he's written. He writes the birth of a person and erases the name of a person when they die. It's the sacred duty of Azrael to summon the departed spirit into the arc, so the journey to the other side can begin.

It's Azrael's responsibility to separate the human body from the soul at the moment of death. He does this with compassion granting the newly released spirit complete freedom.

He transmits a feeling of great love and he makes new arrivals aware of the presence of a friend, who knows what's about to happen, and can explain to the new arrival. Anyone who's had an encounter with Azrael describes him as dark, very quiet and not at all menacing as portrayed by others.

He's not the foreboding apparition portrayed across centuries, probably because of what his name: 'The Angel of Death' invokes. Apparently Azrael is the most sensitive, gentle angel of God's creation.

According to Hebrew and Islamic translation, Azrael means 'Whom God helps'.

Apparently he was given the number of eyes and tongues to equal the population of the world.

He is commonly known as the Grim Reaper, The Angel of Death, The Dark Angel, Azril and Izrail. When you consider that Azrael is a writer, it seems ironic that he wishes to use the same medium to contact the world of people in pain, which is partly what has made me a believer.

I can't help thinking about the film, 'Field of Dreams', the baseball film, starring Kevin Costner and James Earl Jones. Kevin keeps hearing a spiritual voice talking to him saying, "If you build it, they will come!" It turns out that the message was for Kevin to build a baseball pitch on his new crop farm, at the risk of losing everything. He'd find out later that the baseball pitch, referred to as the Field of Dreams, would bring back all the American baseball heroes, who'd passed away, to play baseball together.

I've watched the film around 10 times since it was first made and I've cried rivers associating it with my parenthood.

"Ease his pain!"

The next message Kevin kept hearing was, "Ease his pain!" It's referring to his father, an average professional baseball player who pushed Kevin into baseball. But as a youngster, Kevin tired of the constant baseball practice. They fell out when Kevin was a teenager and they didn't speak for years; but then his father died before they ever made up; just about that time when Kevin realised that baseball was a major part of his life.

The pain ironically turned out to be Kevin's: never being able to make up with his father, to play some 'ball' before he died. Kevin's pain was 'missing the love of his father'.

Unknown to Kevin, his father would appear on the Field of Dreams as a young man at the height of his baseball career. Kevin and he played ball together for one last time. James Earl Jones's pain in the film was that he never got to play Major League Baseball; and he finally got to play with the greats on the field of dreams.

I'd highly recommend this film to anyone who can associate with wishing they could turn the clock back, to get that love from a parent.

Although this is a film, the resemblance to my quest is uncanny. I've been asked to 'Ease their pain'! And just like Kevin Costner in the film, I don't really know or fully understand what I'm doing. And just like the message that Kevin got: "If you build it, they will come," my message was, "I will send them!" Can you believe it? I'm even sat here (With a broken leg.) shedding tears as I write this? I'll see if I can persuade Jill to watch Field of Dreams with me tonight... again!!

Here's a thought: If you're estranged from your parents, don't wait until it's too late to make amends. It doesn't matter if you still think it's their fault. Let it go! Go and see them. If they were loving people before, chances are they still will be. Life's not a dress rehearsal. Time waits for no-one. Next week may be too late.

If they never had the love to give in the first place; then welcome to the club. Learn to give your love to others and you'll find it comes back to you.

6: Spirit are coming, thick and fast

4th August 2005.

It was around 8.30 in the evening. Jill was cuddling with me watching T.V. Once again, she was in a relaxed state as a young spirit girl approached her. Jill wanted to tell me about her. Her name was Luciana (Loo chee anna). She was seven years old with long, flowing, thick, black hair; down her back to her waist.

Jill: Oh Glenn; she's ever so thin, and her clothes are like rags. Slow down. Slow down. She keeps going into Spanish... Cordoba! What's Bodegas?

Glenn: It's Spanish for a winery in Spain or Spanish speaking countries.

Jill: She's around you all the time. She tugs at your clothing; and you think you've caught it on something. She pulls on your left foot at 3 o'clock in the morning. That's why you wake up sometimes. She's drawn to you because you had no love as a child; but you've found love and given love to your children. The kind of love that 'she' wanted.

Her father died in 1552 and soon after her mother died. She went to live with her aunt. There was a great famine. Her uncle couldn't afford to support her. Ohhh Glenn (She said with a quivering voice.), she's showing me her uncle leading her into a barn. He took a scythe and cut her throat. (Tears start to roll down Jill's cheeks.) She's all skin and bone, yet she's so beautiful. She wanted so much to be loved. She feels so close to you because you're giving the love that 'you' missed, to your children.

She's with you all the time. (Jill chuckles.) She touches your face because you have such soft skin.

(Jill shudders in despair.) Ohhhhh Glenn...behind her is a growing queue of young children. It's about 100yards/90m long. They're all waiting to talk to you. They're all so young. They're dressed so poorly; in rags; skinny with malnutrition. They all feel unloved. They're searching for the love they never had from their parents. They want you to write; for all the children that were never loved. "Ease their pain!" they keep saying. Glenn, I can't do this. I'm so tired. It's draining me so much. I've got to let them go. There are spirits queuing all around to get to talk to you. It's overwhelming. I've got to shut off.

www.anewbelief.com

Glenn: Let them go Jill. 'Bye Luciana, and thank you so much. If I could kiss and hug you, I would.

A little while later Jill startled me.

Jill: Good God!

Glenn: What's up?

Jill: There's a huge negro just appeared.

Glenn: Where is he?

Jill: Right there, in front of us.

Glenn: What's he want?

Jill: His name is George. "Not Chicken-George before you say it", he's just said. (Jill laughed.) He knows you've got a sense of humour. He was a black slave in 1516. He wants you to write about the oppression, from the black slave's point of view. "Ease their pain. Write about their hopelessness," he's saying.

At this point it was difficult to understand where George was 'coming from'. Was he just tapping into the fact that I was writing and wanted to get into the act for some free publicity about slavery? Or maybe, his angle was similar, in that he wanted me to ease the pain of all the people who were slaves, that never had the love and affection as children; due to the oppression and splitting of families, both from Africa, and in the countries they became slaves; such as the USA and the Caribbean islands.

I got up and hobbled on my crutches to the toilet for a pee. I've still got a badly broken foot and ankle from the bike crash. I'd just finished fastening my belt as Jill appeared at the door. It was dark, and she startled me.

Glenn: Bloody hell Jill! I nearly shit myself! Don't creep up on me like that. (She was smiling with a bemused smile.)

Jill: You need to see this!

Glenn: See 'what' now?

Jill: This huge Red Indian in ceremonial headgear. He looks so important. He's trussed up like a peacock, and he's huge.

Glenn: What's he want?

Jill: To talk to you!

Glenn: What about?

Jill: He says you're related. Hold on! 1823! 1823! Red River! He's a Sioux Indian Chief. They made a treaty with the Americans; but they were betrayed. You're his relative. He wants you to write about the lost love in children. You were a General in the Army. You made a truce with the Sioux Indians; but the Government betrayed 'you' and the Indians. He's giving me the date 1812.

Glenn: Jill you just said 1823 earlier. Make your mind up.

Jill: Yes! He's giving me two dates. 1812 and 1823. Slow down. Yan... Wan... he's giving me Indian words and it's too quick for me to understand them. 1812! 1823!

We didn't get much after that, so we went back into the lounge to finish watching a movie. We went to bed around 10.20pm.

As usual, we read for a while. Jill settled down to sleep. As she was drifting off she started to blow a little and I thought, "Here we go!" But rather than last time, her face didn't distort too much. She opened her mouth and spoke in a soft voice:

Jill: We meet again my friend. She is weak!

(I quickly reached for pen and paper from the side of the bed, so that I could remember most of what was about to be said. The palest ink remains longer than the faintest memory.)

Glenn: Hello Azrael. Please speak clearly.

Azrael: It pleases me so to speak to you, because you are a son of my own blood. Oh I do love you my son. How sad it is that as humans we don't know what we have within. In the Spirit World we have already sounded out our trumpets to rejoice your presence. You must write about the pain of this world. I want you to be strong. Give some respect to the people who help you. You ask for contact from spirit; but it is not in the way that you expect. You have the ability. You must 'feel' your way and then you will 'find' the way. The woman beside you weakens; but in turn, you will grow strong together.

Glenn: Please don't call her woman. She's my wife. Please call her Jill.

Azrael: Write about your pain. Your pain is what connects you to the rest of the world. Many children are feeling oppressed and not heard. What can be achieved through love of self and the love that you give out; will eventually be returned. You may feel like a piece of sand right now, but 'not' a 'piece' of sand; 'you' are a dune. You will write a children's book about the adventures of Max in a magical land. There's much more to this world than just the physical. As you; as a child. Better than Harry Potter. Better than The Wind in the Willows. To a land where anything is possible. Your heart was the first thing that was conceived, and the last thing that will survive. The heart will always be pure.

Glenn: Azrael; where are you from?

Azrael: Germany!

Glenn: But I understood your name to be Hebrew or Islamic?

Azrael: Yes, I spent much of my time there and then much in Germany. It is written in the Holy books.

Glenn: Where can I read this in the books?

Azrael: You cannot read them. They are not available for people to see.

Glenn: Why not?

Azrael: The Catholic faith hides many truths. They do not like to give away their power. Their imperfections harbour many secrets. The Indigo Child: Max, along with others, is here to pierce the illusion of what is. To sidestep ways of what mankind has set up. Many people accompany him. Mankind will want to drag him down. He's a leader. His knowledge is vast. He thinks so much quicker than the human mind. He thinks from the heart; not from logic.

Your father is sick. But he decided long ago to be a victim. He is not long for this world. He gave up on his ambitions and his dreams long ago.

You want to 'sing'? You can still sing. You can still fulfil your ambition. There you can bask in your true love.

(An explanation is needed here about the singing. From a young child of 6 years old, I was a good singer. At the age of 10, I was lead singer in the school choir. I sang a solo in front of 400 parents in a Christmas show. I sang 'Mary's Boy Child'. This was 1964. The birth of pop music. The first Beatles' hits. At this time, to become a pop singer, it was really a case of who you knew. The city where I lived; Sheffield; was, at the time, far removed from the London and Liverpool birth of pop music. I was with a 'working class' family living in a Council Estate. I've lived my life with the shoulda, coulda, wouldas of wanting to sing. In 2004, Simon Cowell introduced 'The X Factor' to the UK. Like Pop Idol or American Idol, only with the addition of bands and 'over 25-year-old' singers. In 2005, Jill entered me as a contestant. She was so proud of me and my voice, and had great aspirations for me.

Everyone who doesn't make it, has their story, and I'm no exception. Strange thing happened when I auditioned. The first question I was asked, was how old I was. Bearing in mind I was in the over 25's group, and I was 51, it seemed a strange question to ask. I wasn't expecting the question, so I told them my age. In hindsight I would have just said over 25.

When I started to sing, two judges turned to each other, raised their eyebrows and smiled. I know enough about body language to know that that was an unconscious gesture of pleasant surprise. When I finished singing, I was told I wouldn't be invited back. I was devastated. I'd had some singing lessons before the competition and the coach had coached a number of people for the same competition this year and the year before. He told me I'd sail through the first two auditions. As I wondered where I'd gone wrong, I kept gravitating back to the 'age' question. As I've watched the show progress I've noticed that no-one over the age of 40 moves through. I guess we're not considered saleable enough. I was convinced that the judges were eliminating people over the age of 40. Well; that's my story. It makes me feel better, so I'm sticking to it.)

Glenn: Azrael. This is all well and good, but we need resources. We have this large house to run and pay for. We need income. We have to keep earning until we sell the house, so we can move to the 'States'.

Azrael: Jill is your angel. She is here to guide and help you. She chose you to fulfil your prophecy and dreams. She forgave her dreams of dancing.

(When Jill was 5 years old she started Ballet. Until the age of 17, she danced 6 days a week. She went to the Royal School of Ballet, which at the time was the British Ballet Organisation. She danced with Nuriyev, Baryshnikov, Margot Fontayne; and was tipped for Prima Donna until her dad was made redundant in the decline of the steel industry in Sheffield and Rotherham in the late 1970's. She got the highest marks on all her certificates: Highly Commended.)

She 'chose' you. She tries 'so' hard to please you. She tries 'so' hard to fulfil what is expected. She operates through true love, for you and your children. We must have faith. You have a new contract to come to you as proof of my word. It will earn the passing of your time until you find a person to take your home.

Glenn: How long is this going to be?

Azrael: Up to two years. The time is not right for you to go to America yet. It's not safe for you. There will be further bombings in America.

Glenn: Where?

Azrael: New York, Washington and Los Angeles will be hit tragically. But there will also be much tragedy from hurricanes and earthquakes. Within 2 years you will be overseas and find your true happiness. I must go now; she is very weak.

Glenn: Let me help you find the books.

Azrael: The books will not resurface for many years. For in them it is written of the female strength and the rising of the female. Mother Mary was the first fear. Man resented this and rebelled. To rebel they created Catholicism and Christianity to control this fear. The feminine form is to have love and compassion for all. I must go. Keep writing. Ease their pain. We will talk again.

Glenn: Thank you Azrael.

At that point Jill stirred and her eyes opened.

Glenn: Were you awake for that?

Jill: For what; I'm so tired, I feel so drained.

Glenn: Azrael's been to see me again. Listen to what I managed to write.

And I shared the information with her.

The following day I was coaching Stephen Rolphe here at our home and offices. He was being coached on emotional intelligence and behavioural skills to enhance his leadership skills, managing a team of ten sales people in a company called Bistronics. It was tiring for me, working whilst nursing my broken foot and leg; but needs must when there are hungry wolves at the door.

I was drained. Outside, in the back garden, the sky was a beautiful deep blue, hosting a few cotton ball clouds which were gliding slowly across the sky. A bit of a rarity in the UK. The sun was warm on my skin, as I hobbled out of the house on my crutches. Jill came to greet me and we sat outside together on sun lounge chairs, watching the two boys bouncing up and down on the trampoline. Cooper was teaching himself cartwheels and handstands.

Jill walked back into the office, a few feet away from where we were sat. I reclined the sun lounge to feel the warmth of the sun on my face and to get my foot in the air, to drain some of the swelling. I lay there trying to remember the name of the Spanish speaking girl from the previous night. I say Spanish speaking, because as I surfed the net today, looking for clues for Bodegas, 1552 and famine. It seems there was a great famine in 'New Spain' in 1552. So she may have been one of the early settlers in South America, Mexico or North America.

The sun was beaming warmly on my face.

"Phoof!"

   www.anewbelief.com

It was like someone had blown in my ear. There was no 'blowing' sound that you hear from someone's mouth; no wind; not even a gentle breeze. It was just like air rushing into my ear, but without the blowing sound. I just got the feeling and not the sound.

"Luciana!" I exclaimed softly. "Thank you Luciana."

I lay there for a while before I went into the office. Jill had already given me a sheet of paper with something printed on it as Steve was leaving. It didn't seem appropriate to look at it in front of Steve. It might have spooked him. It was about the Red Indian chief. I sat down at my desk to read it:

Red Thunder. A chief of the Pabaska or Cuthead band of Yanktonai Sioux in the early part of the 19th Century; also known as 'The Beaver'.

Lieut. Z. M. Pike saw him at the great council at Prairie du Chien (French for Prairie of the dogs.), Wisconsin, in April 1806; and pronounced him as the most gorgeously dressed of any chief he had ever met.

With his famous son Waneta, he enlisted with the British in the war of 1812, and fought at Fort Meigs, and at Sandusky, Ohio. He was killed under tragic circumstances by the Chippewa on Red River of the North in 1823.

Colonel Robert Dickenson, the British agent in the West during 1812 – 1815, married a sister of Red Thunder.

www.accessgenealogy.com/native/tribes/
siouan/siouxchiefs.htm

WOW!! There comes a time in a doubting Thomas's life, when you just can't ignore the truth. It seems that Red Thunder wanted me to know that in a past life, I was Colonel Robert Dickson and I was related to Red Thunder.

7: 5000 verses the 6,500,000,000

15th August 2005 7.20pm

Jill and I are sitting in the front room relaxing. Jill's content; cuddling up to me on the sofa.

Jill: He's back again.

Glenn: Who?

Jill: Azrael; who'd you think?

Glenn: What's he want?

Jill: He's very pleased with what you're doing. The Council of Elders are very happy with you.

Jill took hold of my left hand with her left hand, and placed her right hand over my left hand, patting as though she was patting a child in endearment. I laughed out loud. This was Azrael's sign that I recognised for the first time. Azrael was pleased with me, and this was his way of getting physical contact with me.

Jill slowly went from channelling into trance:

Azrael: It's a pleasure to be with you again my son.

Glenn: Nice to be with you too.

Azrael: We're very pleased with your progress, but we want you to include more of what people can do to ease their pain.

Glenn: In what way?

Azrael: Write about belief. Belief in themselves and belief in the after life. There are so many that don't believe.

Glenn: Why am I doing this?

Azrael: You are the chosen one my son.

Glenn: But why not Jill? Why me? Jill is the one who's gifted with channelling and trance to the spirit world. She's also a good speaker and she's had her pain too. Why me, when I can't communicate with you direct and Jill has so much knowledge of the spirit world?

Azrael: All in good time my son. Jill is there to teach you. She's a good woman. She's there to help you. You have the ability to reach the people and as you know, Jill is not long for the earth plane. You are destined to be there much longer; to heal and spread the world; to ease their pain. You must learn what you can from her. She's very special.

Glenn: But why can't I talk to you direct?

Azrael: You can my son.

Glenn: How?

Azrael: Learn to. Jill will show you how. You have too much negative energy at the moment for us to get through. First you must learn to meditate and clear your mind.

Glenn: What's the real purpose of all this?

Azrael: When the time comes and we lose two thirds of the people on this earth plane, many of them will not cross over because they don't believe. There are more people now than ever that don't believe in the afterlife. They have nothing to believe in; and first they must learn to believe in themselves.

Glenn: Just how many others 'are' there like me?

Azrael: 5000.

Glenn: Great! That makes me feel 'really' special. I thought I was your 'chosen' one.

(I'm starting to feel like Eddy Murphy here in the film 'The Golden Child'.)

Jill stirs and briefly comes back into channelling to tell me he's angry.

Glenn: Well that's OK; but first I'm the chosen one, and then he tells me there are 5000 others.

Azrael: Yes my son, there are 5000 others, but the vast majority don't possess the knowledge and the skills you have, to reach out to the people and make a change. Few of them are good at writing. This is your destiny. The Elders of the Council are looking to you to start the movement.

Glenn: This is going to take a great deal of my time. What about the contract you promised us? You promised us a contract to keep us stable.

Jill comes out of channelling again.

Jill: Glenn, he's getting really angry. He says you won't like him when he's angry. You're just like 'him'. 'You' say that to people too.

Glenn: Well that's OK, but we can't survive in this house without bringing in some money to pay the bills.

Jill: He's angry now that you're bartering with him.

...and she drifts off again.

Azrael: I promised you I'd not let you down. Have we let you down before? Do you think it's a coincidence that work suddenly comes in when you're at a low ebb with your business? Have you ever gone without?

Glenn: No; but we've lost a lot and we don't want to lose all we've worked for and invested into this house.

   www.anewbelief.com

Azrael: The house is a material thing. You can survive without material things. I promised you there would be affluence to come with this venture.

Glenn: That's not what we agreed earlier. You accepted that I needed the material things and that you would provide for us if I worked at this.

Jill: (Channelling again and very alarmed.) Glenn! He's really angry. I mean really, really angry! He's saying you shouldn't bargain with him. He's not used to people bargaining with him.

Glenn: No Jill! I'm not having this. Azrael; what's good for you is good for me. You've already bargained with me with Jill's life here on Earth. You bargained with her extension of time here, for the continuation of my writing and my help. I won't have this! You're changing the rules. If I'm to trust you, when we agree things we follow them through.

Azrael: I won't let you down my son. I won't fail you. I want you to start speaking in churches and ministries.

Glenn: Why?

Azrael: Because there are many people that go to them that don't believe. They're lost! They want to believe in God and the after-life, but they're distracted by others and they're confused.

Glenn: You're going to have to help me here. There's very little budget in churches and ministries to give us an income and this is going to be very time consuming. You already know that we won't give up our material needs and we want to live comfortably. I don't agree that worship of your God, and belief in the after-life should go hand-in-hand with poor income, humbleness and poverty; or even giving everything away.

Azrael: We won't let you down my son. We won't fail you. We won't let you go without.

Glenn: OK, I'm happy to put the time in, if you're prepared to look after us.

Azrael: It's time for me to leave my son. We're very happy with you. We'll speak again.

Glenn: Look forward to it Azrael.

8: Soul training

17th August 2005 12.00pm

Jill and I are sitting in the sunshine in our back garden, taking a break from work, discussing the channelling and trance she'd experienced two days earlier with Azrael.

I asked her how she knew that Azrael was angry. She described the surge of heat that started in her toes and surged through her body, up to her neck; like an increasing electric current being forced through her body. She said it was really frightening.

I couldn't get my head round The Council of Elders and asked Jill to explain. As she started to explain, and I started writing, I suggested it might be easier for her to put it straight into the web site; and I'd fit it into the appropriate chapter later.

So into the office she went; which was only a few feet away.

When I went in a few minutes later she was rattling away at my computer keyboard. Max came in to talk to her and Jill quickly asked me to take him away as she told me she was channelling. So we gave her the space.

17th August 2005 12.40pm.

First, Jill asked for help:

Jill: Baysarayla; I need your help to help me explain the process of what we do as souls before we get here on this earth plane.

(This is the unabridged version of what Jill typed as Baysarayla spoke to her.):

Baysarayla: I'm glad that you are a seeker of truth. To explain how life and the soul's evolution works, we must first consider what a 'soul' is. A soul is your unique character:- your feelings, your drives, values, wisdom and experiences; and even when you leave your physical body behind to return from whence you came, you are still the core personality that you were in your lifetime on the earth plane. Now with that behind us, let us now turn our attention to how a soul, (you), charts a human experience.

It takes many earth years to arrange an incarnation (That is to become of the flesh.). You will look at the experiences that you have yet to discover and plan what you can achieve in your lifetime on the earth plane, with the help of an Ascended Master. (Ascended Master is a soul who has experienced all there is to be experienced on the earth plane.)

It is similar perhaps to creating a perfect recipe: too much here, or too little application there, can mean the difference to a dish not worth eating, or a dish that tantalises and teases the taste buds in a wonderful array of flavours.

From time-to-time, some souls can seek to 'fast-track' their evolution, i.e. perhaps experience murder or a life-debilitating disease. It is essential that during these 'fast-track' experiences that a soul does not try to take on too much. So, once a rough draft of your chart has been put into place, your Ascended Master and you will appear before The Council of Elders (These are a panel of Ascended Masters.) who will hear your plan and decide whether or not it is possible for the soul to accomplish what has been mapped for the life's journey. It is not unusual for a soul to have to rethink their chart or make amendments for a further Council hearing; before finally being given the blessings of The Council to fulfil their soul's purpose.

You must understand this takes many earth years to plan; for as well as charting what is to be experienced, the soul must also work alongside other like-minded souls who together will ensure that all souls achieve their purposes in their charts. This includes choosing parents, teachers, friends, partners and also how you will interpret the lessons that are to be learnt.

Once you have charted all this, you will then have a final meeting with The Council of Elders, whereby you appoint your guides for this lifetime. It is the purpose of a guide to ensure that you follow the chart.

Now I hear you say, what of free will?

The soul 'does' have free will. You are given a choice. To you, this would be whether you take the long hard route or the easy route. Either way, you will accomplish what you set out to do. This is where your free will kicks in. There are no coincidences. All things happen for a reason. If a soul, whilst on the earth plane tries to deviate from the chart, certain occurrences will be put in place by The Council of Elders to give you a helping hand back to what you should be doing. As is the case with your husband here.

We had tried in our usual manner to get him to take up his calling, but due to the negative effects of the earth plane, he was sitting on the fence. We had to put him in the position whereby he had nothing else he could do but follow his destiny. Hence the broken leg.

For some the lessons may seem hard in this lifetime, but rest assured, they were chosen by each and every one of you. It is not our way to force a soul to do something they have not already agreed to do in the first place. Integrity and love are the firm foundations of our creation and reason for existence. Therefore, if we commit to something, we must uphold our agreement. For without integrity we have no firm foundations on which to continue our existence.

Whilst this may be hard for some of you to comprehend at this moment in time, try to take things a step at a time. Search out the knowledge for yourself.

If you are reading this, you are here as a reminder for you to find your own calling and seek enlightenment.

This message I hope will clarify the confusion of spirit and the soul's journey. We will talk again, but in the meantime, many blessings to you all.

Bayserayla.

9: Man of hugs

19th August 2005

Jill and I went to the cinema in the Meadowhall shopping mall in Sheffield. I'd promised to go with her to see a 'chick-flick'; 'Bewitched'. Jill wanted a break from the kids. We were 4 weeks into the summer break. After the film we went into an Italian restaurant called Amalfi.

8.05pm.
The waiter had just poured us both a glass of red wine, from the bottle we'd just ordered. Jill looked across at me and said, "We're not alone!" I asked her if Azrael was here. She said Luciana was by my side, holding my little finger on my left hand.

Glenn: Is she pretty?

Jill: Yes; in a way. She's almost 'pixie-like'. Very cute. Big black eyes. She's so thin. She's wearing a tunic. No sleeves; up to her neck, and down to her knees.

Glenn: Is she clean?

Jill: No! (As she shook her head and giggled.) She needs a good bath. Her tunic is made of a brown sack-like material. She's very poor.

Glenn: Aaaahh!

Jill: She says she wishes she could sit in your lap, so you can cuddle her; like you cuddle me, and the boys. You are the 'Man of Hugs'. (Jill laughs.)

Glenn: The 'Man of Hugs'?"

Jill: Yes. You give so much love. The love she never had, and always wanted.

Glenn: I wish I could see her, and give her a hug. Where's she from; Spain or Mexico?

Jill: Mehico!

Glenn: I thought so. That's where the famine was in 1552; in New Spain.

Jill cocked her head on one side a couple of times. I looked confused. She did it again.

Glenn: Why are you doing 'that'?

Jill: She's stood at the side of you, with her head snuggled onto your shoulder.

Glenn: Aaahh; tell her I wish I could hold her.

I took my right hand and imagined where she was stood; and stroked her head and long hair, down to her waist.

Jill made a wriggling gesture; like a child when they're full of excitement. Jill was showing me that Luciana was giddy with happiness. My eyes were welling up; just as they are now as I'm typing this. What a sop I am!

Jill: She was very close to her aunt, for the short time they were together. She'd not been there long, before her uncle killed her; partly because they couldn't afford to feed her because of the famine, and partly because of the attention she was getting from her aunt. He didn't like it. She's with you a lot!

Glenn: Does she like our children?

Jill: Max. She likes Max. Sometimes she curls up at the bottom of his bed to watch over him.

Glenn: Why only Max?

Jill: 'He's' the strong one. 'He's' in control.

Jill: She's leaving!

10: Trust and truth

24th August 2005

Jill was sat waiting for one of the computers to 'virus check' and 'killed' the time asking her guide for some answers on the true meanings of 'trust' and 'truth'.

This is what she wrote, which was partly from her guide and partly from her own thoughts:

Jill: Trust is 'reliance on' and 'confidence in' the truth. Truth is the quality of being true; genuine; actual.

When people put their trust in religion, they're accepting the religious statements as being 'the truth'. Yet in reality, religion is merely a concept, or a system of concepts, written, or passed on, by mankind; regarded as representing some aspect of the world or universe.

Why do so many people take these concepts and adopt them; without taking the time to check whether the concepts are accurate and representative of their own thoughts and feelings?

It's a scientific fact that no two things can occupy the same space and time; so if you doubt God, then you don't believe; and to you, God doesn't exist.

It was interesting watching a Catholic Nun protesting on National T.V. yesterday saying, "If I get to heaven, and if I get to meet God, I'll..."

Isn't it strange that a Catholic Nun would say "If"? Surely a woman who's giving her life to serving God would believe that she's already made the 'goody list' and will get her VIP ticket to heaven?

Does she feel unworthy?

Does she feel that heaven might not exist?

How many people have been born and programmed into a religion, without questioning if it's the 'right' religion for them?

How many people have taken the time to learn about other religions, to learn about the values and beliefs of others? Until we do; we won't (in my opinion) find the truth.

This is where spirit interjected and Azrael spoke to Jill:

Azrael: Until we understand our brothers and sisters, we can't hope to comprehend living in union.

We all possess the divine spirit. It's our mission to expand our mental and spiritual horizons, until we can attain the 5 levels of human consciousness. Then, and only then, can you ascend to the next dimension.

The soul's journey is to obtain experiences and information; and apply it to that particular incarnation (to be of the flesh); to see what works and what doesn't work for you. Hence the variety in religious and non-religious beliefs; yet you all experience the same pain; and still you do not bear each other more compassion. Instead you eye each other with suspicion, jealousy and hatred.

Metatron bids you hello. He is watching you both closely and will shortly oversee your journey of evolution.

Jill: Why is Metatron here?

Azrael: Metatron is the Supreme Angel of Death and the teacher of all prematurely dead children. And by this we don't just mean unborn or early children. This includes children whose lives were cut short one way or another.

(Glenn's thoughts: This is why Luciana is with me, and brought so many children to channel through Jill, to talk to me.)

Metatron will help you fulfil your divine purpose. It is the children we are so concerned with; for their pathways are being blocked in so many ways. Hence Glenn's writing. Through his writings, he will be able to touch the hearts of many parents and authorities; which in turn will affect the lives of children now; and those yet to come.

Metatron can teach you many things, but through the next coming years you will meet many entities, and not just me; that will each bring you lessons.

However, it is important at this time, that I stress to you both, the importance of meditation and relaxation. But I talk not of just watching T.V. There are many things to be done, so we need you to be relaxed, so your energies can attune themselves to the lessons being given.

At this time, it is also important to mention your friend and your 'tester': Christopher. He will not like being called this, but he has many truths; and also many questions; yet he fails to listen to answers. He too must trust in God as he would call his spiritual pathway and meditate. For it is only in meditation that we can truly access the soul. He will find his own answers in time. Together you would find them much quicker. Yes?

Now time grows short. It is not our intention to take over, but merely to help your active search for the truth and enlightenment.

Continue to write; but also look to Australia for a contract. You are limiting yourself, when you do not seek a wider audience. Apathy will kill a soul's journey we wish to guide. Also, Canada will bring much luck too for a short period; but it is the contact side which needs a boost. You have many contacts that could be called upon to help you. Look to the settings of programmes for self-actualisation and providence where children and teenagers are. The churches need many hands; and through churches, eventually a wide-spread collective thought, along with a book, will advance Glenn along his way.

It does not help you when you drink such good wine. (Azrael is laughing here, whilst Jill is drinking a very large glass of red Rosemount Shiraz wine.) When I work with you we need a level head. Yes? Good! All in fun; but remember: too much allows negative energies to be drawn to you.

Assalamualaikum!

Jill: What's that? Spell it for me please.

And at that Azrael did; and he left.

We had no idea what these letters meant, or even if it was more than one word; that is until we searched it on the 'net'.

Assalamualaikum is a very common Arabic phrase for, "May peace be with you."

11: Life-force grids

16th September 2005: Azrael and Luciana

Once again I'm in bed reading, would you believe 'The Da Vinci Code'? Interesting book about the Catholic conspiracy theory.

Jill's been asleep about 20 minutes, laid at the side of me. She's laid comfortably on her back, with her right hand crossed over her left, almost like the 'burial' position. She has a happy, content look on her face. I notice her right index finger starting to tap up and down on her left hand. It catches my eye. Her mouth is moving around slowly, as though she's moving a sweet/candy around in her mouth to get the flavour. Then she starts to slowly contort her face to make it look more hawk-like.

Glenn: Yes Azrael!

Azrael: You've been very good my boy.

Glenn: Nice to hear you.

Azrael: I write; like you... so much. It's a job we have to do. You need direction. Your direction needs focus. Your writing grows; but now you need to talk about how you cope with your pain: What it is that you do to cope. You must write as to how you overcome this. As a child; how did you compensate for how you weren't loved? This will give people answers.

Glenn: I'm worried about our finances.

Azrael: We will send people. You must be patient. It takes time to work miracles. Do you have any questions?

Glenn: People are warning me that you may be Satan.

Azrael: Have I done you wrong?

Glenn: Not that I'm aware of. What is God?

Azrael: The problem we have is what God is to human beings. You create a being, and you create it in one place. This is wrong. God is an energy. Energy combined, is a creative energy.

Glenn: And explain the Germanic accent to me again.

Azrael: Energies lie in life-force grids. Angels are assigned to certain areas. My grid is centralised over Germany. Michael is assigned to Manchester.

Glenn: Manchester? Is that Manchester, England or Manchester, USA?

Azrael: USA!

Glenn: Manchester!

Azrael: No, Manchester.

Glenn: Manchester!

Azrael: Mant.......Chester!

Glenn: Spell it for me please.

Azrael: M O U N T ...SHASTA

At this point I'm rolling around laughing because of our lack of communication.

Glenn: Right! Mount Shasta. Where's that?

Azrael: California! These are the areas we are asked by God to keep. You have great humour and you can use your humour to heal; but that will not give you the credibility to heal.

Glenn: Tell me more about what God is.

Azrael: God is a universal energy. The one thought. The one conscious mind. Humans here created God as an idol; a being; in a particular plane. You will spearhead this proper understanding along with your son, Max.

Max is individual. His heart is pure love. Max needs to understand this, so he may change the world along with others.

Religion is a conspiracy of mankind. The Bible speaks of many truths, but many things are not true. Human beings do not seek to be poor like some religious people would portray.

In 'your' lifetime, you will not be able to change the beliefs of all the millions of people that have had thousands of years of programming with their religion. You can't expect to. You are the beginning. Many will follow.

Glenn: What is my direction?

Azrael: Keep your direction going. How you overcome pain. How you have turned your flight of pain to find recognition. Write about overcoming pain. Implant roots. You will build an organisation.

Show people how to have faith in one's self.

Glenn: When you said that people would not pass over, what did you mean by this?

Azrael: It will affect the construction of the Universe. The Universe is a perfect balance of energies. If the human race refuses to embrace change; the Universe will fail. The human race needs to embrace all that can be created; not resort to destruction. With no hope, no belief and no faith, people will not pass over. They won't transcend to the next dimension. If they believe, they will transcend; to keep the Universe in balance.

Write about your pain as a child; not being loved. How you strived harder, to be noticed. Some give up. YOU fight to strive. YOU are strong.

Impetuousness of youth we understand. You failed in one lesson; you didn't recognise the admiration of others. If you'd seen this, you wouldn't have needed the admiration of your parents.

You used your pain as energy to drive you forward. You were willing to face your challenges. Understand that and write about it.

We need to watch your wife. She's tired.

Luciana will help you. She's always around you. You need to listen to her.

Glenn: How?

Azrael: You will!

Glenn: How will I know when she's there?

Azrael: You will smell her. Smell the almonds.

Jill suddenly starts speaking to me in fluent Spanish. JILL CAN'T SPEAK MUCH SPANISH!

Glenn: Luciana?

Luciana: Siiiiiiiiiiiiii.

Glenn: Luciana; is that you?

Luciana: Siiiiiiii mi piqueno.

Jill is speaking to me in a high pitched, soft toned, musical voice, like a seven-year old girl. Her face has changed again. She looks so youthful. Her face is glowing and there's a big smile on her face. But she's babbling to me rapidly in Spanish.

Glenn: Luciana! En Ingles; en Ingles!

Luciana: Si; perdon; I will try. Azrael has allowed me to speak through Jill, but I have so little time to speak to you. How is your ankle?

Glenn: It's healing; but it's weak.

Luciana: No! No! You are strong; so strong! I like you sooo much. You remind me of my Papa. My Papa was killed.

I love Max.

Glenn: Why Max?

Luciana: He's so funny.

Glenn; I wish I could hug you.

Luciana: You can't. I'll be at the bottom of your bed, every night.

Glenn: I wish I could see you.

Luciana: You will!

At that she faded away and Jill fell asleep again.

The following morning I asked Jill about Mount Shasta. She'd heard it was some kind of spiritual retreat. I asked her about the Mount Shasta relationship with Archangel Michael. She didn't have a clue. We went to look on the web. Whoah! There's an incredible amount of information about Mount Shasta as a spiritual retreat, and reference to Archangel Michael's presence.

Yet more validation?

September 17th 2005

As I was sat on the sofa in the lounge, watching T.V. in the evening, my left ear 'popped' open and there was an electronic type noise sucked into my ear. If you've ever seen the film 'Poltergeist', it was a similar sound to what they portray as entities calling out. It lasted for about 2 seconds. I guess it was Luciana.

Jill tells me that this is how it starts, and now that it's started, it will accelerate with a lot more to come over the coming months.

12: What is God?

**According to what the Angels tell me;
God is...**

- **Light.**
- **The one thought.**
- **The one super-conscious mind.**
- **Universal, creative energy.**

Energy combined is a creative energy. We are all part of the creative energy; as are all things that we are aware of.

People try to perceive God as a being, in a particular place 'out there' or 'up there' or 'in here'.

God; light; The Creator; the universal creative energy; is beyond human comprehension. We cannot communicate with God directly. We have to communicate with God's messengers: the angels.

No-one has 'ever' been spoken to by God.

God has used angels for voices and as messengers.

God is not a being as we know it.

We can only comprehend God when we pass over to the 'other side'.

To be able to pass over to the other side; the next dimension; we have to believe that we do. We have to believe that the soul continues to exist.

If you don't believe in 'anything'; then to 'you' it doesn't exist. So if you don't believe in the soul and its existence in the next life, then you can't pass over to something that doesn't exist.

This, for the vast majority of the people in the world, is a new belief.

Imagine trying to comprehend this 200 years ago; let alone thousands of years ago, when the books of the Bible were written. It would be like asking people to comprehend mobile phones, digital camcorders, space travel and special effects on films.

God has been traditionally based on whatever mankind could conceive in the past.

Many people in the UK; far more than in the USA and the rest of the world; have been turning their back on religion. But the interesting thing is the rise of spiritual awareness that's taking its place.

www.anewbelief.com

What does that tell us? Maybe that millions of people have lost faith in religion, but still want to have faith in 'something' and are aware that there's an 'intelligence' that still can't be explained. And they're right.

Take a look at the following picture. This is what most people who believe in God, visualise what God or Jesus looks like:

This is how it's been since the first scriptures were written. People have been programmed with this, or a similar image. The youth of today are fast moving away from accepting this. They just need to understand what God is; and learn about the structure of the way God communicates to us, through angels.

Many people need to understand how to pray properly, in meditation.

Many people need to be educated so they can believe.

The children of the world are the ones who are losing belief the quickest, as they evolve in a technological, media-driven world. They are being programmed with super-heroes, aliens and special effects, which detract and even conflict with a spiritual world. My children at the ages of 5 and 7 can't differentiate between the special effects and reality. They can't understand that the dinosaurs in the film, 'Jurassic Park' aren't real. Because they see them, they believe they are real.

The media want to sensationalise the spiritual world by portraying spirit as evil. This gets the ratings and more viewings. Look at the T.V. programmes such as 'Haunted House', 'Most Haunted' and 'Derek Acorah's Ghost Towns'.

Just think about this. People are fascinated by the unknown. They are fascinated by fear, as long as it's confined to a T.V. screen. People like the controversial. People like to look at other people's misfortune. We gravitate to the negative, instead of the positive.

Now try telling the youth of today to look at love, peace and harmony; and to them; it's not 'cool'. Is it any wonder that the youth of today are not accepting the belief of The Creator? Science has overtaken spiritualism in a big way. So it's up to the adults who are becoming more spiritual, to pass on this belief to the children.

The Christian churches want to depress the spiritual world by preaching from the Bible about the wrong-doing of speaking to the 'dead'. Yet if those preachers would read the Bible properly, they would see many chapters which say it is OK to speak to angels. But because people are so negative, they gravitate to questions like, "But is it really an angel speaking to you?"

Imagine a Christian leader, who's given their life to the church. They meet me; an atheist for 50 years; who is now talking to angels. Come on! Put yourself in their shoes. Do they really 'want' to believe me? Might there just be a 'little' jealousy there? Wondering, "Why him, when I've devoted my life to God?"

Now ask yourself, "How many female religious leaders do I know?" How many do you see? Surely that must be representative of the early Christian conspiracy to suppress the rise of women?

It took until 1971 for the first two Christian women to be ordained in Hong Kong.

It took until 1974 to ordain female priests in the USA. There were 11 initially ordained.

1975: Four women are ordained as priests in Washington

1976: Six female priests are ordained by the Anglican Church in Canada.

1977: Five female priests are ordained by the Anglican Church of New Zealand.

1987: Women are ordained as deacons in Australia.

1987: A woman deacon is ordained in England.

1990: Women are ordained as priests in Ireland.

1992: Church of England voted to allow women to be ordained. About 470 male clergy left the church in protest; 58 subsequently returned.

2000: There remained about 1,000 congregations in the *Church of England* who refused to accept the authority of women priests.

God created men and women to have separate tasks so they could work in harmony. In its simplest format; man being the hunter, food provider and protector. Woman being the child bearer, educator and short range nest protector. They had different complimentary roles. Woman was the natural 'people person'; the educator. Woman has the natural leadership role, yet has been suppressed. God is aware of this.

Some people may say, "If God is almighty, why does he allow poverty, cruelty and despair. Why doesn't he just change things? Smite people down if necessary and allow us all to live in harmony and be happy. Why does he allow catastrophes which devastate the human race?"

Well I'm beginning to form a picture from the angels that God 'isn't' in control, and can only guide our fate through contact with the angels. I may be wrong.

This is just a beginning for me. I didn't choose this. I was chosen. Apparently I'm to have many lessons from many entities as the path unwinds.

My first has been with Azrael; the Angel of Death. Apparently, I'm a son of his own blood. He will guide and teach me. Other entities will give me the lessons and Azrael will help practically.

My second entity meeting was with Metatron. He wants me to write about the voice of children; in that children speak the truth, yet are programmed into negativity by adults.

The journey has just begun.

13: Metatron makes his presence

17th September 2005

Jill and I were travelling in our car on the way to Sheffield town centre. We were meeting friends at a restaurant called Martini's.

I was driving. As we travelled Jill told me she was channelling. She tried to shut it out, but the presence was too strong. It was Metatron.

Jill described the immense power she felt from Metatron. More imposing than any other entity she's ever channelled. Overwhelming!

She says she felt that at any time he could wave his hand, in a dismissive gesture and 'put her candle out'. She was mildly frightened of his presence.

Metatron, as forecast, had come to introduce himself. He talked about how we needed to get our messages to the children, both directly and through parents.

The children are the speakers of truth, yet they are being programmed by parents to 'know their place'; speak when spoken to; be seen and not heard; know that elders know better; do what elders say, and not what elders do; laugh only when it's appropriate; be polite and not tell the truth; and 'grow up' way too soon.

Metatron spoke of the lack of belief in the new wave of children and that we needed to help them or they wouldn't transcend.

I asked him many questions; but he forcefully told me that I was too impatient and that Azrael was my current tutor, who would answer all my questions. He also told us there would be many other entities that would be giving us lessons to pass on to others.

Then he told me of Luciana. He said her name meant 'light' and that she has the powerful radiance of a shining beacon for all children to see and be drawn to. She's to be with me always to help me with this eternal quest. To draw the children close.

Metatron's visit was very brief. An introduction. Jill said he was curt and to the point. Not a presence to be messed with.

As he left, Jill's new guide, White Cloud appeared with us. He told us that I would write many children's books.

14: Jesus and the Bible

21st September 2005

It was a little after 6.00pm. Jill was getting irritated because spirit wouldn't leave her alone. We were making dinner, when she said she needed to be alone at her computer because she was channelling. What you need to understand here, is that Jill types at 130 words per minute (wpm) if she needs to. She once did a test for the fun of it. Her fastest constant speed is 145 wpm; with 15% errors; but she managed 15 minutes at 130 wpm without errors. This is the competitive streak in Jill.

If you want to measure yourself and friends with a Dictaphone, you'll find that the average person speaks between 120 and 140 wpm. Very slow is 70 wpm and extremely fast is 200 wpm. Both extremes are rare. So Jill is able to type the words as fast as the average person speaks. This is what she typed.

Metatron: At last, we are able to commune together for the betterment of mankind. May the North, South, West and East bring forth the energies that are able to assist God in his plan for humanity.

We are pleased with your progress; yet it seems there are many mental blocks, or should we say negative levels, that you allow to affect your ethereal layer.

Despite our promises to you both, you still lack faith. Faith is the one true constant that must be attained to ensure your connection to spirit. This is why so many people fail to see or hear the word of God.

We understand Glenn's reluctance to utilise the naming called God, but it is the only way that we can get people to begin to listen to the lessons that must be learnt.

You ask of Jesus and his role, Jesus was a mere mortal, who was and is the one constant link that connects humans to God. He was a channeller far beyond his time. His healing ministries were not magic or supernatural as portrayed by the writers of that time. He was a special soul chosen by God, to bring forth the lessons that needed to be learnt.

Alas with time, these lessons have been eradicated for man's own use and power. We are aware that people who follow the Christian faith will challenge what we say. But let it be known,

www.anewbelief.com

that we are from God. We bring forth his new teachings. As people must evolve, so God learns too, that changes need to be made. What worked then, perhaps does not work now.

Jesus was chosen specifically by God, to bring forth God's hopes and desires for mankind. That they learn to have compassion and tolerance for all living things.

Unfortunately, the religions of this world have become so chipped in stone, that humans neglect to connect with their hearts and feel what God wishes them to know.

Humans, as God's creatures, must realise that the way they have worshiped him is no longer the way. Mankind must learn to look within. For only when they know themselves, for they are of God, will they find God. So many souls are searching for God, yet like the blind, they do not see.

Let us begin with how the world was created, and why....

The world was created by God, as a form of expression and dreams; the one thought consciousness had. Bit by bit, the world took shape and to help nurture and grow this conscious thought, mankind was created.

The Garden of Eden did exist but on a worldly scale. Many beautiful plants, animals and visions. All this creativity was dissected and imparted to each and every human being. Along with this, emotion was given, so that humans could experience varying ranges of feelings. It was these feelings of love and creation that connected humans to God.

Unfortunately, as times have progressed, humankind has strived to be 'as' God, therefore to take control and power over others. God does not wish to dominate. The rules given to Moses were meant as a 'just' way of living, to ensure that all human kind could experience life in happiness and love. By disregarding these commandments; jealousies, lust and hatred were born.

God has tried many ways in which to reconnect with human kind, yet they do not see; they do not feel. Instead they choose to indulge in mere immediate gratification; not seeing that by connecting to spirit, they can in fact ensure the continuation of their existence.

We understand that at this time, we may cause confusion; but to embrace a new belief and a new connection to God, one must challenge and help others to see that their perception of God, is perhaps not the true image it should be.

To see God in totality is beyond human perception. However, to connect to the Godhead energies, is quite another thing.

Currently the vast majority of the human race do not face, and cannot accept truth. The truth of who they are. For as children, they have been denied, ignored and categorised, so they no longer know who they truly are. Children are currently told to respect elders, be quiet and act accordingly. God's teaching has always shown that the way to connect with God is through the eyes of a child. Their innocence and willingness to face the truth is what connects them to the Godhead, the one universal life force energy.

Children see many possibilities to a situation; they believe that all things can be so. They do not question their own abilities. It is only as time continues and the elders affirm to them that they are not as good as they think they are, that the rot set's in.

The human race must learn quickly that to deny a child, is to deny God. Children can teach the human race many things. Humans say that children can be very cruel. We would interject and say, "No, they are honest. They're not afraid to show hurt. They're not afraid to show their vulnerability. They're not afraid to give love, even though it isn't returned. These dear souls are the unique aspect of God. They must be cherished, encouraged, and heard."

Do not shatter their true calling. Once this lesson and change has occurred, the world truly will be a better place. But for this to happen, it starts with one person, ministering to others, asking them to just consider for one moment the possibilities of what is being said, is the truth of God.

As humans, you like to label and classify people: Christians, Muslims, and Jews. All humans and spirit are one. We ask that what has been learnt be put aside, for the betterment of human kind. Just be willing to reconsider the possibilities; to try something new; to feel with the heart; instead of the head dictating what has already been learnt, in that something new might not be the light all humans have been searching for.

I suspect that some of you will question who I am that talks through this medium *(Jill is the medium.)*. My name is Metatron. My purpose here is to bring forth the truth. The connection with this medium is brought about to bring change.

Your Bibles that contain the elements of truth would say this connection with the medium is the works of Satan; but let me ask you this: If what has been brought forth is the work of Satan, I would ask you to consider how come you know what Satan is? For you must know him well to ascertain I am he.

My work is to help the continuance of the human race. The only way to ensure this, is through the development and nourishment of children. For anyone who shall harm a child of God, shall upon the day of judgement, be cast out and forbidden to enter the Kingdom of God.

I am the 'Angel of Presence'. My purpose is to assist you to connect with your higher self. To connect with your higher self, you must first learn to 'know' thy self. To do this, one must learn Truth and Trust. I ask that you give prayer to God and meditate to receive the divine answers. Be willing to learn and accept new truths. Be aware of the spirit within, and be willing to accept the ways of God as the truth and the only way to eternal life.

Many blessings are brought forth. Until next time, may the North, South, West and East points of the universe be connected only in truth, love and light, for the betterment of mankind.

Azrael: Hello we meet again. It brings much joy to my heart to know that you have reconnected with Metatron. He has many plans to help you achieve your way.

Now; as time grows short, as always, we must look to what is required next. It is important that we now look to showing the people who access your knowledge, how they can begin to grow... and move forward so they may enter their designated dimensions.

For you see not everyone will ascend to the next level. Some will, how you say, 'skip a level', due to the vast advancement of their soul and its purpose in this lifetime.

You will find that you and Glenn are one of these gifted souls. We must however look to the lessons that you need to bring forth.

Glenn's behavioural expertise is one way; but you must also look to how this can be incorporated and passed down to the children. Shine a light and they will follow so to speak.

I know that there will be many questions. But all in good time. We are aware of your concern for financial liabilities; but these I can assure you are being dealt with. Again it is your faith that is being questioned and nothing else. True faith is also known as blind faith in that The Creator will not see his children fall.

Now, we come to a very important point that we need to do, to ensure that this flow of information is maintained and developed.

We have asked that you take time to meditate and yet, you have failed to comply with our wishes. We understand your desire for financial security and that you work diligently to try to bring everything together; but the key to eternal life and happiness is balance in all things. We must make time for prayer and also time for meditation to receive the answers. We must make time for work, to ensure that our efforts are rewarded; and we must also ensure that we have fun and laughter to ensure that relaxation and the pleasures of life are experienced.

We know that you are asked to complete many things; but we do so, due to your ability to endure great highs and great lows. Your souls have been through many experiences, but it is through this that you acquired wisdom.

Take time to watch the world around you. Watch the workings of minds, and then you will see the challenges that the spirit world has to overcome.

Once you do this, you will see that all humans are searching for answers. But for most, the answers are those they are unwilling to face. Do not judge those who are different to you. Just accept that they are different and perhaps need a different approach.

To minister to those, we ask that you help them by beginning to get them to reconnect with their heart and their soul, and get them to understand, or perhaps ask them, what do they feel God would want for them?

Ask them to feel the love and proudness that God has for each and every human soul. The problems lie in their own disbeliefs; their own reasoning; that they are unworthy and they cannot truly connect with God.

They themselves are the block to connecting with God, not Satan. Nothing can stop you from finding God, if you believe in yourself. For each and every one of us is of God, made in God's own image, which is the inner divine beauty and creativity in all.

Create classes to bring this creativity and learning in a new way. Although radical you will find it like a common cold, easily catchable. We shall talk again soon, but for now, we feel we have given you much to think about.

We have been sent by God to spread forth the word. We understand Glenn's reluctance to accept the term God, but for now, ask that you use the name created by human kind to give identity to this great force; this one consciousness; that most humans cannot understand.

Blessings until next time.

One last thing. You will find that Chamuel will be entering your energies. Take time to converse. His teachings and lessons will manifest many truths. Remember, when you doubt, look around you. The beauty of God's world cannot be denied. The intricacies of nature are created to bring balance and pleasure for all.

After that, Jill was drained. She printed the document for me to read. As I read it I felt the immense power from these angels and the immense challenge that lie ahead. It was an emotional watershed and I couldn't help crying. Some of the tears were for the love portrayed in the message, and some were for the fear of the journey that lies ahead.

Blind faith is a phenomenal request. Do I know of anyone who has true blind faith? It's frightening. I have great belief in myself, but now I'm being asked to have belief for entities that have so far shown me nothing tangible, other than channelling through Jill. Yet we're asking for tangible things, to keep our head above water.

Jill rarely remembers what she's channelling. Around 8.00pm she sat with me and picked up the document to read. As she progressed through the paragraphs, her eyes started to well up and she cried continuously as she continued reading.

I asked her for her feelings and she virtually repeated the same feelings that I'd felt of the immense power and compassion within the words; but also the seemingly insurmountable task that the angels were asking of us.

We discussed why me? Why not just Jill? She's the medium; the gifted one. Then Jill set me straight. She told me I was chosen, because I was a staunch non-believer. Jill's believed in the after-life, all her life. My life's experiences are a model for those who feel they can't overcome adversity in their life. Also, we've just had a mild bollockin' for not meditating; and we've been told more than once that I need to meditate to break down the negativity so that the angels can talk to me direct.

That night as we went to bed, spirits were hounding Jill, and she was determined to shut them out. At one point, she started to shape into the position which Azrael takes of her. I was just about to set the tape recorder going and she shut him out.

22nd September 2005

Jill didn't sleep much, and my sleep was disturbed with vivid dreams. You know the types that just keep repeating themselves? Jill is worried that she might be on the verge of insanity. She made a bold statement this morning that she's not channelling anymore. She wants to live a normal life. She finds this too overwhelming. I didn't comment. Free will or no free will; from what I've seen or heard, I don't think that Jill has a choice. Time will tell.

Let's just get a handle on what's just been said by Metatron. Jesus was a mere mortal. A great channeller, like Jill, who was given the task of speaking to people to bring about compassion and tolerance for all living things. He wasn't supernatural and wasn't magic. He didn't perform miracles.

Just think of the impact on Christianity. If you don't believe in something; it doesn't exist. Sure he was the Son of God. But now we understand we 'all' are. Jesus has been used as an 'idol' to support the structure for power and control in Christianity. The image of him being the 'only' son of God, sets him apart from other mere mortals, in that we're programmed we couldn't possibly be his equal. Yet the angels are telling us that's exactly what he was preaching on their behalf; that we are all equal. We don't need the power and control of religion to be at one with The Creator. We are part of The Creator. We just have to learn how to tune in.

15: The making of a psychic believer

8th October 2005

Two weeks ago, Jill decided she'd had enough of spirit. It was draining her and she felt as though she was going insane. The build up of spirit contacting her was getting her down. She'd no time to think without spirit talking to her. She also saw that the emotions of dealing with these new entities were overwhelming me; and she didn't like to see me so emotional, so often.

I didn't want her to do this, but Jill is very independent and she'll do what she wants.

She told me a few days ago that she just needed a break. She was having mixed feelings as to whether she was really channelling angels, or just going insane.

Meanwhile I've started to meditate, in the hope that the angels can get through my ethereal layer and talk to me direct.

Jill did a reading yesterday for a woman in the USA and ended up channelling the angel Uriel for the woman.

I need to explain: At this time, we're living in the UK, in England. Jill doesn't have to be with someone to be able to give them a psychic reading. She doesn't have to see them, or even hear their voice. People from all over the world email her and ask her for a reading. They normally ask two or three questions that they would like answered.

Jill will sit at the computer with her Tarot cards, angel cards, Native American cards; and more recently her sacred geometry cards (Metatron is teaching her sacred geometry.). Sometimes she will use one pack; sometimes two. She sits and meditates for a while. Then she turns the cards over and faces them, face-up on the desk in front of her, one-by-one; and she's away. She starts typing.

As a previous logical, non-believing male; it was difficult to accept at first. But when you see the continual feedback she gets from people, all over the world, it seems irrefutable. She reads for people all over the world without seeing or speaking to them: England, Wales, Scotland, Ireland, Australia, New Zealand, Russia, Spain, Portugal, USA, South Africa, Malaysia, Hong Kong, Canada, Denmark, Tobago, Singapore, Germany, France, Ireland, Venezuela, Iran... Her feedback is amazing. It's the feedback that makes it difficult for you not to believe. A lot of her feedback is posted on her website:

www.anewbelief.com

www.psychicwoman.com. Check it out. If you're a non-believer; prepare to be challenged. So; back to the woman in the USA.

I was sat at the side of Jill whilst she was doing the reading. Our desks are in parallel, in our second drawing room, facing a side window in our house.

Jill asked me to search the internet for the Sirian Council. She wanted to know what it was. Apparently, the woman she was reading for, according to Uriel, in a past life, was a member of the Sirian Council. Neither of us had any idea what it was.

Lots of information came up on the internet. Apparently it's a Galactic Council of Ascended Masters. Yet another piece of the jigsaw of evidence that Jill channels spirit and angels.

I guess the most memorable reading that I'm aware of, that Jill did, was with friends after we'd entertained one evening with dinner. We were chilling in the lounge after dinner. I was about to become a confirmed believer in spirit, channelling and mediumship.

Steve is a real sceptic. He openly said that he thought that spiritualism and mediumship was, "Bollocks!" He challenged Jill. "Come on then. Do me!" Not much graciousness about that was there?

Jill sat for a while before she spoke. Then she told Steve of an older woman who was coming through. She'd died in an unusual way, which Jill portrayed to Steve. Jill told Steve that she said it was time he stopped leaving his dirty underwear on the floor. At that, Steve's girlfriend choked on her wine and burst into laughter. "He does!" she shouted. "I'm always having a go at him for leaving his dirty knickers on the bedroom floor. He never puts them in the wash basket."

Jill continued with the messages from the woman. Jill told Steve that when he was young, his mother didn't allow him to play with the other children on the street. He had to play in the back garden. There was a tree at the bottom of the garden he used to play in. He used to paint faces on wooden spoons. There were two black dogs that he lost to spirit. He once tied one of his front teeth, which was loose, to his bedroom door knob, and then slammed the door closed, to pull his tooth out. Then a man came through who said he was his uncle Alex. He just wanted to say hello.

Jill asked Steve if he connected to the information. He'd just sat there and kept quiet. Steve said that he lost his mum the same way that Jill had described, but it could have been anybody she was talking to. He said his mum wouldn't let him play with the children on the street because she felt they were too rough; and that yes, there was a tree at the bottom of the garden that he used to play in all the time; but most boys would do that. He did have two black dogs that died, but then most people could have had two black dogs. He did use to paint faces on wooden spoons as a child, but didn't everybody? He did have an Uncle Alex, but lots of people do. And Jill was wrong about the tooth and string. It wasn't him that slammed the door shut; it was his brother. So he wasn't convinced.

Can you believe that? What are the odds of all those unusual situations occurring for anyone else? I was stunned by the accuracy; and stunned by Steve's resistance. This was the day that I had my paradigm shift and became a believer.

Why am I telling you this? Simply as more validation for the gift that Jill has, to access the universal creative energy. For some mediums, their gift stops at this level. As I understand it, there are different vibrational levels for entities. The higher the ranking, the higher the vibrational level. Jill has the capacity to access the highest vibrational levels, which only a select few have the capacity to do. Other prophets in the past with this capacity have been Jesus Christ, Abraham, Moses and Mohammad; to name a few. According to Archangel Azrael, there are around 5000 people who may have this capacity today, but most don't have the ability to get the message out to the world.

www.anewbelief.com

16: Metatron explains our destiny and who he is

9th October 2005

I'm sat with Jill chilling after our evening meal. Jill notices Luciana stood behind me. Luciana is the 7-year-old spirit who is always with me. Her name means 'light' in Latin and Hispanic. She's the beacon of light for all children's souls who have had premature death.

She asks Jill why I don't notice her, often touching me, to let me know that she's there. Jill tells me she touches my face and it feels like cobwebs brushing across my face.

I ask when I'll be able to see her. She misunderstands me and says that it will never happen because of the bond between Jill and me. (Luciana thought I meant to see her again as 'an item'; a 'couple'.)

She goes on to say that we used to be together in 2 past lives. We're strongly connected. Once in Spain and once in Mexico. We were together, but not officially. We had secret meetings because I was very important, from an important family, with a family of my own; but my love was for Luciana who was from an unsuitable background in the eyes of my important family. We were lovers.

I explain that I meant: when can I talk to her. She said when I've learnt to meditate properly, to be able to let her energy through.

We were having a laugh, the three of us, about many things; when Jill was interrupted.

Jill: Metatron wants to speak to you.

Glenn: That's OK. Let him come through.

Jill: It's not a case of 'let him'. This angel has such a powerful presence. I've no choice. I've put him off enough times recently and he's not happy with me for that.

Jill went quiet. I could see her drifting off into the stars. It took ages for her to channel. Much longer than before. I rushed to get the Dictaphone to attempt to record her.

This is what we got:

Metatron: At last we have the ability to speak. You have many questions and we will do our best to answer them, but only if it is in the realm of God's will. I feel it is important at this time, that we look towards what fears you so.

You have pre-ordained the path that you must take. So why do you fear it so now? Why mistrust us, when the feeling within you is so strong?

Glenn: Who am I talking to?

Metatron: My name is Metatron. I have guided you since birth. I have watched over you. I have presided over you. You have chosen a hard task in this lifetime. You have chosen many, many hardships; and through those hardships you have become strong, which is what 'we' agreed.

It is important now that you follow your destiny.

Glenn: 'What' is my destiny?

Metatron: To be a teacher of the world. As you well know, but yet you deny. Do not look to the past, but look to the future. Look to what you can become. Look to where you have achieved. Your standing in this life. It has been through your own pre-determined world that you have become a reckoning; and yet, you do not believe so.

Glenn: What is it you want me to teach?

Metatron: The truth!

The truth of pain, and of the ability to change one's pain into triumph. For when one believes in one's self, one has the power to predestine their future. For so long now we have advised and tried to cajole human kind, into the forwardness of the future.

Glenn: Cajoled?

Metatron: Cajoled... We have tried to guide; to advise. Unfortunately, not in a detrimental way that free-will is 'bad' for human kind, but we would say it has outlasted what we thought would be envisaged. It has outgrown and manifested itself into something far greater than we envisaged; and we need for the sake of the universes that exist, for it to continue; but not develop at too fast a pace.

Glenn: How do you want me to get this message across?

Metatron: Your writing is the first way forward. That will give you the credibility you need. It is very important that you continue with your diary. We are very pleased with the manifestation and the way it has taken and we will continue to guide people towards you. And what we want you to do, is look towards the manifestation of the self, the ability to prophesise and create. You are of The Creator, you 'are' of God; and I know you struggle with this word God, but it is important for all human kind. They have the ability to create a better world; but when the world reveres itself towards negativity, it will create a negative environment. When the world looks towards the positivism that is available, then it can manifest many great things; including heaven.

It can re-heal the body entirely. Your cancers; your arthritis; aids; it is a man-made disease. It can be cured through the purity of the mind, heart and soul. There is no need for medicine. It is the belief systems that are withheld within the body; the human mechanism as we call it; that will manifest the well-being of the human species.

Glenn: You need to give me a strategy. Right now I have...." (Metatron cuts in.)

Metatron: (Loudly) Your problem is not a strategy. Your problem is a lack of belief.

Glenn: No; I won't accept that. I believe in Jill, her channelling and her belief system and I believe now in the after-life. You've misread me."

Metatron: I did not mislead you.

Glenn: You 'misread' me.

Metatron: I did not mislead you. Please listen. (With a deep demanding tone.) Do not be frightened of ridicule. Do not be frightened of the doors that will be closed before you. Human kind will fear the truth; and you 'do' bear the truth.

Glenn: I'm not.... (Metatron cuts in).

Metatron: Your soul and the strength you have within you, is far greater than most mankind.

Glenn: Metatron I'm not frightened of ridicule, but I need a pathway, I need a strategy, I need a plan, I need an action plan. (Metatron once again cuts me up and talks over me.)

Metatron: Your plan: write your book. Divulge your feelings and your experiences to the world. This will manifest in many interviews; many media thoughts. From that media will come very many speaking engagements; but also the ability to talk to governments, to change the education of the world. But first you must write of the pain that you have experienced and how you have grown from that.

Glenn: You talk of changing the education of the world. OK. How do you want to achieve change?

Metatron: The children have to have high self-esteem and a belief in themselves. Without this the world cannot continue. So many children are down-trodden and told they are not worthy. We must change this, and the way that we must change this, is only through education.

Glenn: Metatron, you know that I've just read many things about you. I've just read for many moments today, about you; but they are only things I have 'read' of you, Metatron who are you?"

Metatron: Bear in mind that these things that are written are not always as they seem.

Glenn: I know that; and you also know I've been waiting to talk to you... (Metatron cuts me off.)

Metatron: I am the soul of Elohim.

Glenn: Who is Elohim?

Metatron: I am the one that is 'will' of God, of The Creator. I am your one true connection to The Creator. Without me, there 'is' no Creator; there is no connection to The Creator.

Glenn: What is your connection with the other angels?

Metatron: I'm their overseer. I was chosen by The Creator to oversee the connection and the bridge between the angels and mankind.

Glenn: So it's true you 'sit beside' The Creator?

Metatron: Yes!

Glenn: Which I know I can't comprehend.

Metatron: You have no comprehension of the vastness.

Glenn: I understand.

Metatron: The energies are drawing very, very tightly now.

Glenn: What does that mean?

Metatron: It is hard for the medium here to continue her existence and control the power and the energy that I bring forth. She will struggle with this; but she knows her 'given', her permission to allow this to be.

Glenn: So how do we overcome this?

Metatron: Overcome what?

Glenn: Overcome the fact that this medium, which is my wife; I wish you'd call her my wife. She's Jill. She's my wife. If she's going to struggle with this, how am I going to be able to communicate with you, if this is the case?

Metatron: Let us clarify this. She is more than a mere wife. She has far more communication with the spirit world, than she lets on. Her energies are very finely attuned and they are not meant for this world. The negative environment does her harm. She will guide you. She will help you to achieve what needs to be done. But what we ask of you, is not blind faith; for we have shown you in many ways, what has yet to be achieved.

Glenn: Your ways of showing me are often vague.

Metatron: No they are not vague. It depends upon what you expect. You may be shown a grey sheet of paper, but you expect black. A grey sheet of paper to some, may appear black. You must be willing to face the things that we wish to fix.

Glenn: I am very open to this, but there are many things that are grey areas that you give me, for example... You asked me to meditate, but you've not taught me 'how' to meditate. I'm listening to different things. I'm listening to Jill. I 'want' to meditate. I want to be able to communicate with you, but yet you do not give me the signs. (Metatron cuts in)

Metatron: Listen to me! The way to meditate, is through your breathing. Through the prana,"

Glenn: What is prana?

Metatron: The breath of life. If you control the breathing, you will control the mind and you will free the mind to allow it to connect with you. This will be shown to you.

Glenn: How?

Metatron: The medium here, as you wish us to call her, your wife, will show you how.

Glenn: "She 'is' my wife". (Loudly)

Metatron (In an extremely assertive tone): **We.. do.. not.. take.. kind.. to your tone.** For us to show you the way, you must be willing to 'allow' us to show you the way."

Glenn: I'm happy.... (Metatron cuts in)"

Metatron: We sense your frustration.

Glenn (laughing): I'm very frustrated.

Metatron: But we also sense within you, the depth of emotion that still yet needs to be revealed.

Glenn: I'm not sure I understand that.

Metatron: It may be that you need to cry many tears for many days to release the emotions and the hurt that you still withhold within you.

Glenn: I'm almost cried out.

Metatron: But to open, we understand this and we love you. You are very special to us.

Glenn: Why?

Metatron: And we are proud of you.

Glenn: Why am I special to you, I don't understand this?

Metatron: You are special because you are unique. You have many gifts; and the gifts that you bring forth to human kind, touch many souls. You do not have to be a special 'way'. It is the very essence of you that you give to others, that brings a smile or a cheer to someone's life in a daytime.

Glenn: You were in Asda today then (smiling)!

Metatron: Hmhmm, (smiling) we are everywhere. You have a unique gift; and it's using those gifts for the betterment of mankind: a kind word, a kind deed, five minutes of your time. Not necessarily your money; of your 'time' that makes all the difference. Which is why you were chosen.

Let us look at your parents. They are hard, they are cold, they are calculating and yet if was not for them you would not have achieved half of what you have become today.

Do not look at what they have 'not' given you; look at what they have made 'of' you. They will re-enter this earth realm. They will re-learn their lessons. But you have risen above that. You have risen yourself and learnt that a soul's creation and its purpose is more than from what it was created. And there will come a day, not far from now; I will give you specifics, as you request specifics. In six years from now you will have so many friends. You will have no need of family and the yearning of what was. But to do so, all we ask of you is to be strong. You have the belief in yourself. You are good at what do, as you so say, and we do believe this in you. But what we ask is you manifest your strength in your writing to inspire and encourage people to be all they can be.

Glenn: Give me some titles.

Metatron: The leader within. Aspire to be your best. Manifesting the simplicities of life. Moving from 'being' to 'doing'. Living from the heart not the head. These and some of these titles we have given you, will be used in the future, but for now we need to look at manifesting and changing the thought processes of mankind. Bridging the gap from here to there. Helping people to cross the path and move into the light.

Glenn: Metatron, my big struggle with this, is that this is... this is intangible; it is a wish, not even a want or a need. It is a spiritual thing. And my struggle is how people will come to want to listen about this. I know you just said that if I write, the media will come, but you're asking me for blind faith in this. What is the time period over this?

Metatron: 12 months. We ask 12 months of you.

Glenn: I will give you that 12 months Metatron, but at the same time you have to understand that we need some support. We have to find some way of supporting what we have right now.

Metatron: I acknowledge your need. Are you not surviving now?

Glenn: We've just reached the non-surviving point. We are at the point now where our money has gone.

Metatron: There is more money to come.

Glenn: Thank you.

Metatron: And quicker than you realise.

Glenn: Thank you.

Metatron: You must focus your energies upon the contracts you have, and the contacts you have, but you also need to make contact with those who have used you before.

Glenn: Anybody specific?

Metatron: You will find to the South-West of the country is where you must go. Do not bother with people like Estimation who you have used before. Their time is not yet. Also though look towards the media. You must contact radio stations and television studios.

Glenn: And say what Metatron?

Metatron: Advertise yourself as someone who has knowledge of communications.

Glenn: For them it has to be controversial.

Metatron: It 'can' be controversial, if you can show people why they're going wrong; why they are not making their lives as they wish it to be. Take the strong approach, the strong spiritual approach. Look towards Dr. Phil. He's spiritual. He's enthusiastic in his approach; in his belief. He has made people believe that his way is right. You may have to give free time, but the rewards will come.

Glenn: Metatron, I will give as much free time as you want, as long as you we continue to have a reasonable lifestyle; and not lose everything that we've built before us. I know that this is just a material thing for you; but I have to hang on to that.

Metatron: You have to understand that for us, there 'is' no material.

Glenn: I understand that, but there 'is' down here, (or up here or across there) in this plane that we live; and Jill and I and our boys enjoy that.

Metatron: And you will be fine. We will always provide for you, for that is what has been ordained.

Glenn: Thank you. How long with my meditation, before I'm able to talk to you.

Metatron: That is 'how long is a piece of string?'

Glenn: That's a human trait.

Metatron: True, but if you show a willingness at a particular time, every day.

www.anewbelief.com

Glenn: When's the best time for me?

Metatron: You must decide that, it is not for us to tell you when.

Glenn: I'm asking your advice.

Metatron: When do you 'feel' a need to connect with spirit?

Glenn: Many times during the day.

Metatron: When is your feeling strongest? If you look within your heart you will find it.

Glenn: Probably evening time.

Metatron: Well that is when you must meditate.

Glenn: What of Cooper?

Metatron: He's a loving soul, but he fears you so.

Glenn: Yes he does.

Metatron: You have much strength and you're quite foreboding. A softer approach will help you. A more gentle and giving approach with your time; your touch.

Glenn: What is his spiritual destination?

Metatron: He's of the crystalline children. He is here to bridge 'after' your Indigo Child Max has been. His extreme sensitivities, whilst may annoy you, show you of his attunement to the energies and the awareness of what is around him. He is more in tune with the feminine energy because it is softer. He does not understand yet, to use his intuitive guidance of where he needs to be.

Glenn: What is Max's destiny?

Metatron: He's a great healer. He will have many trials in his life; much hardship; there will be much heartache, but he will reach the objective and his alignment with mankind. Such an expressive child. It is important his expression is allowed to continue; his creativity to be allowed to continue. He has the ability to be a great artist, a great writer, a great theologian.

Glenn: What of Brett?

Metatron: (He laughs) We may say at this time, at the moment, he is a lost cause. He has the intelligence but lacks the ability. As of your daughters they have great ability but lack the drive and the enthusiasm to continue on their pathway. But that is their choice. It is not wrong. It is the impetuousness of youth; and the lack of guidance. Do not blame yourself, they have chosen these paths. They are not you. They are not from you, they are 'of' you; there is a difference. Max and Cooper come through you, but they are not you, they are old individual souls and entities, with their own agendas which they must complete.

Glenn: Will Brett come with us to America?

Metatron: He will come with you. He is lost at the moment; he lacks direction; he lacks guidance.

Glenn: Do you have a time yet, before we move to America?

Metatron: Within six months you will move. The sale of this house will go through very finely. It will not be without its problems. Two hurdles and then you will have closure. But it is our intention that you do not leave behind what you are doing here. There is still life in what you have here, with your training and your speakership."

Glenn: And that speakership is ordained to be what?

Metatron: One of motivation, which is why you were given Motivational Training in the first place. You are a motivational person. You have the ability to inspire and recreate within people The Creator; The Oneness; Godness.

Glenn: Is it true that you in a life you were Enoch?

Metatron: I was many names including Yehwah.

Glenn: Yehwah?"

Metatron: Yehwah!

Glenn: And we understand Yehwah in Hebrew to be God?

Metatron: God comes in many forms: The Creator, Allah, Buddha. They are all one.

Glenn: I understand that, but why would you be given the name Yehwah?

Metatron: It was ordained with the one thought, the one creation, you cannot comprehend.

Glenn: I understand (Laughing.). There's an oxymoron: I understand, I cannot comprehend. I understand, I cannot comprehend, so what is your relationship to The Creator; to God?

Metatron: I am the true connection. Without me there is no connection.

Glenn: Meaning?

Metatron: I am the vein; the capillary that connects you to The Creator.

Glenn: But that would be said of Michael, Azrael, Gabriel... (Metatron interrupts)

Metatron: No! They are intermediaries, and will remain as so, as they were created as such.

Glenn: In the Bible... (Metatron laughs.) You mock?

Metatron: You must be wary of this.

Glenn: I am wary of this (Laughing.). I've not even read the Bible, but I have the tester. (The tester is our friend who has phenomenal expertise of the many Bibles.) You're aware of the tester. In the Bible it refers to people 'speaking' to God.

Metatron: The word of God has been misconstrued throughout time. For political and power usage. More so than you can imagine.

Glenn: Probably not!

Metatron: It has become a depth which has created your downfall. So much implication has been put 'on' this word. Instead of feeling the God and The Creator that we designed within; you are 'of' God, internally. Your entire being is of God; and together collectively creates the one God thought; The Creator, the universe; the entire intelligence connection.

Glenn: Azrael spoke to me of not just children, but adults; and if they don't believe they won't pass over?

Metatron: No they will not.

Glenn: How does this create an imbalance in the universe?

Metatron: When the souls pass through that do not believe; they are held in a hell (corrects); a holding area.

Glenn: Did I hear a Freudian slip there with the 'hell'? (Laughs out loud.)

Metatron: Yes! It's not hell. Mankind creates its own hell. They are held within an area, and through time; and through work; the angels; the archangels; they eventually help those souls reconnect with The Oneness. Some souls are beyond help.

Glenn: I'm not sure that you answered my question. How does it create an imbalance in the universe?

Metatron: The energies of human beings and the energy of the earth plane reverberate to a certain speed; dimension; as you wish to call it. And it is from this dimension that creates the energy to sustain and maintain the universes and galaxies that unfold before; and are not of human understanding. And when you have a lapse in one, it creates a deficit in the other or a positive in the other. Let's just look at energy. We have to be balanced. We have to have a negative and a positive. Too much positive or too much negative creates an imbalance. It cannot be sustained.

Glenn: Metatron I understand this and yet, I also understand that in the greater scheme of things, mankind has now suggested that there are 46 billion galaxies in the universe; so why should one tiny planet, with such few people, in comparison to the rest of the universe, have any effect on the universe whatsoever.

Metatron: How would you feel, if one cell within your body turned against the rest? How would that one cell within itself create disease and distortion within your very own body?

Glenn: Good analogy! Yeah I like that.

Metatron: And all it takes, is one cell, or as you call it, one bad apple, to turn the others bad. Now... Azrael wishes to speak with you, and I will leave you for now, but I will return.

Glenn: Metatron, it's been wonderful to talk to you, thank you.

Jill goes quiet. Once again her face starts to distort for Azrael. Once again she clasps her hands in the endearing way of an old, loving person with endearing words to say. Imagine that I am sat to her left. She turns her left hand, palm facing upward and places it on her left thigh, close to her knee, as if to be able to hold water in her hand. She puts her right hand, palm down, over her left hand, mirroring her left hand; and she opens and closes her right hand as she speaks; hinging from the far end of her palm. She pats her hands together like an older person would endear to a child when talking to them.

Azrael: We meet again my dear friend. You do me proud.

Glenn: Thank you.

Azrael: You write from the heart, and that is what matters. It is so important that you write from the heart, but you have not written as much as you should do mmm?

Glenn: No I haven't, but I have written today and yesterday.

Azrael: But we still need to address the real pain don't we mmm? The real pain within.

Glenn: Then you need to give me some very strict guidelines.

Azrael: Let me talk to you, plain and simple, yes? And that is the way you like it mmm?

Your pain is very important. If I was your Papa I would put my arms around you and tell you I'm so proud.

Glenn: But my Papa wouldn't do that.

Azrael: He's not your Papa. It is the needs to your creation, and what you miss is a connection, but the connection you have, is with us, your wife and your children. It is not from where you have come, it is from where you are going."

Glenn (Crying through being overwhelmed): But it's still hard. I see all these people and their parents are 'so' proud.

Azrael: They may be proud; but do they have the love and the compassion you have inside? They may seem very happy on the outside, but if you look at some of these people on the inside, they may be cold. Very cold. They have no belief. They have no love. They may be close to one another, but they despise one another, they're jealous of one another. So do not deceive yourself. There is no perfect family out there.

Glenn: (Despairingly) What do you want of me?

Azrael: I am here to give you guidance and love. It is not what 'I' want of 'you', but what 'you' want of 'me'.

Glenn: I don't know what I want of you. I have a wonderful wife. I have wonderful children, I'm happy to spread the words that you want me to spread, as long as we are happy. I'm fed up of being unhappy. We're happy 'now', but I've been unhappy most of my life.

Azrael: Now that you have happiness, it will continue. Happiness is what is created from within. You have within you a sense of pride, and a sense of direction. Many great leaders have no one but themselves to believe in.

Glenn: It's this blind faith that I can't get to grips with.

Azrael: Instead of blind faith, think of faith in one's self.

Glenn: I'm a person that needs direction.

Azrael: You've always had direction. You've always found your own way; so why are you looking to an outer source like me or Metatron to give you any more direction?

Glenn: We're at an all time low, where we have no work; no income. We were expecting to leave here, to be in America. It's not happened. We don't know which way to turn. We don't know how to start. We don't particularly want to start, because we're expecting to go; and it's like a vortex. We feel like we're being sucked in.

Azrael: You're not. Re-create what you have here. It is not a case of starting something to let it all go. You can take what you have with you anywhere. And people will pay. The problem is you dropped the stirring spoon that re-created for you, everything you had. You gave up and expected to move on; and this is what is your problem.

Glenn: But you now want me to take a new direction; and the direction seems vague.

Azrael: Why does it seem vague? In what way does it seem vague? We have asked you to speak of your pain. To write. And as you are writing, it will bring you the openings that you wish. From that we have also indicated that we wish you to approach, as Metatron has asked you; the radio stations; the media; to get the message out. It's controversial. It is something that will bring distinction.

Let us look at another mortal here that is trying to bring much change to the world. Mister Oliver. Jamie Oliver. You know him, yes? He is rising against many great odds, to get a message through. And he is using whatever means he can. And that is the way for you too. You see, people do not respect things if it is handed to you on a plate. If we suddenly opened a communication channel; and say for example you were on Oprah; more people would listen; but they would ask, "Where has this man come from? From what experience does he speak?"

People need to see other people suffer, to understand and connect; that you too have suffered, know their way. And only through this medium of suffering; as did Jesus Christ have suffering; believe, and we get the message across.

We are not asking you to be poverty stricken and we are not asking you to be without; but we cannot allow you a full open door.

Your credibility will be questioned and ridiculed beyond your dreams. You have to prove from where you have come from. The pain you have suffered. And how you have belief in yourself; you have created for yourself and in the world.

Glenn: But what's the message? There's always got to be a message for people to want to buy into.

Azrael: The message you need to give is that if you want to change your life, you have to change yourself.

Glenn: But there are hundreds of people doing the same thing out there Azrael.

Azrael: Yes, but in the wrong way because they do it for their own needs, and not for the needs of mankind. And they do not talk to children. They talk to adults.

Glenn: And now I have a misnomer, because Metatron wants me to talk to the adults, to get the message to the children, and now you're telling me... (Azrael cuts in.)

Azrael: No, no, no, no, no! I am not telling you just to talk to the children; but the people that are speaking or talking the same or similar language that you think they are; are expecting the adults to change. What we wish you to do, is to speak to the parents, to get them to understand that if they want the best for their children, they must help to change the children; and themselves.

Glenn: In what way?

Azrael: Write your book, about your pain. Let the parents identify with that pain. And then speak to the parents and say to them, "You are not happy where you are now. But you can make your children better happier people, by helping them to see they do not have to be the way that you have become. Now do you understand, mmm?

Glenn: Aha!

Azrael: It is a slow process; and yes we understand it is a hard process. In between that, you will get many engagements and many speaking engagements.

Glenn: About what?

Azrael: About your communication and your behaviour. You must not let that go. It is a means to an end to help you provide for your family; but also until such time; and unfortunately until you are 60, you will not reap the real benefits of this, but look towards regenerating as you have the children.

Glenn: What happens when I get to 60?

Azrael: Oh you have 'much' before you at 60, but for you the realisation of your dreams, or as you call it; the glory: it will be 60 my dear.

Glenn: How long do I keep Jill?

Azrael: We cannot say at this time. Whist ever you write and whilst ever there is a need, she will be here.

Glenn: I love her so much (crying).

Azrael: We know that. She loves you too. But she also has another calling.

Glenn: Does Max; does Cooper have a calling?

Azrael: He does, but not as great as Max. He is sensitive to the world's environment. But it remains for him to decide the pathway he must walk.

Glenn: Will Max be successful?

Azrael: Very successful. You have no fear for Max. He is a true survivor. We leave you now. We will speak again.

Glenn: Azrael, I need you to answer me some questions.

Azrael: You have two questions and then I must go.

Glenn: You're limiting me?

Azrael: Yes, for tonight. The energies are growing weak. We can only sustain your wife with the energy and she is growing very weak.

Glenn: Tell me your thoughts on religion.

Azrael: There is no religion for me.

Glenn: Tell me what your thoughts are of the religion of mankind.

Azrael: For that we do not have enough hours. (Laughing, and I laugh out loud too.)

There are many conspiracies and many theories that is so, so wrong for human kind; yet we cannot go into this at this at this moment in time. But I would ask that you be very wise and very prudent when you look at what you see when it comes to political and religious instruction, for they are 'one'.

Glenn: OK. You asked me, and this is my second question; you asked me to speak to ministries and to churches, yet the other day I spoke to a friend of mine, and I've already had a block.

Azrael: Do not worry where he is concerned.

Glenn: How do I approach the churches and the ministries? With what kind of speech, and what kind of message that you want me to get across?

Azrael: How to communicate with God. You see, for many people they pray to God, "Help me this; help me that," but they're not specific, and like communication, as you very well know, you must be specific. It's the intonation, the words that you use, the language, the body language that you use when you talk to someone. And it is the same with the universe.

Glenn: And the meditation?

Azrael: The meditation for you and the prayer is important; but you need to grasp it before you can preach it. But for now, you could market yourself and put yourself towards the churches and ministries; and offer yourself as a way of how to communicate with God. How to communicate with the angels.

So many people, they question, "Can you help me?"

Help you what? There are so many areas, and you have free will. You were granted free will. We cannot interfere with this free will of yours.

Glenn: So Jill is here to help me how to get this message across and how to pray to God?

Azrael: Your wife here, she can help you. But also, look at what you have learnt with your communication when you wish to communicate to another. As you so rightly say, "Write not to be merely understood. But write so you cannot be misunderstood. And that is the same with prayer mmm?

Glenn: Mmm.

Azrael: Now. We have to go.

Glenn: Azrael. I want to be able to communicate with Luciana. When am I going to be able to communicate with her?

Azrael: Today is not the time.

Glenn: I know. Not today. (Crying) I want to be able to talk to her.

Azrael: You and her have a very special bond; and time and space cannot break that. But we must reconnect the energies of your wife. Yes?

Glenn: Yes. Thank you.

Jill was ages coming back around.

Glenn: Jill? Jill? Jill?

Jill; Ohhhh (With tears streaming down her face.) I didn't want to come back. I was sohhh happy. So happy. Uuuuugghhh. So at peace. Ohhh I didn't want to come back. It was lovely. I was at peace...fabulous. Ohhhh. I don't want to be here.

Oh Glenn, if you could go there. I could die. So beautiful. So peaceful.

The following morning Jill was really depressed. She explained that the channelling not only drained her, but each time she channels for the angels she goes to a place of peace, serenity, beauty and happiness. She's so at peace. The more she goes, the more depressed she becomes when she returns; so she doesn't want to do it anymore.

Jill has free will; but it seems that the will of these angels is stronger.

17: Jill's input from her spirit guide

12th October 2005

Jill: Still feeling doubtful about the validity of what I was channelling, I asked my guide if Yehwah, was really correct and how could I validate this with proof. My guide, White Cloud said to go to Exodus 6 in the Bible and read versus 2 to 3, where I read the following:-

2. And God spake unto Moses, and said unto him, I am the Lord:
3. And I appeared unto Abraham, unto Isaac, and unto Jacob, by the name of God Almighty, but by my name JEHOVAH was I not known to them.

When I read this I didn't understand. My guide, White Cloud said JEHOVAH should be pronounced Yehwah.

13th October 2005.

I was getting the children ready for school and noticed Glenn was sat down, reading. I thought nothing of this, and carried on, when White Cloud said to me, "Go and see what Glenn's reading." I went over and casually glanced at Glenn who was reading a book called 'The Holy Scriptures', trying to find alternative names for God in the index in the back. I was directed to one of the pages. White Cloud said, "Look for Moses." I searched on the page and found his name and asked White Cloud, "Now what?"

White Cloud said to me that the stories about Moses were myths and that this was just the start of the controversy to come. He said that the Bible was originally kept as sacred text by a sect of Jews. Their aim was political control.

The Greeks had their gods; but the Jews at that time didn't. They saw how the Greeks held control and power over the people. So they created something similar. It was about the same time that Amenoteph; a great Egyptian leader, who was the scribe who built the first pyramid, introduced Monotheism; and it is a fight now between all these powerful religions for supreme control and domination of the world.

Each religion has used, abused, tortured and pillaged; in the name of their own man-made god.

It was originally forbidden for lesser mortals to read and interpret what had been written. The reason for this was to bring about propaganda that if they read the text, they would suffer the wrath of God. This was a measure of fear and control, to ensure that the power and wealth were maintained by the elite few who had decided to control the crowds; and also to ensure they learnt to think a certain way.

The sacred texts were, at the time, withheld from common men and women to read and interpret for themselves, as this would give the possibility of questioning what was written. But it is now spirit's intention that truth sets us free.

White Cloud said the Egyptians were renowned for their collating of historical facts; and numerous papyrus and stone carvings bore witness to the truths of that time. By researching we will find that in Egyptian history, there is not one piece of Egyptian historical data that speaks the name of Moses or the exodus of the Jews at that time.

My guide tells me that those who follow the Bible 'literally', in fact worship a false god, a man-made god; and for too long now have we killed our brothers and sisters in the name of this false god.

White Cloud then directed me to the '10 Commandments':

Commandment 4: Thou shall not make unto thee any graven image, or any likeness of any thing that is in heaven above, or that is in the earth beneath, or that is in the water under the earth.

Yet people worship the cross, the Bible, Jesus and the Madonna; which according to God; are all false idols.

To put this into perspective: God is the one thought; the infinite intelligence; the creative energy. Not an idol! God is within. We are our own temple; to worship, nurture and develop. Belief has to start in ourselves. One collective thought. No idols.

There are no Roman records of Jesus being crucified on a cross, whereas they kept records at that time. Jesus 'was' crucified; he was tortured and persecuted; but not on a cross. Yet we worship the cross, another false idol.

The truth is that it is the religious societies that are the evil; not the good people that run their ministries; they act in good faith. The organisations above them (If the truth is known.)will lose all power and riches they have amassed through torture, propaganda and wars fought in the name of The Creator.

www.anewbelief.com

White Cloud said we have yet to (as we would call it) 'Rock the Casbah'.

Many more truths are to be revealed.

Jill: These are not my personal thoughts. These are the words that I'm given. Whilst I find this intriguing, at the same time I'm fearful of what the spirits will reveal to me through time; and whether or not it will jeopardise my family and I.

18: Bible or babble?

If you took a census with Christians in the Western World; it would be interesting to see how many people have read the Bible.

If you go to www.adherents.com there may still be a wonderful pie chart on the distribution of religion in the world.

It shows the major religions; of which as far as we can establish, in 2005, there were in the region of 2.1 billion Christians, 1.3 billion Islamics and 900 million Hindus (The big three.); in a population of 6,446,131,400 according to USA CIA records in July 2005.

So out of 2.1 billion people, how many have read ALL the pages of the Bible? I suspect less than 1%. Then we need to consider; which Bible did they read?

Did they understand it? Were they even literate enough to understand it? I'm not intending to belittle people here; but it's a fact that the youth of today, on average, have a poor vocabulary. The average adult only has the vocabulary of a bright 12-year-old. This leaves much to consider. Just how many Christians are Christians because they're expected to be? How many Christians will stand by and support the Bible, simply because they are Christians, even though they may have never read it themselves?

As I'm correcting the spelling and grammar in this book, it's my birthday; 6th February 2006. There is currently an uprising around the world because two newspapers have published a cartoon which denigrates the prophet Mohammad. Millions of Muslims are protesting in anger. Yet I've spent time in the Middle East these last few months and the Muslims told me that to read and understand the Quran, takes virtually a lifetime. So here is another religion where the vast majority of the followers take the word of Islam at face value from others.

There are three main methods of translation of the Bible.

Literal translation: attempts to keep the exact words and phrases of the original. It's faithful to the original text, but sometimes hard to understand. It keeps a constant historical distance. Examples are: King James and New American Standard.

Dynamic equivalent translation: attempts to keep a constant accuracy of history and facts, but updates the writing style and grammar to attempt to give us the most natural, easy to understand translation. Examples are: New International Version (NIV) and New English Bible.

Free translation (to paraphrase): translates the ideas from the original text, but without being constrained by the original words or language. This seeks to eliminate old words and phraseology. It's very readable, but not always exact, because interpretation depends upon the translators. This makes the Bible more readable; but is subject to how the author understands and interprets the text; which must give the translation the author's behavioural opinion and slant. Example: Contemporary English Version (CEV), "The Message."

Add to this the many different styles of the above translations and interpretations. Here are 'some' of them:

Traditional: Text only. Minimal footnotes.

Study Bible: Sometimes called a Student Bible or Learning Bible. Study Bibles usually have extensive footnotes and explanatory notes at the side of the page, or embedded in the text. They may also have extensive cross-references, a narrative commentary, and maps. (Some also have a cyclopaedia index and/or a concordance—see Reference Bible below.)

Reference Bible: Usually has a cyclopaedia index (Like an encyclopaedia with a reference to the verse where the word or thought is used.), a concordance (Like a dictionary of common words, with examples of their usage and verse references for each example.) and maps.

"Place in Life" Bible: Has meditations and thoughts about issues of concern to people at a particular stage in life. There are versions of these Bibles aimed at men, women, sports players, recovering addicts, new believers, converted Jews, small group members, and many others.

One-Year Bibles: Are divided into 365 readings for each day of the year, usually with each having a portion of the Old Testament, New Testament, Psalms, and Proverbs.

Pastor's Bible: Includes protocol outlines and recommended verses for hospital visits, weddings, funerals, and other events. It often has answers to frequently asked questions.

Children's Bible: Usually includes colour drawings, maps, and simplified stories.

Parallel Bible: Has from two to eight translations side by side.

Chronological Bible: The entire Bible in one continuous story, with narration to cover gaps and make everything flow.

The four gospels are harmonised into one, for example, and the writings of the prophets are placed in the proper place.

The Serendipity Bible.

The Quest.

Key Word Bible.

Leadership Bible.

Hebrew-Greek Keyword Bible.

"Here's Hope" Bible.

Serenity Bible.

Now take into account that there are over 140 translations of these Bibles into languages other than English.

Are you starting to get the message?

Each time a Bible is re-translated and re-interpreted from the original writings, there has to be a loss of some kind from the original text.

Let me give you a few examples, just in the misinterpretation of English. (Now is that English USA or English UK I hear someone thinking.):-

The buck stops here: It's my responsibility.

The buck stops here: This is where the buck stays.

The buck stops here: The young animal stops here.

The buck stops here: The buckwheat stops here.

The book stops here: This is where the book will stop.

The book stops here: This is where the book stays.

OK; here's another:-

I didn't say she stole my money.

It wasn't me!

I **didn't** say she stole my money.

I definitely didn't say it!

I didn't **say** she stole my money.

I might have inferred it, but I didn't say it.

I didn't say **she** stole my money.

It was someone else.

I didn't say she **stole** my money.

But she's done something with it.

I didn't say she stole **my** money.

She stole someone else's money.

I didn't say she stole my **money.**

She stole something else!

Seven words in a sentence, allowing seven different interpretations of the same sentence. The emphasis on the word creates the interpretation.

Here's yet another one to look at:

Woman is now here.
Woman is nowhere.

Just by closing the gap between two words gives us two almost opposite meanings from the same letters.

Here's another; only this time, if you're a man, ask a woman to place commas in the right place and read it out aloud:

Woman without her man is nothing.

The vast majority of men read; Woman without her man, is nothing.

The vast majority of women read; Woman, without her, man is nothing. Try it out with your friends and family.

So a man interprets things differently sometimes, than a woman does.

Women are more emotive and are more likely to give a more emotional account of events, whereas men are more likely to 'report' on events, without the emotion. My understanding is that the Bible has been written in the main by men.

Here's an email that was sent to me in 2002 which will give you a feeling about the difference in the way that some men and women think; and communicate events.

Her side of the story:

He was in an odd mood on Saturday night. We planned to meet at a pub for a drink. I spent the afternoon shopping with the girls and I thought it might have been 'my' fault because I was a bit later than what I'd promised; but he didn't say much about it. The conversation was very slow going, so I thought we should go off somewhere more intimate, so that we could talk more privately.

We went to a restaurant and he was 'still' acting a little strange. I tried to cheer him up; and started to wonder whether it was me, or something else. I asked him; but he said no. But I wasn't really sure. So, anyway, in the car on the way back home, I told him that I loved him deeply; but he just put his arm around me and said nothing. I didn't know what the hell that meant, because, you know, he didn't say it back to me or anything. This is really worrying me.

We finally got home and I was wondering if he was going to tell me he was leaving me; so I tried to get him to talk; but he just switched on the T.V. He sat with a distant look in his eyes, that seemed to say it was all over between us.

Reluctantly, I told him I was going to bed. Then, after about ten minutes, he came upstairs and joined me; and to my surprise, he responded to my advances and we made love. But he still seemed really distracted. I wanted to confront him, but I was afraid of the rejection, so I silently cried myself to sleep.

I just don't know what to do anymore. I mean, I really think he must be seeing someone else; and that our relationship is about to end. I feel my life is turning into a disaster; and I'll be left all on my own.

His side of the story:
England lost at football. Managed to get 'laid' though!

Just imagine what it would be like if we'd got Mary Magdalene's version of events whilst with Jesus.

And if you think 'that's' interesting; take a look at this:

THE IMPORTANCE OF CORRECT PUNCTUATION

Dear Glenn:
I want a man who knows what love is all about. You are generous, kind, thoughtful. People who are not like you admit to being useless and inferior. You have ruined me for other men. I yearn for you. I have no feelings whatsoever, when we're apart. I can be forever happy – will you let me be yours?
Kim

Dear Glenn:
I want a man who knows what love is. All about you are generous, kind, thoughtful people, who are not like you. Admit to being useless and inferior. You have ruined me. For other men, I yearn. For you, I have no feelings whatsoever. When we're apart, I can be forever happy. Will you let me be?
Yours,
Kim

From Games Magazine (1984)

"Don't write merely to be understood.
Write so that you can't possibly be misunderstood."
Robert Louis Stevenson (1850-1894) Writer

Here's a scenario which might make you smile. This is what might have happened many years ago:

Jesus Christ: I'm so happy to be spreading the word of God. I need to take his word to as many people as possible.

Next person: Jesus has decided he's going to start speaking about God to everyone.

Next person: Jesus has been thinking about telling everyone he's talking to God.

Next person: They tell me that Jesus thinks he's the only person who can speak to God and he wants to tell everyone about it.

Next person: If Jesus keeps telling everyone he's the only person that can speak to God, the priests will crucify him with their heckling.

Next person: Jesus won't stop saying that he's the only one that can talk to God; and the priests want him crucified.

Next person: Jesus is going to be crucified for talking to God. God will be angry.

Next person: God's angry, so he's having Jesus crucified for talking back at him.

Next person: Jesus had a go at God while he was being crucified and made him angry.

Next person: God's really angry that Jesus has been crucified. All hell broke loose. By the way, have we met before?

Next person: No I don't think so. Jesus! Jesus Christ.

What message am I trying to deliver here? That the vast majority of people who call themselves Christians, have never read the Bible. Those that have, may have read 'one' of the many different versions out there and it may not be the best translation. Those that haven't but have listened to extracts from the Bible, have listened to someone reading from one of those many versions; giving their 'own' interpretation of what it might mean.

When the people who wrote on the papyrus scrolls, which became a part of the books of the Bible, were writing; what were they thinking at the time? Did they get their message down in the way that they 'meant' to? Did they get the message down in the exact way that they heard it? If they saw it, did they interpret what they saw correctly, or did they make the same assumptions that many people do?

Example: Someone drives past the aftermath of a road accident that's just happened. They didn't see it, yet they tell people they've just seen a horrific accident and explain who hit who. They mean well, but aren't always right.

How often have you read something yourself and interpreted it one way, only to have someone say to you, "But I didn't mean it to 'sound' like that! This is what I meant!"...

The written word is so fickle. It's easily misinterpreted without the emotion, feeling, mannerisms, 'slang understanding' and correct word emphasis that went with the writer's thoughts.

Now consider that all the written words about Jesus were written at least 130 years after his death. There was no-one around by that time, to tell the nearest possible to the truth. So all we have are generations of accounts of Jesus; stories, with 'some' truth.

Most people who are Christians, and indeed for other religions, are too lazy to delve into the truth and are happy to accept that which was written. It makes for an easy life.

Just consider how easy it is to blame God, when people don't have their prayers answered. Now consider the threat of knowing how to be able to talk to God; and how to connect to God. This means that if they can't, they will consider themselves a failure and not be able to put the onus failure on a God, who perhaps was too busy to listen to them before.

Another example of how a message is misunderstood:-

The UK and the USA are two nations divided by a language: Fag in the USA is slang for a homosexual, yet in the UK it's slang for a cigarette. This gets Brit males into a lot of trouble asking for fags in US bars. In the USA the English bonnet of a car is a hood. The boot is a trunk. A sun roof can be a moon roof. The gearbox is the transmission. Silencer is muffler. Spanner is wrench.

The pavement is the sidewalk and the road is the pavement. Lifts are elevators. Petrol is Gas. Oil is Lube. Lager is beer. Trousers are pants. Pants are briefs. 'Pants' is a recent expression in the US for something you don't like. Lycra is Spandex. Cling-film is Ceram-wrap. Courgettes are zukini. Aubergines are eggplants. A US gallon is 17% smaller than a UK gallon (Imperial gallon.) Biscuits are cookies. A bun is a muffin. I daren't tell you what muffin' means in the UK.

A bread roll is a bun. Bum is butt. Backside is fanny. Fanny in the UK is a vagina. Headmaster is Principal. Shoe-lace is shoe-string. Film is movie. Lady's finger is okra. Wardrobe is closet. Lorry is truck. Toilet is bathroom. Loo is John. Flat is apartment. Braces are suspenders. A queue is a line.

A rubber is an eraser. A condom is a rubber. (Young people from the UK get into hot sweats with this one in convenience stores in the USA.)

Chips are fries. Crisps are chips. Moulting of hair is known as shedding. UK ground floor is a first floor in the USA. Autumn is fall. Underground is subway. Dummy is pacifier. Women's tights are panty hose. Dustbin is a trash can. Rubbish is trash. Nappy is diaper. Caravan is trailer. Estate agent is Realtor.

Jam is jelly. Jelly is jello. Marrow is squash. Football is soccer. Garden is yard. Tap is faucet. Articulated lorry is tractor-trailer. Trainers are sneakers. Treacle is molasses. Waistcoat is vest. Vest is undershirt. Porridge is oatmeal. People-car is van. Van is truck. Estate-car is shooting-break or station-wagon. 4X4 is SUV.

You get similar local differences in language the world over. This is where interpretation breaks down.

The Bible was written by men (Maybe women too; I can't be sure.), not by God. Perhaps if God wanted us to have a God Manual; a Creation Manual or a Life's Journey Manual; he'd have dictated it himself/herself/itself.

What if some young Hebrew scholars got together at a 'frat party' a few thousand years ago and decided to write a few books, just to see what might happen to them in the future; write them separately, so there were different accounts; pass a chain letter on to the Greeks to do the same; chuck a few in the Dead Sea, and leave a few around for people to find? It's not impossible! Unlikely, but not impossible.

There are other books written at similar periods to the Bible; yet they didn't make it to print, in the Bible.

So what we 'have' to go on, is 'seeded' information. We only get to read what some Religious organisation 'wants' or 'allows' us to read.

Taking all those interpretations apart, with what's left for us to read in the Bible, it's reasonable to apply the 80:20 law.

The 80:20 law, discovered by Vilfredo Pareto in the late 18th century. He discovered that the Law of the Universe dictated that mankind never puts in 100% of effort all of the time; and that there is always a disproportionate amount of reward from effort put in: 20% of effort often brought in 80% of the reward.

80% of the time, man is idle; but the 20% of hard work brings in 80% of the reward.

Pareto applied this to business in Italy, and then all over the world: 20% of customers give 80% of income. And then he applied it to life: You won't see all of the carpet in the room all of the time. 20% is covered. 20% of all road traffic accidents are caused by people under the age of 25, which results in 80% of the cost of 'all' accidents. 80% of the cost of all criminal damage is the responsibility of 20% of the criminals. Only 20% of the clothes in your wardrobe are worn regularly.

And so it goes on. In this case we can say that 80% of the interpretation and translation of the Bible(s) has the same meaning.

But please don't look at any Bible and think that every word is 'chipped in stone'; sacrosanct.

Treat it as a guide; and remember, there are lots of other great books out there to help you with your life. The books in the Bible are thousands of years old. Times have changed. We've moved on. The pace is faster.

Is it any wonder that people don't read the Bible in the archaic way it was written?

Here's another thought for you about how we can get history wrong:

Heard of Shakespeare? The playwright? What many people aren't aware of, is that he never recorded his name the way that I just wrote it. Apparently there are 12 other recorded ways he wrote his name e.g., Shackspear, Shuckspear. Shakespur; but never recorded as Shakespeare.

He used supposedly old English words such as thou, thee, art thou, dust thou. We seem to have interpreted these plays as though 'well educated' people were supposed to use them.

So here's a thought. What if Shakespeare was writing about the 'common man'?

I came from a 'rough' 'common man' area of Sheffield in Yorkshire in the UK. I'm going to try and phonetically (as it sounds) write some Yorkshire slang:

"H'art tha doin thee?" "Dust tha no wot thart doin?

How are you doing you? Do you know what you're doing?

Shakespeare may have written: "How art thou doing thee? Dust thou know what thou art doing?"

Get the picture?

Last night (14th September 2005) I flicked the T.V. over to see how many religious channels there were on Satellite T.V.

I was curious, because 10 years ago when I looked, there was only one: The God Channel. Last night there were 11 religious channels.

God is big business. The Bible is big business. It was interesting to see a very good presenter on God Channel 2 interpreting the Bible to a huge crowd of people.

He DIDN'T say, "This is what this verse 'might' mean." He proceeded to force his ideas and opinions on the crowd of people, as to what 'he' thought it meant. There was no discussion. No 'what if?'. Just preaching.

Mankind has free will and can veer or be veered in whichever direction they please. I just wish that more of us would 'wake up and smell the roses'.

The Bible is a history book. There are other great history books. There are great spiritual books. And there are great books on self-awareness, self-improvement and self-esteem.

Most people who attend Ministry speaking events and churches are seeking salvation. Salvation starts from within. You have to find 'yourself' first. Who 'are' you? How do you behave? What are your values? Where do you want to be, or go in your life? How will you get there?

Most people are drifting. There's an old saying. "If you're on the road to no-where, you'll get there. There's another! "If you don't know in which direction you're going, you'll get there."

Here's another: "If you keep on doing the same old things, you'll get the same results; or worse."

The Bible is a tradition. A very old tradition. Treat it that way. Take some things with a 'pinch of salt'. Challenge it!

My Archangel mentor, Azrael, tells me that salvation has to start within you. You have to learn about self-reliance and self-esteem so you can help yourself. God isn't going to help you. Even in the Bible there are words from God saying not to look to him for help, you need to help yourself.

Here's an interesting question I came across on a web site:

"I was reading your web page on the King James version of the Bible. I'm hoping you can answer a question for me?

Is there a difference in the King James Bibles? You said that you use the 'authorized' KJV.

I have a Spirit Filled Life Bible, a Thompson Chain , a 1917 Schofield Reference edition, and a Full Life Study Bible, all in the KJV. But only the Schofield says "authorized". Is there a difference? I have been very confused about Bible versions, to the point where I felt tormented with doubt. I have purchased so many different ones trying to find peace as I read. I have the NIV, NAS, RSV, LB, NLT, and NKJV. (All in all, I have 21 Leather Bibles.). How's that for confusion?

My husband has always stuck with his King James, but I had to read everything and now have a whole sack of confusion and heartache.

Can you help? Which one do I use?

I want to know and receive every word God has to say and I don't want verses missing or changed anymore. I'd really appreciate any advice you have. Thank you."

This lady is really 'lost'. I hope she finds her way to this book. Her name or contact details weren't available.

She seems to be putting all her faith in finding the original words of God in a Bible.

If she really wants to know and receive every word God has to say; she's going to have to live for a very long time.

There's an argument that no-one in the Bible references has 'ever' spoken to God. It seems there's a lot of confusion about whether people were speaking to an angel acting for God, or even acting 'as' God. Archangel Azrael tells me that mankind is not in a position to communicate with The Creator. We can't comprehend the communication channel; so the communication is via the angels. But then again, Jill and I just might be verging on madness: Jill for channelling, and me for listening. Time will tell.

My recommendation is that this lady gets in touch with her spiritual side through meditation. Done right, she should be able to communicate with angels; the messengers of The Creator.

But here's another old saying: "Be careful what you ask for, because you just might get it."

Getting in touch with angels may be too much for the person who's unprepared. The unprepared person may think of it as a sign of madness. Be prepared.

This lady needs to recognise that the Bible is the writings of mankind, and not God.

Scientists are finally having to admit that they keep coming across an intelligence that they can't account for.

The world used to be flat; or so we believed.

We BELIEVED the world was flat.

We BELIEVED that mankind would never fly.

We BELIEVED that we'd never be able to run a mile in less than 4 minutes.

We BELIEVED that man would never be able to get to the moon (But there's another conspiracy debate.).

Beliefs are programmes in the sub-conscious mind.

Beliefs are very powerful.

It will take a long time for people to eventually get round to believing that what most people call God, is an energy force that we can't comprehend; that angels are the messengers of this energy force; that the soul is part of a complex balance of the universe; and that without the belief in the soul, the after-life, The Creator and angels; the soul doesn't pass on; which upsets the balance of the universe. This is The Creator's concern; so Azrael tells me.

19: Archangel Chamuel; our third angel encounter

23rd October 2005

Jill is channelling.

Jill: What is Faith?
Chamuel: To experience connecting with The Creator, you must examine this moment closely. Just focus your attention on the 'now'. Ask yourself, what is it that's different about this present moment from anything else you've ever experienced or will experience in the future? We're well aware you may have an infinite number of answers, but your experience 'now' is something completely different.

To be at one with spirit is a state of 'knowing', which you may prefer to call faith. You see, most things you claim to be true or know, is actually just opinions you have formed and chosen to believe in. It's important you learn to differentiate between your beliefs and your inner knowing.

It is human to question your beliefs; but tapping into your inner knowing is connecting with your heart and with The Creator, God. You don't need to dismiss your beliefs and opinions, for many of human kind's opinions can contain moments of truth, beauty and validity.

Jill: What's the real reason for the Bible?
It was meant to help you learn mistakes of the past; to help save you from repeating these same mistakes, but unfortunately through mankind's desire to be a god themselves, and wield power over others, they have taught human kind that the only way to heaven is to believe in death and the resurrection of Christ.

History is meant to save you from repeating the mistakes of your brothers and sisters. Yet the church instead has made you believe you should live to the Bible code literally; and this is wrong. When human kind creates differences which divide people, they create a devil. The devil is not some 'one' or 'greater entity'.

The Bible was channelled through chosen prophets such as yourself to guide and assist. Now I know I stress this point many times; but the Bible has now become a devil in so much as it causes mankind to take it too literally. Human kind is too busy looking for God; The Creator; which ever suits you. They miss the 'knowing' that they are already 'with' God.

It is not a question of faith. It is an inner awareness; an inner knowing. Just like the inner knowing of what's truly right and truly wrong. There wouldn't be enough tears in the galaxies for the times we've tried to help those who blindly refuse to be open to receiving the God within.

You must ask yourself this question, "Why did the Bible only come about once mankind had learnt to read and write?"

You don't need a book or a set of rules to follow and connect with God, for you see, one way for one, may not be the same way for another. For you are all unique aspects of The Creator, God. Now we know you will have some people protest that before the Bible, 'everyone' was evil. But this is wrong. You see the Bible is a record of a person's moment. You can never know the truth, for you were not there. All you have is the person's accountability. Yes, parts are true, poignant and valid. Yet a lot in the Bible isn't.

To have faith in The Creator; God; is to know that you possess many unique beautiful qualities which The Creator, together with you, experience. Look at the greatness of human kind when they put aside their differences and work together as one. When you work in an awareness of love and compassion you are working through the divine purpose. Yes you are all different in looks, colour and beliefs; but together on the inside you are all one; and all together the power of The Creator is complete.

We are sure you'll need to ponder what has been brought to you. But this knowledge is given by us for the betterment of mankind, this blessed planet and its part in the universes.

We will agree to confer for a few more minutes, as we're well aware of your resistance to long drawn out channelling. This isn't meant as a criticism, but a mere observation; and we sometimes forget the heaviness of the physical body which makes the transference of energies even harder.

Blessed be.
Chamuel Elohim Gabor.

Later...... More on faith...

Chamuel: Whilst ever mankind continues to see themselves as separate entities, and have the mind-set that they're fighting against each other, the planet will continue to be one of fighting and evilness.

We're here to help you connect with The Creator; God. You know the difference between good and bad. You have free will to consciously choose which way to live your life. If you wish to be free and connect with God, you can do so by changing your unconscious patterns of thought and behaviour; by recognising these patterns and choosing to change them.

We are asking the human race to undergo personal transformations, which will require total honesty with themselves about their negative thoughts and negative actions. This is not about teaching you to feel unworthy, but to help you recognise your weaknesses and change them into your strengths. Work from the heart and not the head. Life was meant to be a journey of transformation to help bring about your evolution.

Learn to experience the now. The pleasures of who you're with; what they bring to you; what you have learnt by spending time with them; what you have shared with them in the process. Yes they may be different and have beliefs that you may find hard to accept, but if their beliefs have opened you up to the possibility of considering what they have said, you have connected with another part of The Creator. Put your opinions to one side. Become conscious of the moment and you will experience a great shift in your consciousness.

Free yourselves from the prison of your opinions. If you truly come to know yourself, you will know The Creator; God.

Not long from now; the devil; the dividers of this world, will fall down quicker than you can imagine. The religions of this world that were created by mankind to conquer, divide and control, will have no standing any longer.

Already science has shown the discrepancies; and many humans are in the midst of a transitional phase, where enlightenment is very near. It is important that people learn to adapt their behaviour and thought processes to bring about the radical change that is so desperately needed. To do this, we need human kind to begin to change the way the children of this world are taught.

Children are born without discrimination. It is taught to them by adults. Children are born bearers of truth. Adults teach them how to use deceit and lies. Children are born positive and helpful. Adults teach negativity and to pass by people who need help. Children see the world through the eyes of The Creator; God. Adults see the world through their own eyes, which are full of fear, prejudices, negativity and greed.

     www.anewbelief.com

Harsh words you may say, but truth can sometimes be harsh. Children need to be guided and accepted for who they are, yet time and time again, humans try to mould children into beings completely different from the path they were meant to tread.

Let us explain.... With Max you suffer great anxiety and frustration because he doesn't follow your desires. Yet if you were to be open to his way of thinking and behaviour, you would find his acceptance of your guidance and not barriers. You allow yourself to become frustrated, yet Max is merely expressing his own thoughts. Look at Max's enthusiasm for life; his humour, his desire to be noticed and pleasing to others. These beautiful aspects of The Creator; God that is within him, should not be stifled, but allowed to lead and inspire others. Yes there are times, when perhaps a little moderation is required. A gentle hand will do a hundred fold more good than a heavy hand.

When you have the courage to be open to all the possibilities of life, and to know yourself, then you will know The Creator; God. When you're willing to be charitable to others without looking for a return, you will know The Creator; God. When you have the 'knowing' of your strengths and the power to create your own environment, you will know The Creator; God. When you are willing to build your life without dividers and operate from a conscious and unconscious love perspective, you will discover the world The Creator; God wanted you to have, since the first 'one thought' of your creation.

In celestial joy and love for the betterment of mankind.

Chamuel – Elohim Gabor

20: Joseph of Aramathea, Metatron and Azrael

25th October 2005

When this event happened in the evening, around 9.00pm, we had no idea who Joseph was, so we didn't feel a need to organise a recording of the conversation. It was only when we did an internet search for Joseph Aramathea, that we were stunned and emotionally overcome, when we realised who it was: the uncle and disciple of Jesus Christ who history (or legend) has it, took Mary Magdalene and Lazarus to Marseilles in France, and then went on to Somerset in England, which supposedly became the final resting place for the Holy Grail.

It was just before 9.00pm. Jill and I were cuddling on the sofa, watching T.V. We'd just finished watching the film 'Drumline' for about the 6th time this year. I'd been in tears again; and had a revelation about what is was that reduces me to tears most of the time: 'Achievement'. Even if it's a father and son hugging after making up; that's achievement. As we were discussing this, Jill lunged backwards beside me. When I asked her what was wrong; she started to speak, but then said, "It's pointless me saying 'nothing', because you know what's happening now, when I do that."

I'd previously asked Jill how 'exactly' the spirits contact her. Did they speak to her, call out her name or maybe appear to her? She said that some spirits just appear in front of her, which shock her, like what just happened this evening. Others talk directly to her. But with the Ascended Masters and Archangels, she usually senses them at a distance; say 50 yards/metres away. Then they move in closer if she doesn't shun them. They move a little closer so they are within the room. Then suddenly it's like their face is pressed, nose first, on the side of her head, with their mouth directly in front of her ear.

If she doesn't want to speak to the Ascended Masters and Archangels, they tell her they respect her wishes; that they will try again another time when it's more convenient; and they leave.

Other spirits and Archangels she's not channelled before, will sometimes go straight into this position, 'in her face', which makes her jump. As did Joseph...

Jill: I've got someone called Joseph here.

Glenn: What's he want?

Jill: He tells me, that he comes from God and I shouldn't be afraid. He wants me to know that what I'm doing is right. And that I shouldn't be afraid. I could do without this; I'm tired.

Glenn: No; let him through. Let's listen to what he has to say.

Jill: He's a really nice man. Very calming and serene, with a lovely voice. Arimathea! His name is Joseph Arimathea, he's telling me. He says not to worry. We're doing the right thing and we won't come to any harm. He's here to give us peace of mind as to our quest.

Glenn: Ask Joseph if he feels we're doing the right thing writing the book 'Cashing in on God', bearing in mind Metatron and Azrael's request to speak in churches and ministries. They'll not want to listen.

Jill: He says that it is not for him to make judgement. You must do what you feel.

Glenn: That's OK; but we look to spirit for guidance. Watching the Bible bashers on T.V. giving their interpretation and opinions of the content of the Bible, is wrong.

Jill: He's laughing.

Glenn: About what? What was so funny?

Jill: The Bible. He's telling me it was never meant for the way it is being used. The Bible was a series of books written from prophets who we channelled to. As mankind started steering from their intended direction, we channelled people with messages to allow mankind to learn from the mistakes they were making. After the channelling, these messages would be passed on by the spoken word. There was no-one to write them down or record them accurately to start with.

You know of the expression:- Chinese whispers. Much of our messaging was distorted or deliberately changed. By the time the messages were recorded, there was a lot of distortion of the truth. There were many other messages that were put into books that were deliberately removed by religion. Religion became a measure of power and control over the masses. They used the Bible for control and turned it into a religious manual which was to be followed to the letter.

The Bible was never meant for this. It was our way of recording the mistakes mankind were making, so that you would learn from it and not repeat them. There have been many other messages that have been suppressed by religious orders, which is wrong. The tradition is now so inbred and programmed, that it's now difficult for us to guide mankind back onto the right path; which is why we need you to continue with your chosen path. You are chosen for this.

Start with the Gnostics. They will listen to you.

Glenn: But they already have the same type of belief.

Jill: He says some need reassurance and it will lead to other groups wanting to hear you. There are also churches out there with open minds that will want to listen to what you have to say.

Glenn: Joseph; why are we here? What's our purpose in life? (The meaning of life.)

Jill: He says it's not within his realm to answer that fully.

Jill: Metatron's here...And Azrael... And ... They're all here (As she waves her hands in a dismissive way in front of her face.). Go away! Oh look! (Jill looks down to her hands where her right hand is patting the open palm of her left hand. This is Azrael's physical sign to me.)

Glenn: (Laughing out loud.) Azrael! I love him. He's my Papa.

Jill: Yes he is, he says. Metatron says the reason mankind is on this planet is to further the evolution of the universe. The Creator learns from the development of the different species.

Glenn: Oh, so we're just a zoo then?

Jill: No, he says your place in the universe is part of the balance of the universal life force. The path of mankind is bent on destruction, greed, avarice, jealousy and hatred. These are all driven by negative thoughts. It is the negativity we must help you diminish. As mankind develops; if people don't cross over into the after-life, it will upset the balance of the universe.

Glenn: Metatron; is there more than one universe? It's difficult to comprehend if modern science is stating there are now 46 billion galaxies in this universe.

Jill: Yes, he says there are many universes. You can't comprehend the vastness. There are other human beings also on other planets, in different stages of evolution and in different forms; some even below the surface of other planets that may on the outside appear dead.

Glenn: What's the purpose?

Jill: As we have our experiences, it gives The Creator new experiences to create with.

Glenn: Metatron; what are your thoughts on the book title 'Cashing in on God'?

Jill: Did we not give this title to your wife? We acknowledge your request to call her your wife, rather than medium, so we will use the word wife.

Glenn: Gee thanks (sarcastically).

Jill: Oooooohhh...he didn't like that.

Glenn: Well come on; he was a bit patronising.

Jill: He says they're happy with the direction. He knows you find it difficult.

Glenn: It 'is' difficult. What's really difficult is the trust we have to place. All I have is the words from Jill. I have no tangible evidence; not just for me, but for others that want to test me. Still there's been no evidence such as a contract or a house sale.

Jill: We are working on finding a buyer for your house; and as for the contract: you continue to live in this fine house. You eat well and you don't do without do you? Yet you complain even though we've assured you that we will take care of you.

Glenn: Yes, but your interpretation of time is different to our time. You tell us 6 months to our move to California, but that may be a year, 18 months or 2 years to you.

Jill: No; we are aware of your time frame, and if we say 6 months to you, we mean in your time frame. What is it that you need from us? A miracle? If I was to place a baseball in your hand right now; would that give you the belief?

Glenn: Well yes!

Jill: What good would it do? All that you would have, is a baseball in your hand. It changes nothing. Your belief has to come from the heart. From learning to contact The Creator; through meditation and prayer. This world was designed for mankind to have love and happiness for each other; not for religious groups to fight with one another. Once all the religious groups realise that their skin, religion and cultures are superficial; there is one creator; God is within. You are all God's children; you are all a part of God; then you will find your true belief and develop a better world.

You were chosen because of the pain you've endured and the achievement you've had as a result of it. You've had your highs and you've had your lows. You're now a motivational speaker and there is a uniqueness with your pairing with Jill. She's an exceptional channeller. Together you can make a change. You're not going to change the world. Religion is too steadfast to be changed quickly; but you will be the start.

People will eventually accept these thoughts and turn away from the power and control of religion. You don't need religion. You need to learn that God is within and that you all have the ability to connect.

You too will learn to channel soon. Max will follow you. He sees more than he lets you know.

Glenn: Is my destiny then to speak?

Jill: Yes, of course. Did you not know that by now?

Glenn: Yes. What I meant was, do you want me to concentrate on the training or the speaking, to create income for us to survive on?

Jill: The speaking. Now; Azrael wishes to say a few words.

Glenn: Thank you Metatron.

At this point Metatron signed off. You may have noticed that in this chapter that the dialogue was penned in Jill's name, rather than Joseph and Metatron. This is because Jill has at least two levels of channelling (there maybe more yet). She is able to remain conscious and speak in her own voice, as spirit speaks to her. In this state she can talk to me as Jill; and ask spirit questions herself. Spirit also hear my questions directly and often answer them directly. So sometimes Jill will repeat what they are saying, and other times she'll speak instantaneously 'for' them. You'll be able to tell the difference by the dialogue above.

The second way she channels is when spirit completely takes over her body; like Azrael does now:

Azrael: We are so proud of you my son. So proud of you. As Jill takes my right hand, once again with her left hand, and pats my hand with her right hand.) You are so very special to us, and we are so proud.

Glenn: Thank you Azrael. It's lovely to hear your voice again.

Azrael: We love you very much. Luciana is with me. She is so looking forward to being with you tonight. She will be at the foot of your bed for protection.

Glenn. I so wish I could talk to her.

Azrael: You will be able to soon. Now! I must go. I can't stay. Until the next time we speak.

Glenn: When will that be?

Azrael: Very soon my son. Very soon. Goodbye for now.

Glenn: Goodbye Azrael; and thank you. Thank you Joseph too! We didn't get a chance to say goodbye.

At that, Jill awoke. She'd only been gone about three minutes, but for her it seemed much longer.

We went to bed later that evening; wondering who Joseph Aramathea might be; and whether we might find something about him on the internet in the morning.

21: How's your memory?

26th September 2005

Yesterday evening we listened to Joseph of Aramathea, Metatron and Azrael. Jill channelled them, just like the prophets in the Bible, thousands of years ago.

Here's an interesting analogy. Because we didn't tape this, I was writing 12 hours later; with input from what Jill could remember. We jog our memories with each other's remembrances. But it was only what we could remember from 12 hours (And at a later point; 16 hours.) previous. There was at least 40% more conversation that took place, over about a 40 minute period. We just couldn't remember it all.

Consider this. How quickly does your memory diminish over time? Consider you'd watched and listened to a favourite 'soap' channel, or interview programme; something with lots of conversation. Just think; we remember visuals more than we remember audio. We think in pictures, not in words. Try 'not' to think of a pink elephant with purple spots. The image will appear in your mind as a picture. It's easier to remember the words of a song, if you see them written down. It takes longer if you just listen.

Now you're going to tell your friends 'everything' that happened, and was said in the programme you watched. How much will you remember, word-for-word, 12 hours later? How much will you remember a 'week' later? How much will your friends remember, when they pass the information on to other people? How much will the other people remember? Do you just suppose the really good bits will get embellished? Do you suppose that the vast majority of what was originally said, will be forgotten?

People talk, on average, 140 words a minute. So in a 60-minute programme, or speech, that's 8400 words. On average there are 400 words on these pages. So one hour of speaking would be 21 pages. OK, so halve it for the gaps. Say 11 pages. That's 11 pages for every hour of conversation. Now you can begin to imagine how much information is missing from the bible.

When spirit channelled people 2000 years ago. The channellers passed on what they could remember; to people who passed on what 'they' could remember from the channeller. Eventually someone recorded it in writing. Then

www.anewbelief.com

someone translated it. And now people are trying to 'interpret' it, with their own opinions.

So just how much of the Bible is a true record of what was channelled?

Not a lot!

Here's what might have happened using a different analogy. One that you may of heard of before:

This is a story about a School Superintendent in America.

The School Superintendent met with his Assistant Superintendent and he gave him this information verbally:

"Next Thursday at 10.30am, Haley's comet will appear over this area. This is an event which occurs only once every 75 years. Call the School Principals, and have them assemble their teachers and classes on the athletic field, and explain this phenomena to them. If it rains, cancel the day's activities and have the classes meet in the auditorium, to see a film about the comet."

That's what the Superintendent said to the Assistant Superintendent, who was supposed to pass that message along, word-for-word to the School Principals.

Here's what the School Principals heard from the Assistant Superintendent.

"By order of the Superintendent of Schools, next Thursday at 10.30am, Haley's Comet will appear over your school athletic field. If it rains, cancel the day's classes and report to the auditorium with your teachers and students, where you'll be shown films. A phenomenal event, which occurs only once every 75 years."

The School Principals were to pass that message along word-for-word to their teachers.

Here's what the teachers heard.

"By order of the phenomenal Superintendent of Schools, at 10.30am next Thursday, Haley's Comet will appear in your auditorium. In case of rain on the athletic field, the Superintendent will give another order. Something that occurs only once every 75 years."

The teachers had to pass the message on word-for-word to the students.

Here's what the students heard.

"Next Thursday at 10.30am, the Superintendent of Schools will appear in our school auditorium with Haley's Comet. Something which occurs only once every 75 years. If it rains, the Superintendent of Schools will cancel the comet; and have us all meet on our phenomenal athletic field."

The students had to take the message home and give it to their parents. Many of us have been on the receiving end of a message, and wondered what the original message was meant to be, whether it came through children, or even adults sometimes.

Here's what the parents heard.

"When it rains next Thursday at 10.30am over the school athletic field, the phenomenal 75-year-old Superintendent of Schools will cancel all classes, and will appear before the whole school, in the auditorium, accompanied by 'Bill Hailey and the Comets'."

There are over 2 billion Christians; most of which seem to believe the words in the Bible are all truthful. Perhaps we could sell them all invisible clothes too.

22: Who, what and where we are

8th December 2005

Jill is channelling

Metatron: It has been a while since we last communed, but I am pleased you feel strong enough to retake the mantle handed to you. Perhaps we should begin with teaching others the basics of who, what and where you really are.

In the beginning, the one conscious energy, as in the Bible, created light. Those light shards are what is termed the soul. So in reality, you are light. Your thoughts, feelings and experiences collectively help to create the atmosphere and world you live in today. Which is why, to your every action, there is a reaction, but not just in a singular way. For your actions also have an impact on the collective dimension, therefore this will affect people and the environment you believe to be thousands of miles away from you.

To understand this, we must look at what you term as time. Time is not linear. It cannot be truly measured from one point to another horizontally. Time to us, is non-existent. All things are relative, if instead of time, you consider dimensions.

A table may appear solid, but it's energy. It's light. It vibrates at a certain speed. In another dimension, this could appear as a liquid mass floating in a particular area of space. If you could create a hologram of yourself, we could look at time in a different view. You'd be able to see below your feet was the past, whilst still remaining in the present; and also by altering your view and looking upward, you'd be able to look at what yet has to come, if you continue with your current actions. This is why as light-bearers of the one conscious thought, we can appear to many people simultaneously.

By looking at life, or time: which ever you prefer, you would also see that your actions would very much still affect the past and the future, for they are one and the same. Your past, you must remember, is like the table; it isn't solid. It only 'appears' to be gone. This will be a hard concept to learn for many, but we hope that with more time, the reality of what we say, will become a new belief for all to learn from and understand.

You will see that it is the conscious thought that changes and impacts your environment. Try to think of yourself as light. If you use logic to analyse what is given here, you will not learn, so use your creative energy, your God energy to try to understand.

You may feel it is impossible to change the past, but you can bring back the past, or repeat the past in order to change the direction of your life and that of others, through your actions and deeds now. This is why you have memories, to help you descend back into time and relive those moments, to change your present and future.

Jill: So without time, we have no past or future?

Metatron: That is correct to some extent. You are light, so look at how much light you can spread now. Your whole essence of how brightly you shine is down to how you feel. Your feelings or thoughts, if you wish, will draw to you what you believe to be true.

To understand dimensions better; if thought becomes reality, then there are no laws or limitations on what can be achieved. It is only the belief that imprisons one's ability. Let us say that in the first dimension you were a flower, and in the second dimension you were a caterpillar, and in the third dimension a human being. If you had to return back to the first dimension, you would only have the thought or idea of what it was like to be human. You would have no point of reference on which to share with other plants what you actually experienced. You can never destroy a thought, once it has been thought. It is there, no matter what.

Humans refuse to believe that they have the ability to visit other dimensions. You only see yourself as the physical body. If you take away your laws and limitations, you can go anywhere, be anything and do anything. You don't need a space machine to do this.

The One Conscious Mind; Energy; God; is an intelligent energy that is able to absorb feelings, and create from those feelings. The one true source of this energy is love. The feeling of love, creates light. Once you understand these spiritual foundations of who you really are, it will help you to see that your reality holds no bounds except those you place on yourself.

We will next discuss creation but for now, we will leave you to contemplate what has been given. You will have many people who still refuse to acknowledge that what we say here is the one truth, but hopefully you will see the resemblance to what is given and to those whose life is placed and lived through the words of the Bible... "Let there be light. And there was light."

Until then, blessings of love and light are placed upon you. May you continue to shine your light as a beacon for those who are lost to negativity to enable them to find you and us.

Metatron.

 www.anewbelief.com

23: Our perception of reality

8th December 2005

Jill is channelling

Metatron: We're pleased you have again opened the lines of communication and yet we know that perhaps today, your energies aren't as strong as usual. Take comfort and know that this period of uncertainty will change; for nothing ever is as it seems.

It is important that when you try to understand the history of the earth, that the world you consciously live in, is relatively new in the scheme of things and very much in its primitive state. This will surprise some of you, but whilst the souls that populate the planet have achieved much in technology and evolution ways, the planet itself is still young. For in other dimensions and universes, souls have been evolving trillions of years.

The enormity of creation is hard for human consciousness to understand. But in reality, by comparison to the universes, the earth is so small, it would not be seen with the human eye, which therefore puts the human form smaller than a molecule.

The earth dimension (planet) was created as a learning place, similar to your schools and colleges. Originally before souls chose to come to the planet, plans were drawn up; similar to maps and directions, to help them along their way. Now you may well ask where free will comes in to this. But you 'do' have free will. However; each of your actions affects the planet as a whole. Your thoughts create chain reactions, that others around the planet will telepathically receive at the same time, which in turn helps to bring about change, either positively or negatively. A good example that others will understand, is when you think of someone and the next minute they call you on the telephone.

If it makes things easier to comprehend, think of life as a game of snakes and ladders. Throughout your life you'll take so many steps forward, sometimes you will speed upwards and at other times you may sink, but eventually for most, they finally reach the end of the game.

It is important that the souls of this world, for ease lets call them people; grasp how powerful they really are. Many, many people underestimate their talents.

Now taking this chain reaction of thought, you will see that's why you all believe the planet earth to be a solid mass, and this one conscious mind creates reality. But what is reality? When you're asleep, the world of dreams seems real; the fight you're having, the conversations with people seem real enough, until, if someone hurts you, you can feel the pain. Then when you alter your consciousness to something else called 'awake', you dismiss the dimension of dreams you have just been in as 'unreal'.

Why is it that you question this 'awake' reality and not what you call the dream state? The answer is that in each dimension you're totally absorbed in your environment; therefore there is no 'other' reality but what is being experienced; and how you 'feel' during the experience.

People's perceptions of reality is not what has been experienced, but the emotions they choose to place 'on' that experience, which is why for some, it can be a joyous, momentous occasion; and for others a frightening and bad experience. This is the first area that people need to address. Instead of looking to others to create happiness, it is their own perspective that dictates their experience.

By learning the power of thought that lies within you, you are able to expand your consciousness and if you so choose, see multi-dimensional. Many may ask you, how this can be achieved. As we said previously, they need to master controlling their consciousness to create their own happiness. Everything you are, need, know and have, is already within yourself.

We ask that you start reconnecting with your inner power, remove the word 'think', and replace this with 'feel'. When you first meet someone, feel your way around them when faced with decisions. Does this way feel right, or do you feel you need to go in another direction. Learning to listen to your feelings will help you make better human-life choices.

Blessings to you. Remember you are the light. It is your choice whether you're a bright light or a dull one.

Metatron.

24: Light; darkness; positive; negative:- Your choice

9th December 2005

Jill is channelling

Metatron: We're pleased you have again opened the lines of communication.

It isn't always easy to accept what you experience, so for now, we ask that you feel and experience the impressions and visions that come to you. You will be able to continue to write automatically, so do not worry about remembering what you see, as the experience in itself, will create your memories.

Create for yourself a shimmering white light and allow this to draw around you, so that you become one with the light. You're doing well. Do not be apprehensive. Now what do you see?

Jill: I see darkness and two light orbs. One to the left and one to the right.

Metatron: Imagine yourself as a lens of a camera and zoom yourself back. Now what do you feel and see?

Jill: I feel calm and peaceful, and I see what looks like a galaxy of stars.

Metatron: Look below yourself, what do you see?

Jill: The planet earth. Vibrant bands of energies surround the planet.

Metatron: To some, these are known as auras. The planet is a source of divine energy and as a soul, you are the source of your divine energy. The colours are the energies of feelings. Now remove the light and look at only the darkness. How do you feel?

Jill: Safe because I'm with you, but wary, I can't see anything.

Metatron: Now create the light and planets again. See them reappearing like turning on lights. How do you feel now?

Jill: Happier, I can see things now.

Metatron: Let us remove the darkness so that you have pure white light energy, how does this affect you?

Jill: I can't see anything. The light is too bright.

Metatron: Bring back the darkness. Now, you're wondering why you have experienced this, but we would ask you which felt more comfortable, the darkness or the light?

Jill: The light!

Metatron: Why do you feel that way, when both could be just as blinding in their own way?

Jill: The light was bright and warm. The dark was cold.

Metatron: Was it really, or was it that you chose to experience the darkness and light in the way that you did?

Don't try to analyse things at this stage. As we asked previously, this is about feeling your energies and learning to work with them. Consider darkness as someone who isn't knowledgeable and light as someone who is knowledgeable. When you learn, you grow; you expand your energies. You expand your light. Every human is a sun and they radiate their rays of light and choose to either illuminate or cast shadows. Always remember that your life is full of possibilities and what you hold to be true, will be your reality.

You are the miracle. You have the power to create miracles as so does everyone else. When something crosses your pathway, you can choose to allow it to be your downfall and ruin your day, week, or year in the human world; or you can use your infinite intelligence and creative energy to turn your experience into a learning experience, that will enhance your journey through this dimension. Try to look at the trials you're experiencing now in the material world and see what lessons can be learnt from them.

If your life isn't working, what do you need to change? Is it your emotions and feelings connected with the experience, or is it the experience that needs to change? Learning to decipher what to do when you're trying to push the mule; and whether you should lead the mule, is a valuable life lesson.

Now when you look at the evolution of mankind, the first souls to come to this learning dimension were inspired men and women. They lived their lives according to their emotions. Life was good and the light energy of love abounded.

The channellings of these souls marked the evolution of the sacred texts which would allow souls to awaken to the true power within and experience feelings of oneness and love. At this time certain channellers as yourself, inspired small communities to learn the power that lay within all souls.

Unfortunately the more successful they became and were acknowledged as the knowledgeable ones, the more, over time, they turned away from the light (knowledge) and ignored the true teachings, to become authoritarian organised religions.

The end result was the original messages degenerated into total untruths. Now the Christians of this world focus on the words of the Bible, but miss the point of its teaching entirely. They waste their inner power by arguing and philosophising over what things may have meant, whether or not they are true. They gather together claiming to worship the true word of The Creator and yet have no experience of The Creator which is oneness and love.

Many souls now blindly believe what is written in the Bible and do not go in search of the truth for themselves. They have allowed other ignorant souls (darkness) to cloud their ability to find their own inner light, and in so doing, have created a following based on ignorance. It is this diabolical error that has impacted on the collective energies of this dimension. Souls are being taught to create fear and condemnation of others, if someone else's light does not match their own. By creating this division and conflict, the energies of this dimension are greatly endangered.

Oneness and love is brought about through caring, sharing and creating harmony through learning experiences. The Bible's theme is one of ignorance, division and suffering. The souls of this planet are currently on a collision course which will affect the galaxies and universes.

The original sacred texts, of which most have been destroyed, were to help human souls to understand the complexities of life and death and the transition from one dimension to another. These original sacred texts also taught that as well as being separate bearers of light, collectively we are also one. In other words an instruction manual/map to help you find your way.

We feel that for now, you need time to assimilate your experience and what has been written, your energies are becoming stronger, but we do not wish to go too quickly. We will commune again and continue soon; but for now, blessings our kindred soul.

Metatron.

25: A multitude of angels; with a twist

9th December 2005: evening

Jill is channelling

Jill and I are musical people and one of our highlights for our 'chill' time, is watching 'The X Factor'. If you're reading this outside the UK, this is the equivalent of American Idol, or Pop Idol, with a spin.

Simon Cowell, Sharon Ozbourne and Louis Walsh judge three groups of people to win a £1,000,000 record contract. There were over 75,000 contestants in 2005. The three groups are: the under 25's, the over 25's and the groups or bands.

It's a family gathering for us. We'd just watched the main part of the show and were waiting for the second part of the show. Our young boys, Max (7) and Cooper (5) had just gone to bed. Brett (16) was still with us. Jill and I were sat on the sofa, cuddling as usual. Jill was relaxed; when she suddenly started slapping her right hand on top of the back of her left hand. If you've been reading this diary, then you'll know that means only one thing to us at present.

This was unusual, in that Jill had already channelled Metatron earlier. It's around 9.00pm.

Jill: Your pal's here and he's impatient to get through.

Glenn: What's he want?

Jill: He's worried about you and wants to talk.

Glenn: OK, let him talk.

Jill: No way! He's been hovering around for ages. He can wait. This is my highlight of the week. I want to watch the rest of 'The X Factor'. He can come back later.

Not too long after that, Azrael started to press the urgency of his message. Jill started to drift into a semi-conscious state and finally flopped, seemingly asleep, into my lap. We were cuddling on the sofa at the time. She then sat up, and Azrael came through. He told me that what he wanted to talk about, wasn't for recording. It was just for me. I'll give you the gist anyway.

Azrael told me how proud he was of me; and that he was worried that the plans the spirits had for us were not progressing as they should. He told me that the energies were in turmoil; more than ever before, and it was affecting what they could influence. I asked him about the promise of a contract to support us. He said they were still working on it, but it was more difficult than they had envisaged, with the current turmoil in the energies. He didn't stay long, because he knew Jill was already weak from channelling Metatron in the morning.

So we were really surprised when, rather than Jill coming out of the trance; Archangel Chamuel came through. Jill was already weak.

When Jill is channelling it uses a tremendous amount of her energy. The entities use her energy to communicate, either with her, or through her. There's a sliding scale of 'energy sapping', dependent on 'how' and 'who' she's channelling.

If she's talking to her spirit guide, she uses very little extra energy. If she channels a spirit, she uses more energy. If she channels a spirit who engages her in trance, so that the spirit is using her to speak; she uses even more energy. If she channels angels, she uses yet more energy. If she channels angels in trance, so that the angels speak to me directly; we're into energy sapping 'big-time'. Now consider that the power of the angel determines the amount of energy Jill has to accommodate.

Metatron, according to Jill, is the most powerful entity she's ever channelled; and at first could only stay with him in very small time-frames.

Liken it to walking and running. Talking to her guide is like going for a stroll. Eventually you'll get tired, but you don't really notice it in short bursts. Channelling with Metatron is like running a marathon; except that all the energy goes in a few minutes. When the runners cross the line, they often fall over with exhaustion. Sometimes they're physically sick with the exhaustion; and often they collapse. Many times they're dehydrated too.

This is what Jill experiences. So when Chamuel came through, she'd done the marathon in the morning with Metatron; had half a day to recover; just done an 80 mile cycle race with Azrael, and was now about to do the 2.5 mile swim with Chamuel; to complete the Triathlon.

Chamuel wanted to introduce himself to me. He spoke with a very high-pitched warm voice. Very soothing. He urged me to keep going and approach the media. He wanted me to give out a challenge to take 5 people and use my knowledge and wisdom to teach them positivity. Then he wanted me to take 10 and then 20; but do it through the media.

The world, he said, is becoming such a negative environment, which is having enormous shifts in the energy balance of the universes. I explained that we must have an income stream if we're to do this. Our focus at present is on keeping our head above water. We currently have no income at present and have to generate some income. Chamuel said that 'they' had not experienced this kind of negativity before and needed to re-address the situation. I don't think he was talking about my personal negativity; but about the energy disruption that was happening on our planet.

I explained that Metatron had promised us a contract, to keep us going. He stated that Metatron wanted to talk to me to give me reassurance and explain, but that Jill was too weak to be able to handle it now. Then I pushed Chamuel a little, by asking him if we'd still be emigrating to California by the end of March, and he affirmed that we would. He then needed to leave because of Jill's energy levels.

When he left, Jill collapsed. She felt sick, was dehydrated and couldn't walk. I had to lift her out of the sofa and assist her to the bathroom, where I had to hold her in place to pee, because she was so weak. Then I had to help her to the kitchen to get some water to re-hydrate her.

We then went up to bed. As I was getting into bed she started to doze off. Or so I thought.

As I was moving around between our bedroom and our bathroom, I kept hearing her wittering about the dark and dark forces. I wasn't paying too much attention. She was wittering in a quiet low key voice. I thought she was thinking out aloud about what she'd experienced with Metatron, with the light and the dark. She was laid on her back in bed, very slightly sat up, in the position she normally adopts when she's reading.

I eventually climbed in bed and snuggled up to her, but she brushed me away with her left hand; very dismissive. I asked her what was wrong, but she didn't reply. Then I realised she was channelling yet again.

Glenn: Jill... Jill... Jill; are you still with me? Jill...?

Her face started to contort, more than I'd ever seen it before. She started to look like a gnarled, old witch. She was breathing noisily and deeply. She slowly turned to me on her left side, and started to speak to me in a really deep menacing voice.

Jill: **'I'** have her now.

Glenn: What?

Jill: She will be **mine.**

Glenn: Who are you?

Jill: **Beelzebub.** (Bee-ell-zee-bub) Eh. Eh. Eh. Eh. (A wicked cackling laugh.)

Glenn: (In a very casual voice.) We don't need you. Go away!

Beelzebub: I will **take** her. She will be **mine.** Eh. Eh. Eh. Eh.

Glenn: No you damn well won't. We don't need you. We don't want you. **GO AWAY!**

At that, Jill slowly relaxed back into her 'normal' state; and I really thought that was the end of it for the night. How wrong could I be? She'd still not come back to me. Now I have to tell you; I was scared. I went into a cold sweat on my brow. This is the first time Jill has ever channelled an evil entity; and I was worried; so you can imagine what it might be like, wondering what the hell was coming through next.

 Jill started channelling yet again. But this time it was a spirit who'd passed over. She suddenly sat up in bed and started to bounce around, shouting out in an accent from somewhere between Virginia and Georgia in the USA. Her voice was incredibly enthusiastic, modulating up and down with passion; and her body was extremely demonstrative. She was bouncing around like a rag-doll clown. Keep this mental picture in your mind as you read this dialogue. I've tried to make the spelling phonetic where I can, to give you a feel for the deep southern drawl and the particular accent she was using.

Remember I wrote about the two levels of channelling that Jill does; and that there may be more? Well here for the first time of me seeing it, is the third level of channelling. This time the spirit physically moves 'all' her body around. The spirit is in control of all her bodily functions; except her eyes. Her eyes remained shut all the way through this.

Jill: Mah ohhh mah. Dat sure feel mighty goo-ood! I ain't felt dis good for a lonnng time. (As Jill sits up in bed and stretches her arms up in the air. She wiggles her upper body around as though this spirit is making his body fit into her, and stretching muscles that haven't been used in a long time.)

She turned to me and started to talk. Her eyes were closed and she had a huge grin on her face. She was bobbing around, sat up in bed, like a huge rag-doll clown. She took hold of my hands with hers.

Jill: Do you feel the pahwer within you? Then it's about spreadin' that power. Like a torch lightin' a candle, lightin' a fuse; and it will blow. Mayn, it will really blow. But you gatta believe it, really deep down in the depths of your soul. Do ya believe?

Glenn: (Very quietly, with uncertainty with what was happening.) Yes!

Jill: Now I ain't hearin' that. So well; **do ya believe mayn?** Come on (loudly) **Ahhh believe!!! Ahh got the power!! Ahh got the power to change mah destiny and control what happens to me; from the root of mah toes, to the tip o' mah brain.** (Whispering now) You gatta believe! Tell me you believe. 'Cos 'you' have that power. You have the ability to touch people's souls; and yet; you do not.

Understand the depths of the power you control. Ahh know you, you really do think too much. You create barriers where there 'are' no barriers. Instead of creatin' 'buts', create possahbilities.

(Louder) **Go to the media. If the media won't listen, go to the news. If the news won't listen, go to the T.V. If the T.V. won't listen, go to the people. Someone, somewhere, is gonna believe in you. It's gatta happen.**

It has to start with you being the ignition to the time bomb that 'will' explode.

Glenn: What's my message?

Jill: Pahwer to the people to believe in themselves. Understand and adapt, to appreciate other people's individuality, for whart it is.

Glenn: The behaviour again.

Jill: **Exactly mayn! Ya gart it! Ya gart it! Ya gowin' on the raht ro-ad. You just gatta believe in yourse-elf. That's all it takes. It don't matter what somebody else thi-inks.** (Softly) It's what you feel and know to be true. For the truth within you creates your own reahlity.

Glenn: Tell me who you are.

Joshua: My name is Joshua. I was a servant. I served in a cotton plantation. But my main theme in life: I always remained pahsitive. I always saw the sunshine in everything that came through.

Glenn: Did you just get rid of Beelzebub?

Joshua: Well; Beelzebub was here to test you. But Beelzebub was also part of your own creation. There was a part of you that wondered what you saw, was actual reahlity, or a figment of your imagination; or hell. And you can create whatever you wish it to be-ee.

Glenn: Which I did; and sent him away.

Joshua: Exactly, 'cos part of you wanted to wonder whether or not that was evil, and another part of you sa-aw the goodness in things. And you got rid 'o dat thing as quick as a diddly squat mayn. You did go-ood. But don't **'ever'** let things get you down. When things happen, they happen for a reason, and you can choose, whether or not it be a good day, or a bahd day. But this is the pahssibilities of human kind. If you always see the good in things, you can create new oppahrtunities. So you go forth. But I have to go now. The medium... your wife; they say you like her to be known as; she tires. OK? But I sure as hell know we'll speak one day again, 'cos as I beg mah britches, we're gonna meet again, 'cos me and you are real soul-mates. OK? So you keep smilin' and you keep lookin'; and look for that silver linin', for if you look, you sure as hell are gonna find it. OK?

Glenn: Thank you Joshua.

Joshua: Oh you's welcome sir. You's mighty welcome. It's been a real pleasure.

Glenn: It's been a pleasure meeting you too.

Joshua: Blessings; and the love of the Lord to you and your family.

Jill slowly collapsed in total exhaustion. I couldn't even wake her up to see if she was OK. She hardly stirred that night, from the position she'd collapsed in.

Glenn's thoughts: Having the evil entity come through was really worrying me. I didn't sleep well all night. One part of me was gravitating to the negative; whilst another part of me was recalling Jill saying that when she's really weak, that's when she's most vulnerable to evil entities taking her over. We all have a positive and a negative side. What we perceive in being reality, is not necessarily always the case. Our mind tricks us. The power of the sub-conscious mind is like a sleeping giant. All our fears are drawn from the dark side; and they become as real as we allow them to be.

The following morning we discussed the previous day's events. Jill explained that she'd had no time to surround herself with protective light, like she normally would, if she was going to do a 'reading' for someone, or access the spirit world. This would have given her the strength to keep positive, and not be obsessed with the negative.

Whilst Jill is channelling more, with profound information from the angels, we're still stuck in this 'catch 22' situation. We need income to survive. Even the likes of Mother Theresa and Mahatma Ghandi had support.

Perhaps an explanation is in order. When we put our house up for sale in May 2003, we planned to emigrate to Southern California. The housing market had been booming. We wound our business down, to concentrate on the move to California. There's a tremendous amount of planning to do. Add to that, the planning for undertaking a new business too. We'd let our staff go gradually, and we'd stopped promoting our business. Our business needs a three to six month lead-in time, so there's been no point trying to generate new business, if we aren't going to be here.

Our entire pension is tied up in the house. We have very little savings pension. The sale of the house was going to allow us to have a new start. A new adventure in California; to help grow our pension for retirement.

The government increased the bank base interest rate 5 times in almost as many months. They succeeded in halting the housing boom. We stopped promoting the company 2 years ago. The income we have achieved is from past customers who've got in touch. We're having to start a marketing campaign to raise income, and assume we're not leaving.

But when the angels tell us we'll be leaving by the end of March 2006; where's the incentive to start a marketing campaign? It's a real 'catch 22' situation. If we left and rented, the rent wouldn't cover the costs.

We still don't have any evidence from the angels to give us the faith to push this destiny hard. We had two promises. A contract to help keep us going; and that our house will sell, allowing us to emigrate to Southern California before the end of March 2006.

Now it seems we're getting excuses that these may not happen yet. Our savings have all but dried up. We're into overdraft. Going out and getting jobs won't pay the overheads. We have to generate the kind of income needed to support this house.

This is why we put the house up for sale, and decided to emigrate.

Now we're being 'pushed' to help The Creator; which we're happy with; except we're reminded of an old saying:

"The objective of all the Everglades employees is to analyse all situations thoroughly. Anticipate all problems, prior to their occurrence. Have answers to those problems; and move swiftly, when called to action. However! When you're up to your arse in alligators, it's difficult to remember you originally got into the water to drain the swamp."

We're frantically busy trying to earn money, just to keep our head above water; waiting for the house to sell; and at the same time being pulled by our values to take another direction.

Spirit doesn't seem to have a grasp on the reality of this world when it comes to commerce. Yes, I could approach radio stations and T.V. and get interviews; but that doesn't pay the bills. It's purely PR (Public Relations). The PR gets exposure, which then takes time for paid work to materialise: 6 to 12 months.

Before I do that. I must get a book in print, which I'm currently working on; but you don't write a book overnight which turns into a best seller.

Blind faith is a tremendous challenge and test. With our bills being paid for, I'd be happy to go for it. But until we get tangible signs from the angels, this work has to play second fiddle to generating income to keep the wolves from the door.

26: Metatron on delays of spiritual contracts

14th December 2005

Jill is channelling

Metatron: It is our pleasure to commune with you once again. We bring you love, light and understanding. We're aware that you have questions, but first we ask that you take a few moments to allow us to give you some much needed renewed energy; and help lift your energies, by accepting the light we bring to you.

First we bring you pink light of love. For every soul is loved so; and sometime on this earth plane, souls need reminding that we love them so. Secondly we bring you the green light of healing and calm, to help heal the pain and frustration you are feeling; and lastly we bring you the yellow rays of light to lift and energise you. Take a moment to breathe in this wonderful energising light.

Jill: Glenn and I wish to know who, are what, is Beelzebub?

Metatron: Beelzebub is nothing. It is a name of myth. It is a human manifested entity, just as there are no fallen angels either. This again has been manifested by humans to create fear and enable them to control others. We know at times, you question whether or not what you receive is real; but this isn't because you're unsure we're real. Your real reason is one of fear and scorn from others.

Just as other prophets have had their share of being scorned, it is one of great spiritual learning, to follow your heart and be true to your heart; rather than allow others to redirect your course of life. Look closely into your heart. You know only too well that you hate and fear confrontation, as do most other human beings. This is one of life's lessons to be learnt by all. You need to realise that you're just as important as anyone else; and it is only yourself who decides that someone else, or 'their' words, carry more weight than your own.

What Glenn thought he'd spoken to, was in fact your own conscious mind fighting through fear. You were deeply tired. But at the same time, we brought you energies to lift you too. It is not really ourselves that drain you so, it is the emotions you feel and the stresses of the day that actually take its toll. Had we left you there at that moment, your sleep would have been too heavy to break out of your own creating nightmare.

Joshua was allowed to come through to bring you the positive energies and upliftment you so desperately needed. He was also trying to convey that both you and Glenn at the moment have negative feelings, but are failing to accept what you feel and change them to more positive ones.

At the moment, the world mass energies are extremely low. Many, many people do not have hope. Yes many place their faith in God, but inwardly doubt that anything will ever change. It is as though everyone is expecting failure and doom. We are all working in the spirit world to help change this. Look around you and really see the faces of the people passing you by. As a result, everything is suspended. One cannot move on without intention and a goal.

Along with others, what was spiritually contracted to have happened, is way behind schedule. It's similar to a production plant having a major machinery problem, that will affect the end result of when people get their delivered goods.

We feel it is very important that Glenn and others understand we can only merely guide. We are here to help you; and if it is in our power to do so, we will; but we can not give anyone a step-by-step guide to follow. This would break our universal and spiritual laws. The reason for you being here is to learn like everyone else. Even Jesus was not given a step-by-step plan. He knew the final outcome would be a physical death; as is every other human being's prophecy. But the pathway you take to attain that end, is of your own choice and no other. You all have free will.

As we have said before, you must make the intention and set the goal. Once we know the direction you wish to take, then we will do all within our power to ensure people, opportunities and pointers are placed in your pathway. No-one is being punished. Humans punish themselves. There are no malevolent spirits cursing anyone. Humans curse themselves. We have stressed so many times, that the outcome is what you create for yourselves.

At this time, we cannot confirm when your home will sell. You are all connected. Let me see if I can explain this better; as I sense your confusion.

Imagine that you are a pilot light of a gas boiler that fuels the energy of the planet. You, on your own, would never be able to create the energy to sustain the planet. Together, all human beings are the pilot lights that help create the energy to sustain the planet. If everyone has hope, positivism and intention, the flames burn on full power, and the planet's energies bring renewal and growth. But at the moment, everyone is just coping; living in quiet desperation and hope is at an all time low. So the flames have been lowered. If the heating element is only just managing to keep things warm, the energy of the planet slows down considerably.

When the planet's energies are so slow, it takes longer for the prophesies we've given you to be fulfiled. So contracts, sales, and any changes are all delayed; not cancelled, but unfortunately delayed.

To lose more faith now, in us and yourselves, would only slow things down even more. The more positivism shown and intention to move forward regardless, will help turn up 'your' flames, which will eventually affect the critical mass.

Glenn must not fear he has upset Chamuel, we are angels who bring you love and light; and although we may feel sad when a lesson goes unlearnt, or you feel pain, our only wish is to bring love and light into your life.

Glenn can talk to me anytime he wishes. Whether he hears my answers is another thing. You see, many people ask or plead with God, angels, spirit guides and loved ones who have passed over, but then don't look for the answer, or even wait to receive the answer. It is like picking up the phone, calling your dad and asking him a question; and then before he answers, you put the phone down and cut off the communication.

Another area of concern is whether or not the answer we give Glenn will fit into the tight constraints he puts on what he is willing to accept. We say this with love, for we know that the frustration arises out of things not happening quickly enough for him. He's a very results driven man; but he expends his energies on so many projects that he is failing to allow himself to reach a final destination.

If he was sailing to a particular place, he'd never get there, for he deviates so many times, he'd forget where he was supposed to end up (lovingly laughing). He makes us smile; for his intentions are pure and from the heart. His frustration and ego are what spoil his dreams from becoming a reality.

If Glenn speaks to me; and sits quietly; he will hear me, as a thought, feeling or impression. He just needs to learn to follow through. Although your thoughts that he will take this 'another way' are quite correct. (This is Jill laughing inside because 'follow through' would be another word for a 'shart', or maybe you'd know that as a 'wet fart'. Another example of angelic understanding of our humour.)

Now his book is progressing superbly, he is applying himself, so we need to help him a little more.

It is the Bible that is the divider: the devil. It is through these words of mankind that has allowed a force of evil to pervade, and destroy human lives, with an excuse that the atrocities carried out were in the name of God.

If love, sanity, and reflection of our actions were to replace the Bible, what soul in their own heart would follow or worship someone or something, when it segregated, and killed another soul, human or animal? What is really happening here, is that what they hate in 'each other', they actually hate in 'themselves'. There is no exclusivity on reaching God; the conscious energy; the one thought.

What we're saying here is that your light has to shine brightly to be absorbed by the light, so that you can join the one conscious thought. The only way is through 'being' the light, by sharing, loving and caring about one another. BE THE LIGHT! Nothing more and nothing less. Retaliation only breeds more retaliation, until all the reasons why you're fighting, are lost.

If you keep God; the one universal light, in your heart, and look at how you can make a difference, by teaching others and sharing, you will receive back, a hundred fold, the same. The sacred texts that were destroyed, taught mankind to look to their hearts and learn the knowledge and key to life; and attaining heaven was through divine love.

You will find that those human beings who are the light by showing love, tolerance and understanding to others, are a threat to the powers of the churches. For they truly believe in the power within; and they alone have that power to predetermine their lives. They have no need for approval from a father, priest or religious authority.

If they want to be charitable, they have no need to give their money to the church. There are enough beggars, hospitals, children's homes and charitable associations, who would happily welcome anyone personally handing over their money to help them.

The one conscious mind; God, has no need for gold crosses or elaborate buildings to be built. You don't have to go anywhere, except within your heart, to access true spiritual enlightenment.

If you were to create a new Bible that contained the positive scriptures, you would have a modicum amount of text that was similar to the sacred texts. Currently your greatest threat to the life of this planet, is one that lies with religious fundamentalists who feel that they need to fulfil the literal words of the Bible, into creating Armageddon in the name of God.

What is given here is nothing new and it may seem disheartening, but by being the light and spreading the light to others, each thought affects the critical conscious thoughts of others all around the planet. It is the positivism and love that needs to be taught to the children of this planet; to show that killing or hurting one another only diminishes the light within.

Instead of teaching children to breed contempt, teach them to love unconditionally; to see the Divine Creator in each and every one of us. Show them to create a better world. But the changes have to begin with yourselves individually. Then within families, communities, governments and then globally.

We will commune again. Loving light to you. Be the light and shine within and cast your light out so others may be drawn to the beacon of hope, a new belief and love.

Metatron.

27: Metatron challenges people to test the Bible

15th December 2005

Jill is channelling

Metatron: Greetings to you dear daughter of light. We're pleased to be with you once again. We will do our best to bring you as much information as possible. However, with the time we have, there is no way we can cover the ground Glenn wishes to achieve. We will first perhaps deal with things in sequence, and this will take quite some time. Please know that we are not here to destroy the human soul, but to perhaps put their faith back on track. Currently their direction is that of a derailed train.

What we bring may well cause chaos, but for those who truly believe in a greater being, be it God or the one conscious mind; then those who truly understand the message of creation will not turn to fundamentalist mentality and create more abominations in the name of God, Muhammad, Allah or any other title created by mankind.

What we would ask, is that those who read these teachings, look within their hearts to understand the lessons given; and then go and research. Leave no stone unturned before making your decision as to whether to accept these lessons, or leave them behind.

Mankind has the ability now more than ever to research and uncover vital information for themselves, through the internet, universities and other historical documentation. Those that do so will uncover what the vast majority of the population fear to hear, see and acknowledge.

Abraham is portrayed as a descendent of Noah. This was not so. If you look and research, you will find that there was very little in the area you name Palestine. There were no temples or any great civilisation at the time Abraham was purported to have lived.

We feel it is important that you understand what was happening in that time, to grasp the reality of what we say. The time you would understand as 324BC was when the Jews came into competition with the Greeks. At this time, if you were to speak to theologians and research, you would find the learned, educational Jews often wrote in Greek. Some of the first educational writings of the Jews were in Greek, and at that time a Greek university was built in Jerusalem; and some Jews competed against the Greeks and embraced the Greek culture for a while.

The city of Jerusalem was a place for budding philosophers, teachers, and academics to learn and study life. During this time if you weren't of Grecian descent, you were considered of a lower standing. The Greeks considered any other nation to be barbarians. You'll find through research that it wasn't long after, the Jews followed suit; and created Jews and Gentiles. The separation had begun, through ego and wanting to be considered better than others. The downfall of humanity was to spread like a plague amongst the lands.

As their knowledge grew, the Jews distanced themselves from the Greeks and over a period of time denied that they had learnt their education from the Greeks. At this same period in time, they realised the power of stories. For people would travel far and wide, to listen to the teachings of the priests. The Jew's wished for independence and so in 164BC they created new teachings, new calendars and new rules for the people of that time. It was at this time the birth of the Tanakh came about.

To make their standing more important, the Jews wrote sacred texts, that were able to give the impression of a set of prophecies that had come to light. As there are far too many; numerous errors, it would be impossible for us to recite them to you. We know that for those who desire the truth; if it is important enough, they will go on to discover these revelations for themselves.

Let us take a closer look at Adam and Eve. This mythological couple were to symbolise man and woman. But the underlying message of these passages, is that they were not to ask questions and attain knowledge, or dare to search out the truth for themselves. For to do so would be damnation.

A man at that time: Judas Maccabeus, along with his descendents, desired to rule Palestine. You'll find this referenced perhaps under Hasmoneons in your historical records. To do so, required a reconstruction of history, to bring about a new understanding to others, that they were a specially chosen generation, who God had bequeathed the land to. It was during this time that many atrocities took place. Galileans and others were forced to adopt this new faith, or choose death. Many fled Palestine at this time, and found sanctuary in Rome.

 www.anewbelief.com

To ensure that what had occurred in the name of God was not to be questioned, the Tanakh was to be shown as being created in the second century, so that it would portray prophesies that had become reality, therefore who would dare to question God or what the Hasmoneons claimed was true?

The Tanakh draws together many myths and legends from all areas, which if closely researched will bear a remarkable resemblance to Egyptian, Greek and original Palestine mythology. The Hasmoneans created stories that would help serve their purposes in the present by recreating a past.

We feel for now, you may need to go and research what has been given. These teachings are meant to be short so that you acquire the knowledge given. For now, we surround you in love and light; until then, blessings.

Metatron.

28: Metatron: The laws of life

17th December 2005

Jill is channelling

We're pleased to commune with you again. Before we begin, it's important that we remember to leave ego behind, when we search to connect with The Divine. Remember that no one human is better than another. No life is more important than another. All are children of light, and as such no judgment or belief that one is mightier than another must be harboured.

If you operate from an ego perspective, you will never be able to connect to us. You must wish to share these teachings with others for the benefit of mankind, not the benefit of one's self. The rewards by working from this perspective will be many fold. A souls worth, is not merely measured by their material worth, although we understand the need and importance of such things. All we ask is that we do not lose sight of the end result: To free humankind and create a new belief and understanding of God; light; the one true consciousness.

All humanity has the ability to connect with God; light; the one true consciousness. When you operate from within the heart, and follow your life's path in service to others and love, you will experience the divine within and the real connection with The Creator.

Progress can not be made if we allow ego to build the notion of greatness or importance, for this goes against spiritual and universal laws. The laws of life are:-

- To respect all living entities, no living entity must kill or maim another entity.
- To learn to love all living entities.
- To share information and experiences.
- To learn to understand differences and work together with those differences.
- To serve each other.
- To be honest.
- To be loyal and respect each entity.
- To treat others as you would also expect to be treated.
- To be positive and thankful for life's experiences.
- To attain peace and harmony with all living entities.

www.anewbelief.com

- To be proactive and not reactive.
- To create and manifest the light.

The only real lesson of life that everyone should learn, was first given to mankind through Jesus. Love God:- meaning 'love the light'; and love others as you would yourself. This does not mean that you run around declaring love for someone you don't know and perhaps may not have anything in common with. This love is a respect and compassion that this stranger is on the same pathway as you; and this stranger is an integral part of your life, your world and the universes.

You must learn not to take the Bible literally. Let us show you an example: 'Hamartia' is the Greek word for sin. This is a term which was used in archery and it meant 'to miss the point'. 'Metanoia' which translated as 'repentance', originally meant to change perspective. The Bible has been translated literally as sin needs repentance; but really the lesson given was asking people to learn to stop seeing themselves as individuals and change their perspective; for they were missing the whole point.

Currently, you will find many people do not love themselves. This is because for too long now, the Bible has portrayed that they are born out of sin; that God feels they are unworthy and they must pay for their wrong doings. But for God; light; the one true consciousness, to exist, its continuance can only be sustained through love. Love is all that God; light; the one true consciousness, has for each being of light, for it is one and the same.

There are different degrees of love. The love you have for a partner, is different from the love you have for a child. The love you have for your parents, friends and associates is different from the love you perhaps may have for a cat or a dog. We can not put it any more plainly. Learning to love one's self in a non-egotistical way, and understanding that every living soul are one and the same, is the only way to attaining Nirvana: Heaven; connection with God; light; the one true consciousness.

It would help us greatly if you would have a Bible by your side the next time we commune, so that we may explain different texts and how the misinterpretation has taken place. We feel this may be a better avenue for you, rather than, as you personally feel, that this seems to be manifesting into a declaration of war against religion groups. We are aware that you're frightened, but ask that you remember we come in love and peace. Our words are meant to help bring hope where there is none. To bring light where there is dark. To bring love to those who are unloved and to help those who feel unworthy; feel worthy.

Please be aware the lessons we bring will not be quick. You may well change as we take you through these lessons; but the change will be that your light will shine brighter; and your compassion and caring nature will grow for others. We will help you to overcome your impatient nature. We will help you to walk forward fearlessly. Most important of all we will help you to value your skills and work from a love perspective. For now we will leave you to contemplate what has been written.

Metatron.

29: Truth about Jesus

18th December 2005

Jill is channelling

Metatron: Blessings we bring to you. You have many thoughts at the moment. We would ask at this time that you clear your uncertainties and allow us to guide you. We're pleased that you have your Bible to hand. It's imperative that you remember we are not here to destroy human faith, but to bring to light the real meanings and uncover the truth within the texts given.

Firstly, we will not be covering the Old Testament; as for those who search for the truth, will find it bears little historical truth. Most of the teachings were channelled and narrated to others in story form, to enable people to grasp the understanding of what needed to be learnt. Therefore, as these stories have passed from generation to generation, their true teachings have been lost.

For all those who place their faith in the Bible, we would ask that before they dedicate their life to following its teachings; each and every one of them goes in search, to substantiate the people and occurrences that are said to have taken place. We will guarantee they will find many untruths on their journey; and many will be afraid to take the journey of knowledge.

We will begin with the New Testament. The beginning of the conception of Jesus Christ is taken from a collection of Egyptian, Greek, Syrian and Persian myths. Each myth told of a god who was born of a virgin; became of the flesh; was seen as a Messiah and then brutally murdered by evil wrong doers: Dionysus, Adonis and Osiris are just examples. However, there was a child known as Joshua (Yeshua). He was able to channel and connect to God; light; the one true consciousness. His teachings were simple and in his village he was revered. These teachings were picked up by travellers and passed on from village to village.

If we look to the gospel of Matthew chapter 5, verse 3:-

Blessed are the poor in spirit; for theirs is the kingdom of heaven. What Joshua was trying to teach, was positivism. They had the spirit; the power of belief to change their situation. (If they think themselves poor, they 'are' poor. If they think themselves blessed, they 'are' blessed. Although they may be poor, they are still blessed in spirit, because they have the light within them.)

Blessed are they that mourn, for they shall be comforted. The power of love and light will overcome and ease their pain, if they allow love and light to enter into their hearts. To have experienced a connection of love and light between yourself and the person who has passed; should be a joyful experience to be thankful for, not one to be of sorrow.

Blessed are the meek for they shall inherit the earth. Was meant to teach that to connect with the heart, humankind must set aside their egos and not see themselves as separate from others; for all of you are one.

Blessed are they which hunger and thirst after righteousness for they shall be filled. Those who carry out their life in search of knowledge, truth, love and light, will be filled with peace and oneness.

Blessed are the merciful; for they shall obtain mercy. Those who show care, compassion and understanding, will in turn receive the same. Light will create light. Love will create love.

Blessed are the pure in heart for they shall see God. Those who operate from the heart, in love, light and knowledge, will connect with God; light; the one true consciousness; and the knowing of all things will come to pass.

Blessed are the peacemakers: for they shall be called the children of God. All those who are of the light and spread light, will create peace and harmony. They are an extension of God; light; the one true consciousness; as your children are from you.

Blessed are they which are persecuted for righteousness sake, for theirs is the kingdom of heaven. Truth, love and light can never be destroyed. To be pure of heart and mind, this connection to God; light; the one true consciousness; can never be severed.

Blessed are ye, when men shall revile you and persecute you, and shall say all manner of evil against you falsely for my sake. For all those people who believe in themselves and operate from the heart, there are no words or action of others which can truly destroy the power of the light within.

In verse 16:-

Let your light so shine before men that they may see your good works, and glorify your Father which is in

heaven. Be the light. Shine with love, compassion and understanding of others; so that together you can come together and connect to God; light; the one true consciousness.

So that we encourage open thought and not create barriers to those who shy away, or struggle with the words of the Bible, it is important that you search out, as we have asked before; the truth.

Learn to question what is placed before you. Learn to listen; to ask, "What if?" Be thankful for the opportunity to hear a different point of view. Then go in seek of proof, so that you can discover for yourself without doubt, where truth lies.

Many times people take what is given without question. Knowledge is light. But ensure that the knowledge has been acquired through one's own search for truth, and not that which others feel you should just accept.

You will find very little historical evidence dated during the period of Jesus' life. Of all the historians who lived in his lifetime, none recorded many of the great miracles he was said to perform. We concur that Joshua 'did' live; and his teachings were taught far and wide; but there was no crucifixion. The only crucifixion that took place, was that he was continually challenged and hated by those who controlled the land at that time. Joshua was murdered, but there was no great darkness that covered the earth.

The earth did not shake with such magnitude that temples and buildings were destroyed. Many who read this will not believe what is written. And to those who doubt our word, we ask that you seek out historical data from the historians, that such an event was ever recorded by any one person of that time. You will find many supposedly sacred texts, that were pre-dated, to give that appearance; but none will be found which are accurate, for this occurrence never existed.

For now, we will leave you to consider what has been given. There will be many who will not wish to search to verify what we have given, but we would ask one final question. Those of you who have placed your faith in the literal word of the Bible:- if you really do believe in your God, you will not hesitate to go in search of the facts, so that you may have the honour of disproving what is written.

By this, we do not mean preaching the scripture you already have, but go for yourselves now. Go to historians. Visit the places mentioned and seek out the truth. We assure you that you will be reborn and awakened to the truth that awaits, to set you all free from the blindness you currently are experiencing.

Glenn's thoughts: What's really interesting here is the challenge that Metatron puts forward to Christians and other religious groups. We are led to believe by religions that there is one Creator, who is given different names in different religions. We are led to believe that this one Creator has used people we call prophets, to spread the word of The Creator. All those prophets are dead and can't be challenged as to the authenticity, or the true words that were given from The Creator.

Here we have the direct, almost exact wording from Archangel Metatron; who is the one direct connection to The Creator. For it to be 100% exact would demand that Metatron channels through Jill every time and we record her voice, and then transcribe that into this book. What Jill transcribes from Metatron is far more accurate than any channelled writing in Biblical times. Not only that; she's here to be challenged. But she can only be challenged on what Metatron said; not the validity of 'what' he said. Jill is the prophet; the messenger; and as we should all know:- You don't shoot the messenger.

Core beliefs are not easily changed. The change affects so many other things. A change in core belief ripples change in other beliefs, attitude, emotion and behaviour.

Consider some core beliefs that have been changed: The world is flat. Man will never fly. Man will never set foot on the moon (OK there's some debate here). Light travels in straight lines.

When a core belief is changed, we start to challenge our other beliefs, which creates uncertainty and instability. People in general like the status quo in many things. To expect someone to stop worshipping Jesus Christ on the cross is tantamount to telling them they've been brainwashed all their life; and most people don't like to feel they've been manipulated and feel foolish. Much better to stick with the status quo and turn a blind eye to Metatron.

People laughed at Henry Ford and said the car would never catch on. People laughed at the Wright Brothers and said it would never catch on. People laughed at colour T.V. and said it would never catch on. People laughed at spiritual people, called them witches 200 years ago and burnt them at the stake. Thirty years ago, psychic mediums were few and far between to the public. Five years ago, Jill had hardly any men call her for a reading. Today around 25% of her clients are men.

So why do so many millions of people follow the word of the Bible so blindly? It's time to progress and determine our true purpose in life.

30: A Christmas holiday message

20th December 2005, nearing Christmas holidays

Jill is channelling Archangel Metatron, Michael, Gabriel, Chamuel, Uriel and Rafael

Metatron: Greetings! We are pleased you are communing with us again. Michael, Gabriel, Chamuel, Uriel and Rafael are here with me, to combine energies.

We feel it is perhaps time to actually bring forth a message at this special time; in the hope that those who read this, will look upon their loved ones and take our message to their hearts and minds.

Please spread our words so that they may manifest amongst those who are lost and in need of direction; and also; those who preach in the name of God: consider our words.

At this time when most of humankind is preparing to spend quality time with each other, we would ask that you stop for a few moments and listen within your hearts.

It is time to stop the violence and killing that is justified in the name of God. It is time to put aside your political and prejudiced views and look around you at the other human beings in this world; and ask yourself; why for so long have you and your predecessors continued to follow words that inspire you to take up arms against your fellow men; and view each other as enemies?

Millions of men, women and children have been slaughtered; and yet if you truly looked with your heart, how could you truly hurt another human being? For in doing so you destroy yourself.

Where is your self-belief? Why do you continue to blindly turn away and just accept the atrocities? Some of you will say that you are powerless to do anything; but let us just consider something.

The mysteries of life are just that. Many questions go unanswered. But look at who you are. Once born, you cannot choose to be male or female, black or white. You are what you are. However, the one thing that gives you your power and control; is free will.

Your free will is what gives you the right to live and be who you are. It is your one defining characteristic; nothing else. You choose how to act, how to react. So we are asking of you now

www.anewbelief.com

to choose for yourself the type of person you really want to be; and the world you really want to create for your children, and their children.

It is time that you all woke up and realised that whilst every one of you takes your religious man-made writings to be the word of God, you will never truly see the real glory of God; light; the one conscious thought.

It is time to put away and forget the words that inspire you to turn against each other. It is time you began worshipping the beauty of life and those who share this planet with you.

The whole purpose of your existence was to experience freedom, love and creation.

We're saddened that you have never really questioned if you should follow and give praise to someone, when they told you to sacrifice your children. When they tell you that only you are the chosen ones who will reach heaven and everyone else is evil.

When they ask you to turn away from those who are different from yourselves, look into your hearts. Are these the words that inspire you to be the person you know yourself to be? You all want happiness. Do the writings inspire you to live in peace and create that happiness?

The book of revelations will, if action is not taken, transpire not through God's will, but the minds of men; who are fanatically following these writings and are ready to push the button. For they so blindly believe that they will then sit at the right hand side of God.

This could never be further from the truth. Preaching to congregations that they need to prepare for Armageddon is not going to inspire people to create a better world. It is this type of preaching and misinterpretation after misinterpretation that tells you you're unworthy, you're a sinner, you're evil; when nothing could be further from the truth.

The truth is: you are from God; light; the one conscious thought and therefore already possess the qualities of love and light within you. When humankind works from the heart, humankind can create great monuments, great inventions that assist you in your life on this planet. Together in times of crisis, you can put down your weapons of destruction and come to the aid of others. The energy that this creates and a sense of self-worth it creates can not be matched.

Please consider your future very carefully, when you next open your mouth to speak. Will your words be of kindness and encouragement, or words of darkness and destruction? Each and every one of you, can make a difference. It is time to stop looking for salvation. You already have the power to create and give salvation to each other.

You do not need to ask or pay for atonement. You have the power to give this to yourself, through your actions. If you have done wrong, forgive yourself, wipe the slate clean and ensure your actions are positive ones that help, encourage and assist yourself and others.

This is not a pipe dream. We have told you many times; your thoughts create your reality. We can only do so much. We can only give guidance. It has to be each and every one of you that turns to the light and embraces that light together, as one united nation.

It is time to go out to your enemies and learn all you can about them, and for them to learn about you. Yes you're different, but you are also one and the same. Take away the image, the colour of your skin, the language you speak. You all have blood running through your veins. You all have a heart. You all possess the ability to love and care. You all share the same air and planet. Surely it is time you rinsed out your eyes and looked at the world with new eyes and new hope?

It is time to stop following blindly, laws and writings that are not of your time. Perhaps this holiday period you share with your family, just this once, you take time to stop and think of your future, and how you play such a vital important role in the lives of those people around you and on the other side of this planet.

We love you all and bring you energies of light and healing. We hope it will help those of you in search of happiness. We hope you'll take the opportunity of giving rebirth to yourself, and discover the loving, light person you would like to be and can be; if you so choose.

Angels collectively speaking: We unite together from North, South, East and West, to bring together the cosmic universal life force energy, to assist and heal the rift of pain within the planet, for the betterment of mankind.

We bring the one true constant energy of love. Our only wish is to bring humanity peace and happiness. Always remember we are always here for everyone. If you need sustenance, healing, assistance; ask us, and we'll do whatever we can within the realms of the universal light force energy.

Peace be with you.

Archangels...
Metatron,
Michael,
Gabriel,
Chamuel,
Uriel and Rafael

31: The meaning of life

21st December 2005

Jill is channelling Archangel Chamuel

Chamuel: Hello! It is my greatest pleasure that I speak with you today. I am Chamuel. My purpose is to assist humankind, and help each and every one of you, in finding your life's purpose and how to build firm foundations and maintain relationships.

For the purpose of Glenn, who I know will ask of you where my strengths lie, I lead the 'Powers of Angels' who guide and protect this world from negative energies. I assist those in need of comfort and intervention. I am here for those who seek God; in all its truth and light.

Perhaps we should begin with one of the oldest questions in human time. What is the purpose of life?

So many of you spend hours, weeks, days, years; wondering where you came from, why you are here, where you're going and what your purpose is on this planet?

By listening with your heart, you will discover your origin. Your origin is from God; light; the one conscious thought, which is in fact the one supreme TRUTH.

Unfortunately, most of human kind has turned away from their light within. They have denied themselves the truth for so long, it is sad. For all of human kind's claim of progress, 'what', we would ask, do you call progress? More so than ever, the numbers of wars being fought; murders, people stealing and lying; has never been so great. Your purpose on this planet has and always been humanity.

Instead of creating barriers between yourself and others, you should have been creating and building togetherhood. The reason why so many of you are so unhappy and have lost faith, is that you lack true understanding about yourself and the greatness that lies within.

Your origin is from God, therefore just like God; light; the one conscious thought, you have within you a greatness that needs awakening. Your universe is one energy. God; light; the one conscious thought; created everything from within itself, as you so have the power to do. You're not different from anyone else. You are not different from God; light; the one conscious thought.

It is your understanding of yourselves that has caused you to lose direction. You believe yourselves to be men, women, children; fat, thin, beautiful, ugly, rich, poor, strong, weak, happy, miserable, English, Jewish, Arabic, American, Russian, Catholics, Protestants, Jews, Hindus, Buddhists; and yet you all come from one origin:- God; light; the one conscious thought.

It is time to teach your children to put aside these titles and roles they play. It is time children and adults learn there is only one role in life; to access the divinity within. Then and only then can you truly know that you are all one; God; light; the one conscious thought.

Your free will allows you to define your own life. Do you choose to see yourself as ordinary and weak? Do you choose to just pass through life, accepting whatever is said to you, and then die?

Or, do you choose to see yourself as someone who has the power to be the best they can be? That they can make a difference in their own and others' lives. By your own choice, you can reach God; or descend into your own creation of hell. If you look into your heart and access your emotions, you will feel the power of God within your very being.

By accessing this power, you could if you so wish, become powerful and almighty like God; light; the one conscious thought; for remember 'we are all one'. You were given this ability, so you could discover the greatness you possess; and yet, the vast majority of the population on this planet waste their energy fighting over petty material gains, chasing the pleasure of senses with food, alcohol and sharing brief moments of intimacy; fighting with others, having a family and then they sit back and say they've fulfiled their purpose.

Compare yourselves with animals, for every day they wander into the jungle to ensure longevity for themselves and the ability to provide for their offspring. So too, does mankind wander into the corporate jungle and then return back to their families. So what is it that makes you different?

For were you to not look further than what I have just said, you would feel that perhaps you are no different from the animals.

What is it that makes a human being special; unique?

You have within you, the unique ability to experience your identity with God. You are here on this planet to get to know 'you', the creative being that you are; the being that has the ability to help make dreams come true. The being that has the ability to bring forth and give love to others and also to experience receiving love.

Once you understand, you will see 'YOU' are the temple within which God dwells. This not only makes you someone who is great, but also something to be valued. Do you value yourself? Do you value those around you?

Learn to understand the divine consciousness within yourself, for if you do not truly understand and learn all about yourself, you will never know God.

Every one of you really wants to eliminate suffering, and experience happiness. You all cry out for acceptance and love. Even when you do harm against another, in reality, it is with the sub-conscious hope it will bring about happiness for yourself.

Look around you. What do most people do to attain happiness? They pair into couples, have children, work to earn money so they can buy possessions and experience entertainment. But all these things are reliant on external factors. When you connect with the divine consciousness within yourself, you will uncover the truth; that the ability to create happiness lies within; and not in the possessions and people you have around you.

Perhaps it's time you taught yourself; your loved ones and the future of your world: the children; to look within themselves, for all of you have the choice whether to sow seeds of pain, or seeds of happiness.

What is truly amazing is that despite the thousands of years that have passed, and the amount of historical data you have to look back at, on human kind's follies; no one has stopped to look at how they can change and end this horrible cycle you all seem stuck in. Instead it is easier to whine, complain and point blame at others. You continue to waste your time on 'if onlys'.

How many people do you hear saying, "If only my partner loved me." "If only we had more money." "If only I could get a better job," and so it continues until you run out of tomorrows.

Look at your life with new eyes. Start to discover the God; light; one conscious thought that lies within you. Start to look at how you can access the happiness within. Learn to stop super-imposing your hopes and dreams on something external, for it does not come from there; it comes from within.

Look at your material possessions; the people around you. When your day has ended and you close your eyes, everything that you have, is unnecessary. Whilst asleep you don't need love. You don't need possessions. You don't need sustenance such as food, drink. When you awaken, you have, on your own, renewed your energy. You're strong! For you have accessed the power that was within you.

The vastness that is within each human body, is that of a universe. Your light within you is far brighter than the planet you call the sun. Nothing can compare with the human ability to create, when it is one with the divine energy within.

I hope that what I have given to you today, will resonate within the hearts and minds of mankind. We will bring further lessons to those who wish to reunite the Self with God. We want you all to awaken, so that you may see, and experience oneness with God.

For when you experience God; light, the one conscious thought; you will experience virtue, beauty and most importantly true love. By experiencing and connecting with your inner divinity, you will see a radiance emanate from the very depths of your soul, that the world you see as a beautiful environment, will pale in comparison.

Everything you seek, is within. God; light; the one conscious thought dwells in every human being, and everyone's true purpose is to connect and learn about Self so you may identify and experience God.

In love and light, we will commune again soon. Blessed be you.....

Chamuel.

32: Truth about Mohammad

23rd December 2005

Jill is channelling Archangel Metatron

Greetings dear child of light. Today we will lift the veil of secrecy that surrounds Muhammad; as we look at how Muslims came into being.

Unlike the Torah, which is based on many myths and legends, we will begin by saying that Muhammad did actually walk the earth plane; and in his youth was a great channeller. Muhammad's early life and teachings were amongst the Jews and Christians of that time, which is why you will find in his earlier days he talks of Abraham, Moses and Jesus.

It is sad that as the lessons were channelled through Muhammad, they were never recorded at that time. It wasn't until a decade after Muhammad's death that the Quran was actually completed. It was pieced together from the bits of notes others had written down; in remembrance. This is why, if you were to read through the Quran, it is out of context both in writings and meanings; as so with the Bible, contradictory in many places, For; over the time it took to put together, in the Quran you will find that once again, man's own interpretation of the some of the events and some of the lessons taught, bear little resemblance to the truth.

Originally, the messages channelled, spoke of how man and woman should work together side by side. There was to be, as there should be now, no difference; or one mightier than the other. For each brought their own special qualities to the earth plane that complemented the other. For example: a man's strength would be complemented by a women's softness.

Later you will find that as Muhammad's power grew, the lessons originally taught were changed; and mankind was told that a woman should hide her face, and if she were bad, that she should be beaten.

He instructed the Islamic men that God would allow them to keep concubines. This not only helped justify his own desires, it also ensured that Islam grew in population, so that one day, it would become the greatest nation.

As with Catholicism, Judaism and Christianity, mankind's own innate fears took hold of their female counterpart's strengths. The religious leaders preached exclusivity to the male population and shunned women, despite the fact that you are all created equal in the eyes of God; light; the one conscious energy.

The messages that were originally brought to Muhammad were to serve as completion of God; light; the one conscious energy's advice to mankind. The power that this gave to Muhammad, allowed him to become very powerful, and important to the Islamic community. It was only a matter of time before he began to use, and abuse this power for his own egotistical, self-proclaimed status, to rule the Islamic community through manipulation, extortion and brutality.

At this time, he convinced the many warring tribes to join together and become his army. He then sent his army out to enlist people to his cause. Those that refused were slain. Muhammad's army was a force to be reckoned with, and you will find historical data to confirm the atrocities this army carried out; supposedly in the name of God; light; the one conscious thought.

Let it be stated here and now for all those who truly want to be one with God; light; the one conscious energy: that no one area or country has been specially chosen by God; light; the one conscious energy. Why would God; light, the one conscious energy create a whole world, if only one particular area was supposedly more worthy?

Why would God; light; the one conscious energy, create the earth plane; place upon it human beings with great ability; and then incite these beings to start holy wars, jihad's, ethnic cleansing? Would you build a house, fill it with your children, so they could kill, maim, torture each other and tear down the house?

As with most parents, who are creators, you want your children to search out happy experiences; to live in peace, love and harmony. So why do so many of you follow such teachings that ask you to be so evil and do harm to your fellow man?

No human being has, nor ever will, bring forth the direct words of God; light; the one conscious energy. Those that do so, have done so for no other reason than their own egotistical, pious beliefs. So it is advisable that you seek God; light; the one conscious energy, for yourself, through yourself; and not some self-proclaimed religious leader who tells you that the only way to God; light; the one conscious energy is through them.

Those who read this, may well ask, "Is there no difference between these religious leaders and this medium here?" There is a vast difference. This medium here has not incited you to a holy war; jihad. Nor has this medium asked you to judge or treat others differently than you would yourself. The medium we have used, has only channelled words that ask you to go seek out for yourself and make your own self-informed decisions.

We will ensure that you are shown how to access and connect with God; light; the one conscious energy, shortly; for we are aware that many people profess that it can be achieved, but do not show the how's and why's.

The awakening is starting. The new world; the new belief, has begun; and many uncomfortable changes lay ahead for those who fear, or choose not to search out the truth. The day of reckoning for those who have misled, extorted money from the blind in the name of God; light; the one conscious energy, will come. Their downfall will not be of God; light; the one conscious energy's doing, but their own.

Blessed be; we will commune again soon.

Metatron.

33: Worship yourself first; to find God

27th December 2005

Jill is channelling Archangel Chamuel

Chamuel: Greetings. We have given you much to consider. However, those who read of our teachings, we would ask if they truly grasp the meanings of our teachings?

It is so hard for you all to understand and accept that, unless you know yourself, no amount of practicing religious rites, prayers, or acts will connect you with God; light; the one conscious energy. You will never find God in churches, temples, mosques. For you must remember God is formless. When you discover and accept the truth for yourselves, you will see that all forms of worship, rituals and religions, should be abandoned; for the only thing you should worship is yourselves.

Jill: Why worship yourself?

Chamuel: God exists in every part of you. God is not an external thing. When you understand this and it resonates within you as truth, enlightenment is yours. Presently millions of people pray, fast, and live their lives under the delusion that God is elsewhere. If that is so, does this mean you've been abandoned?

In reality, God has never left you. For God; light; the one conscious energy is you. There are no special methods to contacting God. It is the awareness of God residing in you, that you have to become aware of.

Many of you are trying to find God. You're looking and yet you're not seeing or feeling God. Look in the mirror. Look into your eyes. It is difficult to see God, when you don't really see yourself.

Jill: Why don't we truly see ourselves?

Chamuel: It is your mind that blocks you from finding God. Through years of programming from other humans you have learnt to block and hide your inner self. This is why your mind can be your worst nightmare and your happiest experience. Because of this, yoga and meditation were brought to mankind.

Jill: Why meditation and yoga?

Chamuel: For when you truly experience stillness, and you free yourself from the thoughts that hound you, you connect with your inner soul. There you find true liberation, knowledge and light. It is the way you can connect with the one conscious energy; light, which you call God.

To meditate, it is important that you understand the mind, its worth to you and the vast ability it possesses to manufacture, devise, ponder and bring forth knowledge. The mind cannot be forced into meditation, you have to understand your mind and slowly learn the art of letting go of thoughts.

Jill: How do you do this?

Chamuel: By realising the mind is nothing more than pure energy of consciousness. All the time, your thoughts come and go, even whilst asleep you dream, consciousness is constantly creating. When a thought is created in your mind, you create words, pictures; and then together you give the words, pictures meaning by adding emotions. It is when words, pictures and emotions combine that your inner energy; God; light; the one conscious energy, affects your human body. Hence; once consciousness has created a thought, it is your choice whether it becomes pain or joy, love or jealousy. It is this same awareness that can help you to attain inner peace and connectedness.

Just for now, breathe deeply, think calm, warm, content. Do you see how easy it is to liberate your agitated mind?

Jill: Yes, yet I still don't quite see how this connects us with God.

Chamuel: You will. We have to get you to first start seeing yourself as already complete and at one with God. To do this, requires you to retrain your mind. Start to be aware of yourself. Think of your choices, before saying something or answering someone's question.

Tomorrow, we will introduce you to connecting with God; light; the one conscious energy, through the use of your Kundalini. Do not worry at this time about the pronunciation, or its meaning. Try to practice quiet contemplation for the rest of the day. Practicing letting thoughts come and go. Do not dwell on them. Everyone can meditate and let their mind free. Anyone who watches the T.V., experiences this, so it is not hard to learn how to connect with God; light; the one conscious energy.

Until tomorrow. Blessed be and remember that God already resides in thee.

Chamuel.

34 The Holy Spirit: Connecting with God

28th December 2005

Jill is channelling Archangel Chamuel

Chamuel: Greetings! We know that you would perhaps prefer to be relaxing and being with your children, so we thank you for communing with us once again. We will first look at what the Kundalini is.

The Kundalini means many things to many people and is known under a variety of names:- In Christianity, the Kundalini is known as the Holy Spirit. The Chinese refer to the Kundalini as Chi. Japanese as Ki. In India it is known as Shakti. To us, it is known as 'supreme energy'.

However; many great channellers, sages and spiritually gifted teachers who have connected with this energy have named it Kundalini. Therefore, to help those who seek to connect with God; light; the one conscious energy, we have called it so; to enable you to research for yourselves. And also if you need to, you can connect with a teacher will who help you through this process of connecting with your inner supreme power.

This is extremely advisable if you find it hard to still your mind, relax or meditate. This source of energy resides in every living thing: trees, plants, animals, birds and humans. It is formless and is the supreme energy that controls every living cell. Without this, nothing would function. To connect with God; light; the one conscious energy you need to awaken the Kundalini within you.

To do this, you need to project your awareness within and not project it outwards, as most of you currently do. Learning to project your awareness inwards can be done in many forms: meditation (Or as some would prefer to call it: reflection.), yoga; through the use of sound, like mantra's (Which is popular with Buddhists.), chanting, physical exercise and also through breathing techniques.

Once you have awakened the Kundalini, you will discover the supreme power to enable self healing, and a whole new perspective on your true nature and the one true connection to God; light; the one conscious energy.

It is very important at this stage that we explain that when you experience and awaken the Kundalini, you will experience manifestation. And for those who aren't quite sure what is happening, may feel that they are becoming ill. It is quite normal for you to experience flashing lights, visions and strong emotions. Although we would advise that you will be quite safe and able to control the surge of power you'll feel. If you wish to attempt the teachings we bring you, please remember that 'you' are in control and try your best not to feel frightened. At times you may experience some of the following:-

- Feeling highly emotional, tearful, joyful, angry.
- Extreme tiredness.
- A feeling of detachment, or negativity towards oneself.
- Seeing of auras, coloured lights, orbs or balls.
- Insomnia or agitation.

If you do experience any of these, then you should be pleased, for you are indeed awakening your inner energy and experiencing a detoxification of energies that are currently affecting your physical body. It is also important that once you venture on this pathway, it is with the right motivation. Your true desire to connect with God; light; the one conscious energy, in its purest divine form.

Whilst it will not affect you materially, it will affect your actions, the way you are and how you travel through your life's journey. It will bring you happiness, health and peace.

To help get you started, we would suggest you find a comfortable chair to sit on, or if you prefer, cross-legged on the floor. If using a chair, ensure that your clothing is loose and that you have no restricting belts or shoes. Place your feet firmly on the floor and ensure that your back is upright. If you slouch, you will not be able to allow your breathing to be full. Ensure you are somewhere, where you'll not be disturbed by your telephones, T.V., family or friends, unless you wish to try this in a group.

Your breath is what connects you with the universe; the cosmic energies. So it is with this thought that we will first begin with breath. When you breathe, you breathe in a rhythmic pace that is at one with the energies that surround you.

Try to focus on your breath as you breathe in. Allow the breath to completely fill your diaphragm and you'll notice that for a short, brief spell, before you exhale, there is a nothingness, where the breath doesn't come in, or out. This is

www.anewbelief.com

the space where your supreme energy is: truth; God; light; the one conscious energy.

When you first try it, you will probably hold your breath. This is not what we want you to aspire to. We want you to become aware of the breath entering and leaving the physical body. Initially practice this technique for 15 minutes, and as you progress, build your way up until you can attain this quietness of mind for one and half hours every day. Learn to follow your breath. Listen to it. Listen for the space in between the breaths. Slowly become aware of this space.

For as you progress, you will find the space in between, becoming longer. Try this for a suitable period of time. Do not rush or force yourself. Allow your natural energies to guide you. When we next commune, we will show you how to incorporate what we have given you today, with the use of mantras for those who are really struggling.

We would ask that perhaps you research mantras and the different methods people around the world use, to assist you with helping others connect with God; light; the one conscious energy. If possible pay particular attention to those that resonate to the voice vibration of ohm, ham, so.

Blessed be, Chamuel.

Metatron 28-12-05.

Metatron: These teachings that Chamuel has brought you are in-depth and need time to be learnt well. We feel it would be beneficial for you to now set aside time in your busy schedule to assist Glenn, he is .....

Interrupted by max.

Max: Can I have a drink Mom?

Jill: Get out Max; you've been told to leave Mommy alone in this room. Go see your father.

It was too late. The connection was broken. When Jill comes out of the connection suddenly, it gives her a big headache and she can't continue. Guess I'll have to wait for the next lesson, to see what's in store for me...

Glenn.

35: First meditation

4th January 2006

It's a new year and it seems like we've so many hurdles in front of us. The kids went back to school today, so it seemed the best time to find quiet time to start the meditation exercises that have been asked of me.

I'm not the 'sit-still, eyes closed and think of nothing' type, so I knew this wasn't going to be easy. Jill and I went to our bedroom, away from any phones, and sat to meditate. I point-blank refused to chant mantras. I've seen the butts of so many jokes about people sitting, going ommmm; ommmm; ommmm. You have to remember that a few years ago; I was one of the people that would make fun and take the piss; just like many people are going to do the same with me, in the days to come.

Still; if I can't get the connection without it, I guess I'm going to have to do what's asked of me. You see; I'm their test bed. A past negative, non-believer, who's wrapped up in the rat-race of the logical, material world of commerce, technology and media. But for now, I'm going to do it the hard way; without the mantras.

Jill tells me that if she meditates with me; 'her' energy will help combine with 'my' energy to help me 'see the light'. Problem with that is, the first time we sat down together, I just burst into giggles. Now you've got to imagine this. Remember back in your school days, when you weren't allowed to talk or mess around in class? Well there were some of us that just couldn't handle it, and would burst into fits of uncontrollable giggles. That was me.

I'd just had a giggle fit the night before. We'd had fresh veg' for dinner and I'd been warned not to fart in bed. When I got to bed around 10.00pm; we were just settling down to sleep, and I let one go. It was knocking me out. I knew I had to keep quiet, or Jill would get naffed off; and I started to giggle. Then the giggling got worse, until finally the bed was shaking. There were tears streaming down my face. I could hardly breathe for the length of the giggles. My face will have looked like a 'first day in the sun' 12-hour sunburn. Jill does her best to ignore me; unlike what she does. She wants to make sure that I know about hers straight away. She's a cover-wafter you see.

So I was in the mood for giggling. I had to pull on all my 'sensible' resources to get going with the meditation. Jill set an alarm for 15 minutes. Now 15 minutes of conscious breathing in silence; for most people; is a big deal. And I'm no exception.

Eventually I held back the giggles and settled down. You have to inhale deeply through the nose, and exhale slowly through the nose. If you do it through your mouth, you end up getting dry-mouth, which will interrupt you after a time, because of your need for water to re-hydrate. It's also important that you go to the bathroom and 'empty' before you start too.

So there I was; sat comfortably; eyes closed; inhale; exhale; for what I knew would seem like an eternity. Jill asked me to notice any colour changes or shapes in my mind.

After about a third of the way through, an image started to appear. I recognised the type of image straight away. Now I don't know just how many other people experience these images, when they're trying to go to sleep at night, so I'll do my best to describe them to you:

When I'm drifting off to sleep, but my mind is still busy, my brain feels tired, but I have difficulty drifting off to sleep. It's during this time that I start to visualise tiny white shapes of people's faces. They usually appear one at a time. It starts of as a tiny speck of light which seems far away. Gradually the light drifts closer and starts to take the shape of a ghostly white, transparent face. The face is still tiny in comparison to my 'mind's eye' viewing area. Imagine looking at a computer screen with Microsoft opened in 'desktop', with all your icons for shortcuts to programmes. Well these faces don't get much bigger than the icons... usually.

Sometimes the faces turn round to the left or to the right. Sometimes they shift shape and distort. Sometimes the same face changes shape several times. Sometimes they become head and shoulders. Sometimes two or three appear at once.

But then sometimes they start to move forward, and they open their mouths towards me. Sometimes they turn into the foulest of ghoul-like figures and monsters. They fly towards me like screaming banshees; except without the sound. No matter how I try, I can't get them to go away. There's times when there's a succession of them screaming towards me, one after another. They always fade off to the outer edges of my mind's-eye vision. As they fly towards me, sometimes their mouths open extraordinarily wide, totally out of context with the rest of their face; as though they were trying to swallow my head.

When I told Jill about this a few weeks ago, she explained that they were evil entities that the negative mind conjures up. I'd always thought they were distortions of previous visions in the memory, that the mind plays tricks with as you drift into 'alpha state'. A way of emptying unwanted images. Jill explained that they weren't harmful, and I simply needed to call on my guardian angels to get rid of them.

When Jill channelled Beelzebub (Bee-ell-zee-bub) the other day, they came out in force as I tried to get to sleep; so I gave it a whirl. I called on Azrael, Raphael and Gabriel to get rid of them. Well! Whadoyouknow; it worked.

So back to the meditation. The little white speck of light had appeared, and it was moving towards me. At first it seemed like another demonic figure. It had a head with what appeared to be solid whisker shapes coming out from its cheeks and the sides of its upper head. It had cat-like features and stripes across its face. Remember, it was transparent too, so it took time to pick out the detail. Also, the shape moved towards me, disappeared and then started the process again; as though it kept trying to 'get through'. On this occasion though, I knew it wasn't an evil entity, because it didn't open its mouth at me.

Eventually this faded away and I had a new vision. Imagine an eclipse of the sun, by the moon. I had sun eclipses rise up in front of my eyes. The crescent of the sun was the same size arc as my eyes. They slowly rose up through my mind's-eye vision, one following another. The halo was a yellow-green colour and the background was a very dark red. This continued for about three or four minutes I guess. It was a warm feeling. At the same time I felt taughtness on my face, from above my nose to my forehead.

After 15 minutes the alarm rang out and I shared my experience with Jill. She explained that the cat-like figure was an entity coming to me to show me strength; like a tiger. The colours rising, was the beginning of my energy vibrations starting to rise. At the moment, we already know my energy vibrations are very low. Metatron made a point of telling me some time ago. Apparently I have to learn how to raise my energy vibration levels to a much faster speed, to be able to communicate with the angels.

Jill also explained that the taughtness of the face that I felt, may have been me accessing my 'mind's-eye'. She explained that sometimes her forehead has a piercing pain in the centre of it, when she starts to channel; and this is why she gets headache if she's interrupted and loses the connection suddenly.

Well; there you have it. My first experience at meditation. I probably made more progress than expected, bearing in mind I was told to expect nothing for a long while yet.

I'll continue to persevere with this, 'cos if I can't connect to the spirit world; how am I going to expect others to believe in this new belief?

There was another benefit though. Both Jill and I admitted that sitting together side by side, breathing deeply, had made us think sexy thoughts, which we both found we had to suppress and empty our minds... until the alarm bell went, that is. We finished our debrief together; and had nooky.

36: Jill visits the Healing Chamber

10th January 2006

Jill's been unwell for a couple of days. Her eyes are hurting and she's been unable to get rid of a headache for around 3 days. She visited the doctor who diagnosed eye-strain from computer screen, and a viral infection.

I've been meditating most days. Some days, if Jill isn't well enough she won't meditate and I've wanted to be with her to access her energies. Now's the time to start meditating on my own if need be. I must keep the process going, even though it still feels alien to me. I'm determined not to give up.

Jill asked me to go and meditate with her, even though she was feeling ill. We sat and meditated for twenty minutes. When the alarm went at twenty minutes, Jill switched it off and went back into her meditation. She was channelling again.

When she finally came round, I asked her where she'd 'been'. She told me she'd been to the Healing Chamber. She said that at first she was looking into blackness for ages, thinking, "Oh great, it looks like they've cut me off for good." But then Metatron came to her; acknowledged her with a nod of his head and ushered her to follow him. They flew off through space, to a planet where they approached tall buildings which were made of crystal; hexagonal in shape.

Inside she was led to a chair where a female angel sat her down. Swirling light appeared above her and spiralled down, surrounding her. She said it was wonderful and soothing. It made her feel much better. When she'd had the treatment, Metatron brought her back, acknowledging that she needed to be in better health to continue channelling him.

I told Jill that I'd not achieved much; a few rising eclipsed colours, the odd orb and some flashing lights that were a little like lots of lightening flashes across my eyes.

Jill told me to be thankful, in that I seemed to be progressing well. Then she told me of a friend who meditated for ten years with no results and then it suddenly arrived at once; in that she's now a practising psychic medium and can channel.

Jill used to meet her at a spiritual church, so I'm guessing that maybe she only meditated at the church each week. Meditating daily should produce results much quicker, so if you've been following these chapters, and you've started, or are about to start meditating: persevere. This is your 'only' connection to God and the after-life whilst you habit this planet.

37: Bible myths; and our relation to the universes

12th January 2006

Metatron: Greetings. It is good that you are well enough for us to continue and perhaps bring forth more revelations, to help seekers of the truth find their way.

There are so many thoughts, ideas and questions that run through your brain, it is important that we try to maintain some resemblance of order and balance. So let us take things slowly and see if we can bring some closure to those questions and thoughts you have.

Prior to Christianity, there were many myths, pagan rituals and various spiritual practices embraced by different people. People at that time used these myths and spiritual rituals to bring forth spiritual truths to the masses. For you must remember, that many were 'unlearned' at that time. Just as you now have your super-hero's on celluloid, and you immerse yourself in the characters, it was the same for those who lived at that time. Why were these myths created? To bring forward hope, that all was not lost. By creating such characters as Pythagoras, Osiris, Jesus; it enabled mankind to create a mouthpiece that could not be destroyed physically. Words of wisdom were literally placed into the mouths of these characters.

If you were to study the disciple Paul's authentic letters, you will find these pre-dated the gospels of your Bible by decades. No mention of Jesus will you find in these documents. Paul's teachings originally taught others to honour the Christ (God) within. To become and acknowledge the one awareness that resides in all humans. His teachings of being re-born, were meant to symbolise union; the union of all souls, male and female, Jews and gentiles. His teachings of crucifixion, resurrection; was to symbolise shedding and death of the old self and resurrecting; and being reborn in Christ (God) and become one with all things.

It wasn't long before leaders in Christianity realised this was a way to have a hold on human kind. The cross was used to manipulate the masses through guilt, and ensure they knew their place and keep them down; for to question would mean hell and damnation.

 www.anewbelief.com

Let it be known, there was no water turned into wine. There was no walking on water. No crucifixion. No flogging. Look to the Bible. You will see that Joshua in your old testament, is Jesus again reborn. These allegorical myths have over time become one the most profound novels of all time. So much so, that it now deceives people into believing the accounts are actual historical events.

For most humans who profess to follow the teachings of Christ now; although they are happy to quote scripture to each other; very few lack the ability to really decipher for themselves, what is truth, and what is fiction. They possess lamentable ignorance, and use the written word as a weapon for 'covering' themselves. Very few have realised that by literally following these words, they have already created a world that has suffered a thousand years of misery; and are no nearer reaching the kingdom they refer to as heaven. How many more thousands of years do you all wish to be in misery for?

Do not be afraid of those who may call you a heretic; a Satanist; for those who do decry you and refuse to see and embrace the light, are showing you how weak they truly are. Their traditions as they know it, are doomed, for they are holding onto a medieval world that no longer exists, like sleeping beauty. It is time that the kiss of love; light; God; the one conscious energy, awakens them to the reality of who they truly are. It is time they realised that their continuance of believing in the status quo is what draws misery and suffering. The people who you give your power to: your prime ministers, presidents, religious leaders; are the ones who perpetuate division amongst you all, thus leading to violence, hatred, discrimination, abuse and suffering.

If you all learn to connect with the divine inside oneself, there will be no need for these leaders. For if you were all to realise you are one and the same, you would happily share the food and possessions you have. You would choose love and forgiveness; and peace would create and define for you, the world that God; light; the one conscious energy; actually had originally intended.

If what we teach here resonates within your heart, becomes a part of your feelings and consciousness; pass, in your own way, your beliefs, feelings and thoughts. Show it in your actions. It is possible to create new traditions and bring innovative teachings to others. Come to understand that if even without a trust in the Bible, the message is still the same: a belief in God; light; love; the one conscious energy; but through loving actions and liberation, not guilt, blame and brutality. What is given here, is for the needs of human beings today, not of yesteryear.

Transform your thinking. Understand yourself, your life and what life is all about. Question which is truth. When you're asleep, are you in fact experiencing reality, or when you are awake are you experiencing reality? There are so many insights and depths of life to be experienced, and very few are able to grasp the understanding, that within you is a power that is waiting to surge to the fore, and show you the possibilities of the human form. Discover the indivisible divinity within.

I know that you often struggle with yourself in relation to the world and the universe. Your universe is an energy field, and within this universe are many things: planets, star systems, beings, which together are unified. It is this unified field that creates a very strong energy. By coming together; this unified field (your energies [consciousness]) becomes form. It is this conscious thought that has created the physical.

Although you see yourself and the things around you as solid, you are in fact energy; light. In your universe you're a quantum. You're one of the smallest units of energy. I know that you struggle with atoms, protons, quarks, bosons; so to make it easier, the whole human race on your planet and your universe, when unified with the universes, is similar to a sub-atomic particle. To comprehend your relation to God; light; the one conscious energy, it is similar to you (the whole human race on the planet collectively) occupying the remainder of 99.999r% of empty space.

God; light; the one conscious energy, cannot be comprehended by mankind, but it 'can' be connected; through your words, deeds, thoughts and beliefs. Only by working from the heart, as we have so asked before, can you ever hope to achieve understanding of your place: why, and how there are a plethora of experiences and visions to be seen.

Interlinked with your planet, dimensionally, are four other planets. You do not see them, for they vibrate at different levels. Just as you cannot touch the signals a satellite emits to your planet and T.V. aerials, neither can you touch or cross these dimensions. However, those who have learnt to understand the composition of the body; the 'thought' is what has created you as physical; then you can understand and learn the ability to connect with those other dimensions. You would be able to think of a place and find yourself there. We know this is hard for you to grasp, but only when you can understand how energy works and it transpires and evolves, will you be able to understand evolution and see the universes that surround you.

We have talked at some length and no doubt your brow will be even more frowned as we progress. It is time to leave religion behind for a short while, and perhaps it is more important that we teach mankind about the universal life force grid that keeps everything unified; and how to utilise this energy to manifest for yourselves: total healing, acceptance of each other and harmonisation. It may be time for you to commune with The Council of Elders and perhaps introduce a member of The Council to others; for each of them brings special wisdom and teachings for the elements within a human life. Their energies are strong, so we suggest meditation prior to this. I will still accompany you, so you have nothing to fear. I will continue to be your overseer, for we have much to accomplish.

At this point Metatron took Jill to The Council of Elders, to show her where she would be going. This is how she described it:

Jill: We suddenly arrived at a place where we stood on what appeared to be a high rock ledge, looking out over the The Council and the scenery beyond. It was almost like the scene in the film 'Lion King', where Simba the lion stands on the high rock ledge and looks out over his kingdom.

Metatron had 'thought' his way there. It was instant. I just arrived as soon as he told me we were going. He placed his arm around me and we just 'arrived'.

Down below was The Council. To the left, to the right and at the far end of The Council, were crystal apex roofs about 15 feet / 4.5 metres wide, surrounding The Council. We seemed to be over a building at our end, which completed the enclosure of The Council.

The crystal roofed areas had crystal archways beneath. It seemed to Jill that the crystal construction was there to condense energy. It may have even been a healing area for people to walk under. There were no joins to the crystal. It was seamless as though it had been cut from one piece. The sky above was bright blue and as the sun shined on the crystal roofs, they emitted a rainbow effect from the prismatic effect of the crystal.

The Council was similar to a Roman Villa with a central square. In the centre of The Council, was a large disc, hovering above the ground. The disc was around 7 feet / 2 metres in diameter and only around half an inch / 10mm deep. The surface was mirrored. The disc was hovering around 3 feet / 1 metre from the ground, with no apparent support.

Around the disc were several marble chairs arranged around the radius of the hovering disc. Each chair would seat around three people. No backs to the chairs; more like flat benches. There were four of these benches arranged around the disc, with spaces in between the benches.

I was shown a vision of what happens there: On each bench sat three Council Elders; 12 in all. Except for one; they all wore hooded robes of a fine material in a matt 'turquoise to darker blue' in colour. Each had a waist sash of braided rope, gold in colour. The robes were full length to the floor. I couldn't see any hands, feet or faces. The front openings to the hoods reflected darkness.

One of the Elders was wearing a similar robe, except cream in colour, with the same gold sash. The floor was overlaid with large, cream, hexagonal, marble tiles. Around the chairs were Roman-like columns around 2 feet / 600mm in diameter. The columns were fluted vertically with a wider plinth to the top and bottom. They stood around 10 feet / 3 metres tall. There were around 12 of them, with an opening to the far end, where the Elders walked between the columns, into the seated area.

On the disc were holograms of a spirit guide and an entity. It looked like a scene from the movie: 'Star Wars', where people were communicating by hologram. The spirit guide and entity were asking permission for the entity to be able to reincarnate; to go back to Earth as a different person; usually because there is another lesson to be learnt.

Around The Council was lush plantation; gentle valleys with streams flowing through them. Lush vegetation with colourful flowers and colourful birds in the trees. This is what people may have described as the 'Garden of Eden'.

Metatron stood with me in his 'scaled-down' size, standing about 7 feet / 2 metres tall. He had his arm around my shoulder and his left wing wrapped around my body as if in protection.

Metatron stands all in pure white light with a luminous presence. He wears a long white robe with a gold brocade sash around 4 inches / 100 mm wide; which wraps around his waist and crosses diagonally around his back and chest. He has long white straight hair, swept back from his forehead to reveal a handsome, youthful face. His hair is shoulder length. His eyes are all black: no iris or pupil or white surround; just all black.

Metatron: For now, we will leave you, but perhaps we can commune again tomorrow, for we know there will be many questions when you have reread the knowledge that has been brought forth.

Try to understand and learn about atoms. We know it is something that you shy away from, but it will help us if you can grasp what we have talked about. Perhaps a drawing of an atom may help those who are drawn to this information and are similar to you in their lack of understanding.

May the cosmic forces of the North, South, West and East draw close to impart love and light for the betterment of mankind.

Metatron.

38: The Council of Elders

13th January 2006

Jill is channelling

Metatron: Greetings, you are about to resonate and connect with the consciousness of earth and the entire unified collective solar energy combined. As your journey unfolds, there will be many changes within yourself which you must be aware of. Access and experience of this consciousness will affect your awareness as you move through each dimension; eventually reaching the 13th dimension. Planet Earth is not even half way there at present, so do not have any preconceived ideas of what is to come.

The resonance of energy fields are to be raised so that your solar memory and awareness connect with I who Am; and all that is. I am the one true light that brings forth everlasting light from God; light; the one conscious energy. Be it known that all universes created are in wholeness, so that twelve becomes one.

Since time began, unconditional love is the essence of the soul and portal that allows the profound understanding of consciousness to be connected. For through these universes are many aspects of the soul; terrestrial, intra-terrestrial, extra-terrestrial, upon galactic and supra-galactic levels of awareness; until the soul finally comes to learn the truth of wholeness.

As you now transcend, relativity to your human form and how unnecessary this form really is, will become more apparent, however, you must accept that to return to your physical body, may be uncomfortable; and your aspect and beliefs of humans may dramatically change.

To be allowed to commune with The Council of Elders is not normally granted unless the soul has already ascended. Your relativity to consciousness will be realised and you will see and become unconditional love that brings forth new teachings for all living things.

The teachings that are to be brought forward can be aligned with your scientific counterparts. For already they understand holographics, the theories relating to morphic resonance. However, they should also be aware during their search for scientific fact that unless it is balanced with a spiritual approach, they will miss half the answers. For there are many scales and levels of experience in relation to each solar universe.

All universes together are collectively synchronised, to create harmonic flow. It is not by accident that the power of twelve combining and becoming one, has been brought into being. Just as humans are living entities, so too are the planets and the other universes which together form an energy force dodecahedral grid of love. It is this grid that forever holds the thought of creation and one of wholeness.

As you now leave your physical body, as in death, shedding this physical form will release you from all physical handicaps. No longer will you fear anything. For as you now see, you are ready to ascend and see with the eyes of truth.

Jill's thoughts: At this point I was in darkness with Metatron. I watched my body disintegrate into tiny shining stars. My molecular structure seemed to separate, just like in the 'Star Trek' transporter. The separated particles then dispersed and disappeared, leaving a spherical ball of light about the size of a large grapefruit. This was a really strange feeling, because it felt like my body was still with me, yet all I could see of my body was this light orb, hovering about 3 feet / 1 metre from where my feet would have been. Metatron 'thought' of The Council of Elders' Chambers; and we arrived immediately at their Chambers.

I was hovering by the hologram disc in the centre of the Chambers. Twelve hooded figures were seated around. There were no faces in the hoods; just blackness.

Metatron was by my side at all times. He had reverted back to his full scale self, towering over the chambers. His height was taller than our house, which is tall at 45 feet. I reckon his size to be almost 100 feet / 30 metres. This was nearer to the height when I first ever saw Metatron appear, but even taller today. His height was frightening to me at that first sighting, so he scaled down his size from then so as not to intimidate me; however, it would appear that it was important to him to be his 'normal' size in front of The Council of Elders; which were of a similar height to mankind. It seemed as though Metatron was using his size to energise the meeting. One of the Elders began to speak:

Council Elder: Greetings, we are pleased to commune with you dear one. It is our hope that with what you experience today, it will help bring about the beginning of salvation of your planet, as we wish it to be known that you are to communicate to those who are brave enough to listen and take to heart the importance of what we have to say. You understand, yes?

Yes, of course you do. We know you do. Otherwise, (laughingly), we would have our work cut out for us yes?

My dear; the decline of your planet and those who inhabit it, seem blissfully unaware of the havoc that is taking place. We are most concerned. Mankind has created masses of technological machines and appliances, which now rule mankind with an iron fist. Your social systems are near breaking point and most of mankind feel overwhelmed, and powerless to make changes. With all this bombardment of noise, pollution and fighting for material possessions, there is very little time given for reflection or contemplation of the pathway upon which they are travelling down.

The human form; man and woman, were created to help God; light; the one conscious energy, understand spiritual growth and how each experience affected things relative to that experience. A game of life, you may call it. We do not mean this in a mocking way, but a series of experiences, that together would help you and all of us reveal and understand the wonders; to say nothing of the tremendous capacities of an inner being.

Currently though for mankind, there are many outer and inner struggles that threaten to sabotage everything, as the struggle for survival without caring for the spiritual struggle, has taken over. Let us look at how you're formed, as you can see yourself now for who you truly are. How do you see yourself?

Jill: I am light; one with yourselves. I already possess all that I am. I have no need for answers, for they are here. No longer are there needs to be met. My purpose is to bring forth knowledge and help others through the doorways of knowledge, to become unified.

Council Elder: That is right. But let us look at your physical form on the planet earth. Man's physical form is pure consciousness harmony. Or as some scientific minds would say, a wonderful piece of construction superbly put together. Each and every cell has its own specific function on its own, but it also has a function in relation to the other cells around it. Your blood was uniquely created to bring forth the breath of life and ensure that any toxins or waste were carried away, so that no harm could be brought to the body. You were equipped with a self-heating and self-regulating system, so that if a substance was entered into this physical form, your body could ensure its ability to transform that substance.

Every cell has been created in so much detail, that very little contemplation is given to how unique and special the human form is. The brain was developed to give you divine creation; the ability to experience and sense so many wonders: smell, colour, touch. The ability to create through science, music, art and dance, to name just a few.

And yet, despite these immense abilities, mankind 'has', and 'is' choosing to create viruses, bombs; weapons of mass destruction. The world you live in, in the physical sense, has chosen to create to destroy.

Mankind has made himself so complex that he now is not able to define who he truly is. The answer in reality is, that the more mankind learns, the more there is still to learn. Consciousness is endless. This is why mankind has so many points of view. Many will create for themselves a philosophy for which they feel comfortable with; and through this, they will then feel that they can measure their worldly sense of self.

What is man? (For the purpose of ease, we will use man, although this does relate to women too.)

Man is an element, with two aspects to that element. One being the physical body, the other the spirit. The physical body, or physical mass as we call it, as you are now aware, is just a vehicle that allows you to fulfil your mission. And once the spirit has fulfiled its mission, the physical body will be left to disintegrate back into the elements of nature and replenish Mother Earth.

Jill's thoughts: At this point, the hologram disc powered up to show images in three dimensional form, of what I was hearing.

A physical mass appeared in the shape of a human body, with a swirling mist of energy; the spirit. It then disappeared and I was shown a sperm entering an egg, which represented the spirit and body being merged together.

However, the spirit, the soul, was what created your thoughts, impressions, feelings. These do not have physical mass or material substance which you can touch. Along with these, mankind was also given a conscience to help guide him between the right way and the wrong way. To honour the spirit and connect with the spirit, ceremonies were created. In the beginning, mankind created ceremonies, to connect with the divine, go within oneself, so he could be guided in his life. It is through these ceremonies, that religion was originally formed.

Now blinded through material greed and the vast civilisation mankind has created for itself, mankind has failed to see the need for 'true' spiritual nourishment. Mankind has chosen to blindly follow others, duped into the belief that by following and denying the true self, they will find salvation.

Duality exists in all things. As well as the physical and spiritual form on your planet, you have day and night. During the day, many of you go about your way, experiencing life, and during the night time you rest and sleep. Sleep was created to enable mankind to return to his spiritual self. For us, we call this awakeness 'incarnated', and when you sleep we call this 'excarnated'. During the time of your excarnation, we are able to enthuse, advise and guide you with the choices that are to be taken for your own betterment. A time for you to reconnect with your true home here in the spiritual world.

This context of incarnate and excarnate is also representative of life and death. The only difference is, that you continue to use energy threads to continue the connection between the physical and the spiritual. During death; when the moment of physical death arises, you will experience separateness. Your spirit will arise, free from pain, fear and ignorance and move forward towards the next dimensions, of which we will discuss another time.

It is very important that mankind understands whilst its physical mass receives stimuli from the external world, there are more aspects that affect the spiritual.

The complete making of mankind comprises of the physical body, the etheric body, the astral body; and finally the ego.

Most of mankind do not instinctively use their astral body to guide them on their life's pathway. They have replaced being in touch spiritually, with logic. It is vital that ego is also understood. Every human being has a proportion of ego, similar to a drop of water. This proportion is unique in that it is conscious of itself, and has the ability to grow and develop.

Ego has the ability to direct the astral body. When this happens, the human form transforms. In other words, the ego begins to control the emotions. This in turn, disconnects you from your divine energy; the god within.

Most of the time, the four elements of the human form: physical, etheric, astral and ego, work well together. When in union, the human functions well. When they do not function together, for example: the ego becomes more driving than the rest; illness results.

So far, you may have comprehended that mankind began as two aspects and now those two aspects have become four. We also need to now consider other elements to mankind: the difference between soul and spirit.

Let us just remember, mankind consists of the physical, the etheric, the astral and ego. We now add a different dimension to mankind. This being soul and spirit.

You walk your children to school.

Glenn's thoughts: They seem to be aware that we personally walk the children to school, without us telling them. It's part of our exercise regime.

Whilst walking, your human form is moving, thinking and feeling. Whilst walking, what you see creates your experiences. From this experience, you are creating a world within yourself. This is your soul. At the same time, however, you also have feelings. Your feelings can be positive, or negative. Your feelings are formulated in your mind. This is spirit. The spirit is what comprehends the soul's experiences, similar to your heart feeling and your mind thinking. Duality between the two must exist.

The soul is the innermost part of a human. It is the intermediary between the body and spirit. Your soul is created from your astral body. Hence the ability to astrally project yourself through time and space. It is your soul that carries the memories; experiences of your human form. The soul helps the human form to formulate decisions, to enable the physical mass to react. It is your soul that connects you to the eternal truth. It is your soul that separates you from the animal kingdom. The animal kingdom works only on the spirit, instinctively. The human form, works on both; soul and spirit.

The human form, although physically consisting of minerals and physical substances, also plays a greater part in regeneration of the planet: Unlike rocks; which have density and mass and are composed of minerals, which do not have any etheric force. When the physical body is transposed in death, it contains within it the unique ability to emit energy for regeneration. What you see as a lifeless piece of flesh is in effect, emitting energies through its decomposing, which help reunify the energy fields within the planet.

Glenn's thoughts: This must mean that cremation reduces the reunification of the energy fields.

As you will see, two has become four. Now mankind has become 6, for we have added spirit and soul. Let us now show you how mankind becomes 10, through the addition of temperament.

Similar to the elements of earth, fire, water and air; mankind was granted temperament. These elements were to help with the development of mankind.

The earth element was to bring forth weight and substance, which represented the physical mass. With this brought introspection. Humans who have not embraced their spirituality will be noticeable through their inability to embrace change or see other human points of view. These beings will often feel the world is against them; and despite these beings being avid knowledge seekers, they utilise their knowledge to keep them rooted to the same spot in the physical.

Human forms were also granted water elements. These were to bring about perseverance and persistence, like the ocean, able to rise to the occasion, and find a way round the barriers that stood in their way. On the earthly plane you may consider these human forms as dreamers. But with these dreamers also comes achievement.

To help human forms bring action to their creativity, the element of fire was added to temperament. Humans possess within themselves, force, energy, drive.

The final element added to human form was air, which brought human form the ability embrace change, to create and constantly reinvent. These are the talkative type.

The process of creation is the reply to mankind's question of: "What is man?" All these elements are what you are. God; light; the one conscious energy, has created each constituent part of your being. The final two phases to create 12 were: where human form became aware of its own consciousness and then to take that consciousness and begin self-development.

Mankind must not be afraid of death. The soul and spirit will continue onwards to many other realms.

For now, we feel you must return back from whence you came. Metatron will guide you back. You must also perhaps take time to confer with him of how this information will be represented to your world.

It is with our blessings that you return. The embodiment of spirit that resides within you can never be removed. It is this embodiment of spirit that now needs to be spoke of to those you come into contact with. There are many ways in which to spread a message; not just mere words alone. Remember to use your actions as a way for your soul and spirit to connect. It is wise to caution you that you may only see the purity of the soul in others for a short while, until your energies are realigned. During this time, we will ensure you are well looked after.

Metatron: **I, who am the one true connection to God; light; the one conscious energy; restore within the dimensional energy changes; all that should be as; is.**

You have done well, as we knew you would (smiling). Be it known that those who work in truth, can never fear the outcome of their actions, as I know, you now too know. It will perhaps be helpful, if you can describe what you have seen and what you experienced, so that others too, may absorb the energies you bring forth.

I know that Glenn will have many questions for you; and I know he requires answers. But for now, the immensity of what you have experienced is enough for now. He is doing well with his meditation. He must relax a little more, and allow himself to be absorbed by what he sees. This way, he will meet with Gabriel. Gabriel is already helping to raise his energies. The difference in temperatures will signal him transcending the physical body.

We are conscious of your energies, dear one. We ask that you re-commune in a few days, to enable yourself time to realign with your planets energies. It is The Council's will that you help others to learn and speak of how the physical body mirrors the soul and how the anatomy of the body relates to the planets in your universe.

Once this has been understood, we will show you how destiny relates to human form. You will, through this, then begin to understand the development of human conscience, the relationship of human form, and what you believe as evil.

It is through these teachings, that mankind will be able to merge the physical with the divine, for the betterment of the spiritual foundation of the world. If mankind can learn these lessons, they will recognise the one universal truth which will continue the establishment of mankind and the true brotherhood of man.

Blessed be, Metatron.

39: The Council of Elders: The composition in the design of the elements of Mankind

16th January 2006

Jill is channelling

Metatron: Greetings dear one, we are pleased that we are, yet again, communing with you at this time. We are aware that your time is short, so we shall continue from whence we came. As you now are aware of the process of inter-dimensional travel and the ability to project oneself from one place to another; let us see how well you can put this into practice.

Remember to allow the physical body to be left behind. Hold no fears and allow yourself to embrace the freedom and peace the energies bring to you.

Iajoveh (I yo vay), will talk with you. It is important to remember that we have no real need for names in the spirit world, for we are all one; so do not see ourselves as having any need to be singled out, or recognised, for we all together achieve many great things, and every time one experiences joy, so do us all.

Iajoveh is not of your universe, so at times he may speak in a way you don't always comprehend; but any clarification that is required, will be given to you; as we know your every thought and feeling. So with that said, let us now convene, for The Council of Elders are awaiting your presence.

(Back to the meeting area)

Iajoveh: Ah, lovely to commune with you dear child. You seem to have grasped what was given very well, so now let us bring forth more insights for you. In turn, you will get to speak with us all, but also, you will absorb a little of each of our energies, so your capacity to predict many things will grow.

It is most important that you honour your true feelings and use this awareness of the energy around you. You still haven't learnt to trust it completely. Work on your belief of yourself. Do not be afraid to be wrong, for there is no such thing. Do not always assume that someone else's opinion is more of an authority than your own feelings.

We granted you the ability to see the composition of man. Now for you to understand how this was put into practice, we need to look at physical birth and physical death. Now it may seem strange but we will look at physical death.

Upon physical death, there are a series of energy occurrences that help your transition and the energy of the planet you physically resided in. Firstly when a person breathes their last breath, which we call life sustaining force, it's absorbed by the etheric energy of the planet. At the same time the soul and spirit detach from the physical body. During a three day period, the etheric body dissolves slowly too and is absorbed back into the planet's energies. It is during this time period that the soul and spirit experience the opportunity to view backwards in time, their life and experiences on this planet. They are still at this time, in the energy circle of planet earth and have not ascended yet.

Sometimes, you will come across people on your planet, who have begun this process and then returned back to the physical body, in the realisation that they have not fulfiled everything as it should be, The term you humans use for this is a 'near death' experience.

Those who have fulfiled their purpose; the time then comes for the spirit and soul to cast off, as a snake casts off the skin it has outgrown; the soul body, and transform into pure light energy. During this phase, there is much time for reflection on achievements, imperfections and whether or not it needs to return to the earth plane to correct anything. The pure light energy; just as you are now; the orb of light you see, now creates a new astral body and can now ascend through the realms (dimensions) to reunite with those who have gone before them.

In all, physically in the human world, there should be a period of at least 12 days, to enable the spirit and soul to complete the cycle of life and death, before disposal of the physical body is ideally placed for disposal. We are well aware of the implications of what we discussed last time. Please know that it is alright for the physical body to be cremated, as you call it, but for the process to be complete, it is also important the ashes are returned to the earth, to further continue in the regeneration of your planet.

Granted the breakdown process isn't as nutritional to the earth, but it still plays a vital function. Your marble urns prohibit this. Remember you do not need a mourning place, for if they reside in your heart, they are with you in the spiritual sense and you can honour them from within.

Now, where were we? Oh yes! Now that you understand this process, let us turn to birth. Once the elements of mankind are brought together, we need to look at the process of birth.

We will not reveal to you the missing link as you call it, on how mankind came to be where and what he is; for to do so, would only encourage more negative energies to conspire to overthrow and dominate the universal life force grid; and this cannot and never will be divulged. However, prior to your physical conception, a soul is requested to research a suitable hereditary lineage and the reasons for such an incarnation.

A soul must also provide and ensure that the environment is suitable and that the experiences planned are within the realms of possibilities. The chosen parents must be able to meet the spiritual and physical needs of the soul. Once this has been done, and the other physical entities are in place, then, and only then can conception take place.

When a physical sperm and an ovum are joined, for a while the physical mass is created without the soul. Once the physical mass is at a stage that the soul feels is ready, then and only then will the soul project itself into the physical mass.

You will find that humans who carry the traits of your leaders, pioneers and entrepreneurs will usually enter into the physical mass early, so that they can absorb outside influences from the mother. The soul is already acquiring knowledge and learning. Those souls who enter later into the physical mass, are normally human beings who play a supporting role to other humans and are quite happy to serve others.

It is also important for you all to understand how everything in your lives relates to the universe.

Glenn: The channelling was interrupted by me banging around in the kitchen downstairs, tidying up. The noise carries in the quietness of the house. Jill was upstairs in the bedroom at the time. It was 2.00 in the afternoon. The kids were at school, so the house was quiet. Sudden noises break the connection, which gives Jill a violent headache and makes it almost impossible to continue. I managed to convince Jill to go back later around 3.30 to reconnect. This was a show of respect to the entities for their graciousness in sharing the after-life and universal life force energies with us.

Metatron: We are grateful that you attempt to reconnect with us once again. However, it is with concern for your well being, not ours, that we must stress; you must ensure the energies and harmony is maintained whilst you commune with us.

To bring a soul back to a human physical mass quickly, stresses the energies. So we must ask you to mindful of this, when taking time to commune with us. We shall return to The Council of Elders, and see what can be done to continue.

Iajoveh: Hello dear child. We will continue at a later time with much great details. But for now, let us quickly show you how your physical body and the soul body have duality and that part this plays in the earth plane and the universes.

Firstly when you consider your planet, you visually see this as round; spherical; yes? As with yourself; as you are now, an orb of light; you too are spherical; so too is the physical body.

Although to your eyes, you cannot see this, the body is a series of circles, spheres, globes; you understand yes?

Your head was designed to be slightly detached from the rest of your body, for your brain is where your thinking spirit resides. It is this part of your anatomy that allows the physical body to create thoughts from what it has seen, heard and experienced. The cavity of the body is created to embrace the heart and lungs, for this is the area in which the rhythmic energy encases the soul. This area is the area from which feelings are created. Your outer limbs enable you to touch and connect with the outer world. Nothing within your body works independently. They are all linked. This is the same with humans. You are not independent. You are all inter-linked as one. As is the planet within your own universe.

Each physical aspect of your body relates to your universe. Although mankind likes to think of themselves as individual, in reality each human is inter-dependent on the environment and other human beings around him. Mankind has persevered and created many wonderful things; yet the mystery of life is still as evasive as ever.

Once man learns to accept his environment and his abilities, peace would be much easier to find. To give you all the answers, would bring many ramifications and complexities that you would simply not be able to comprehend or accept. It is time mankind accepted flexibility in his thinking. So many of you have such rigid ideas, that they keep like a rod, in life, unbending, unshaping, until such times as those thoughts and beliefs are what in turn causes you to snap, losing everything you thought you once had.

Often mankind will ask why some die early and some die later in life. Let is be known that those who make the transition early, are often storing up their energy forces for a very special destiny. Mankind will often ask why one person is born whole and another with severe handicaps. Again; despite the fact that the body may not appear whole, it does not mean the soul and spirit aren't. These wonderful spirits bring forth and communicate on a much deeper spiritual level and are still fulfiling a mission here on your planet.

Metatron: We will commune again. Until then, may the cosmic energies of the North, South, West and East be combined together for the betterment of mankind, in love and light; always.

40: The Council of Elders: Science is our undoing; the need for spiritual development

18th January 2006

Jill is channelling

Metatron: Greetings you are now well on your way to being ready to go forth and speak of what you know; and also to inspire others to discover the divine that lays dormant within them.

Whilst we're aware of your many questions, we ask that you bear with us and work your way through these lessons, so that you can bring them to the awareness of others. Sekutet will speak with you today; she is a very enlightened being.

Sekutet: A pleasure to commune with you dear one. We have met before, but you will not remember me. But I remember you. Mankind has lost the ability to penetrate the spiritual world, but hopefully today, with my help, we can perhaps begin to make amends on how to connect with the spiritual world, whilst still occupying physical mass.

Your human brains have many faculties, which when awakened can help you manifest and bring forth much greater spiritual perception than you can possibly comprehend at this time.

There are no great special exercises, which suddenly, like magic, will reveal the answers of life to you. But to bridge the physical and spiritual worlds, requires a human to have the right attitude and a sense of deep gratitude for each experience, whether it is positive or negative. Only those with open minds can ever bridge the gap between the physical world and the spiritual world.

Once a human can accept that they are part of the universe; only then will they have the ability to transpose themselves into how others are feeling; and what actions are required for the situation. Begin to think of yourselves as one. The world must begin to develop and work towards a feeling of unity. As a microcosm within a macrocosm, you are and always will be related to all things. Nothing can exist without the others.

Once a human has developed this understanding, developing their own confidence is of the utmost importance. In your schools, you should be teaching awareness and considerations of others first. Teach your young how their own actions have an effect of those around them. By teaching them to relate as one, they will positively be able to focus on overcoming obstacles that are put in their way.

After this has been accomplished, the children then need to also be taught confidence; to be able to go forward with the conviction that their goals can be achieved. Currently your education system is breeding dry, intellectual, stifling humans who do not have the capacity to help themselves. It is time to stop feeding the minds of the young with materialistic concepts. You destroy their imagination, so that their ability to inspire is lost to all but to those few who are branded as ADHD (Attention Deficit Hyperactivity Disorder) or misfits. One is never too young to learn. Perhaps it is time the young taught the elders the ability of joy; the ability to find joy in new experiences; for it to be alright to laugh and enjoy life to the full.

The ability to bridge this gap is fundamental, for many can see the abyss that mankind is heading for, and yet, those that do see have not joined forces to try and change the pathway in which everyone is headed. Look at your planet currently. Chaos and corruption are by which you govern. Confusion is what rules the environmental impact you play on your planet; and your ability to find the true spiritual enlightenment you all search for, is non-existent due to you still following rules and regulations from a bunch of stories eons ago.

Glenn's thoughts: There's that damn Bible again.

Just as 'you' go through evolution, so does the spirit world. Do you not think that unless we embraced new ways of thinking and discovering different ways of creation that we could have continued our existence? The difference here is that we all accept ourselves as one born into unity. We consider the implications of our actions prior to creating change.

Whilst your scientific evolution is fast expanding, you must also realise that science has no morality. If it did, and it was one with the spiritual, you would not have created your bombs, delved into genetic engineering, interfered with the creation of life: giving you the decision of whether a child should be born, or your ability to choose your ability to procreate.

It is science that is your undoing. For the vast majority of your research is no longer used towards helping mankind; but to creating bigger and better means for controlling humans through bacteriology and how you can pollute a human body, the planet and its atmospheres. Your governments are deceiving you with half-truths and untruths, that you are all becoming so brainwashed and hypnotised, that you lack the ability to switch off and say, "No more!"

When you gave birth to your sons; your divine; your God within, cared and helped develop their identity within the world. But with every child, as with Max now, he is spiritually transforming his own Godly divine energy into now learning to develop on his own.

Slowly he is detaching from your divinity and finding his own way forward. If he is to be free, he must have the ability to reflect on the greatness that lies within him. Once this has been achieved, he then has free will whether to learn from the wisdom of others or through experience. Along with this will also come the quest as to whether he uses his talents in a positive way, or to the detriment of others around him.

If you go forth and talk with others, you have the ability to teach how the main principle of life is balance between all things, living and dying, physical and spiritual, night and day. Too much or too little in one area, causes dis-ease. Mankind must realise that to be in excess in one area, will cause discord in the energies of the physical body. Expansion in one area and then contraction in another creates balance, give and take; it is when one area overtakes completely, you will find evil.

We know that mankind struggles greatly to understand evil. But evil is not an absolute. For at different times, they may be quite the opposite. If mankind isolates evil, it will never really be understood. If you consider mankind's evolution, originally, there were very little material things to occupy him. Mankind connected and was always aware of the spiritual world and spiritual beings. As mankind progressed, through development, they learnt to establish themselves; creating cities, towns, principalities. Whilst this happened, they needed to also understand and have the opportunity of learning what excess would bring, and yet instead of recognising the opportunity of their own downfall, they ignored their spiritual guidance and fell into misery and evilness.

This was never more so learnt than with the souls who inhabited Atlantis and Lemuria. For those who search for Atlantis, you will find it resides in what you now know as the Atlantic Ocean. Lemuria you will find far, far below the Indian Ocean. Up until these two great nations created their own downfall, the energies of the earth were harmonised and well balanced.

So many of you now, live in quiet desperation. It is time that you stopped allowing your lives to be dominated by outside events. Your senses and experiences are in a state of overload; through drugs, alcohol, noise, entertainment, materialistic possessions and food. We ask you to go forth and show others that they have within them the ability, with a little bit of desire and effort, to fulfil their soul's needs.

Teach your children to cultivate their divinity; to work towards improving your social conditions. Nothing can be born without desire, effort and love. It is no use acquiring knowledge if you do not have the capacity to understand that knowledge. To understand requires reflection, contemplation, meditation. Mankind must learn awareness of the self. In doing so, the ability of connecting the realms of the physical and spiritual will become reality.

(Referring to Jill.) It is important at this time that you remember your original role on this planet. Your role was to assist the Egyptians with the 'Temple Sleep Processes'. You often helped others to go into trance so they could be aware of the spiritual world. Your role has never changed. You are still to make others aware of the spiritual world. We are not asking you to teach trance, but to show others in the written word and with demonstrations, of how to find silence, so that they can connect with God; light; the one conscious energy; and follow their true destiny.

Everyone you teach must realise, that like an Olympic runner, they have to develop their muscles before they can win the race. True spiritual development is not easy, but is attainable. Remember that you are beginning to utilise dormant muscles within the physical brain that have lay dormant for quite some time. So the ability to perceive must take time.

We sense your energies weakening. So for now, we ask that you return to your physical body and look to realigning yourself with sacred geometry; and how it was used to help you originally bridge the physical and the spiritual. You will be drawn to books, for a purpose; so do not worry about which books are for you. We would also ask that those that are brought to you, are referenced for others to access of their own free volition.

   www.anewbelief.com

Metatron: we will not commune tomorrow. We ask that you take the time to view what has been shown to you. For not only does the physical body require rest, so too does the spiritual body. You have worked well and we are blessed that you take upon you these tasks to help mankind. There are many lost souls, and it is not your purpose to save every single one. But by reaching out, if you help just a few, you have made a difference.

I AM THE ONE TRUE CONNECTION to God; light; the one conscious energy. Your bond with me and God; light; the one conscious energy, can never be broken. Go forth with love and light.

41: Darwin's Theory; the missing link will never be found

20th January 2006

Jill is channelling

Metatron: Greetings, I am delighted of the opportunity to commune with you once again, and as usual, your emanations and questions are quite chaotic. You must try to focus yourself in one direction and learn all that you can, before moving forward onto the next one.

For today and due to the shortness of your time, we will perhaps recap on some things for those who still are confused, or need further clarification. Glenn must realise that over time, the thousands of questions he has, will become answered, but perhaps not in the timescale he envisages.

So with that in mind, perhaps it may be best to state that for creation to occur, there has to be intention and reason. Without this, nothing can ever be created. Your planet is 50 billion years old. Mankind's constant search for the fossils that will prove without doubt, Darwin's theory; will never be found. For as hard as the truth may be, the reason why your missing link is not available, is because that missing link, you would call it extra-terrestrial. The name human, is taken from hu, meaning the awareness and energy that emanates from energy. Man, is the physical mass that has been manifested to hold that awareness. Darwin's theory is nearly accurate for the animal kingdom, but not for the human race.

Your planet has in fact been occupied by three previous forms of life, but all failed miserably. During this period, there were other life forms, on planets that had managed to sustain life. There are still highly intelligent extra-terrestrial life forms on your planet, but for their safety, they will not be mentioned here, for fear of mankind's scientific experiments.

The nearest missing link you will find is the aboriginal humans. It has taken God; light; the one conscious energy, billions and billions of years to create the thousands of species that occupied your planet. Now it is sad that just over a hundred years, is all it's taken for mankind to destroy half of those. Mankind has currently destroyed 15 million species with more species to be added to that number shortly.

For many of those who read this, you may feel doomed, however, all is not lost. But it will not be your scientists and leaders who will save you and your planet, but your children. For as with the creation of all these species, the unique DNA that lies within each and every form, has the unique ability to transform and mutate into new beings.

To help you understand, let us look at the blood that runs through your veins. Animal and human blood originally was type 'O' only. This was because mankind ate meat to survive. The human body at that time was dense muscle mass and very little fat. As the human race developed and spread further afield, they acclimatised to the different terrain, and with that terrain, also their diet too. When humans began to incorporate vegetables, seeds and grains, their DNA had to adapt.

You will find, if you take time to research, that your scientists already know that by feeding tiny amounts of poison to creatures, they will over time, alter their DNA and genetic coding to enable them to survive the poison. This is the same for human beings. Over time, as you have changed your diets, you have altered the DNA structure of your blood, which thus brought about your different blood types, A, B, O and AB. You may wonder how this actually now relates to your children, and the fact that they are the ones who will save this planet from destruction.

We have already discussed the Indigo Children. These children already have different DNA and genetic structures that are different from the rest of human kind. Already their livers have the ability to handle toxins, which for most would mean physical death. Also you will find that as these children develop and grow, they will have a natural IQ ability of well over 140. These children are already equipped with great reasoning and awareness of the different dimensions, and energies that surround them. It is these children that will be your missing link between this physical world, and the spiritual world. These are the children you should be investing your time getting to know. Not how mankind first came to be on this planet.

We will discuss these things further, but for now, it is time for you to go. For now, may the cosmic forces of the North, South, East and West join together for the betterment of mankind. Love and light be with you.

Metatron.

42: A word about Tithing

"Everything on this Daily Bible Study web site is completely free for the taking, while to make it all possible, donations are gratefully accepted."...

This was the very gracious message asking for a handout, at the bottom of the following article at
www.keyway.ca/htm2002/tithing.htm
Tithe is the English word used to translate the original Hebrew word of the Old Testament, pronounced mah-as-ayr, and the original Greek word of the New Testament, pronounced dek-at-oo. All mean a tenth. Tithing is a God-commanded 10% "flat tax" which is used to support those in His service.
The payment of the tenth to God was practiced early in Bible history, well before the law was given to Moses. The Scriptures record that Abraham paid a tithe to Melchizedek, who was the king of Salem (Jerusalem) and "priest of God Most High." (Genesis 14:18-20, Hebrews 7:4-6). Jacob, the father of The Tribes of Israel paid the tithe to God (Genesis 28:22).
Tithing was formalized in the Law: "A tithe of everything from the land, whether grain from the soil or fruit from the trees, belongs to The Lord; it is holy to The Lord." (Leviticus 27:30)
"The Lord said to Aaron, "You will have no inheritance in their land, nor will you have any share among them; I am your share and your inheritance among the Israelites. I give to the Levites all the tithes in Israel as their inheritance in return for the work they do while serving at the Tent of Meeting." (Numbers 18:20-21)
"The Lord said to Moses, "Speak to the Levites and say to them: 'When you receive from the Israelites the tithe I give you as your inheritance, you must present a tenth of that tithe as The Lord's offering. Your offering will be reckoned to you as grain from the threshing floor or juice from the wine press. In this way you also will present an offering to The Lord from all the tithes you receive from the Israelites. From these tithes you must give The Lord's portion to Aaron the priest. You must present as The Lord's portion the best and holiest part of everything given to you.'" (Numbers 18:25-29)
If someone lived too far to bring his tithe of produce, he could sell it and use the money to purchase produce when he arrived. (Deuteronomy 14:24-27).

Those who neglected the command to tithe were considered to be robbing God and cursing themselves in the process:
"Will a man rob God? Yet you rob Me. But you ask, 'How do we rob You?' In tithes and offerings. You are under a curse - the whole nation of you - because you are robbing Me. Bring the whole tithe into the storehouse, that there may be food in My house. Test Me in this," says The Lord Almighty, "and see if I will not throw open the floodgates of heaven and pour out so much blessing that you will not have room enough for it. I will prevent pests from devouring your crops, and the vines in your fields will not cast their fruit," says The Lord Almighty. "Then all the nations will call you blessed, for yours will be a delightful land," says The Lord Almighty." (Malachi 3:8-12)

Glenn: So there's a little history about tithing. The thought process here is that, if at one time it was law, then why isn't it now? Here's a message that was sent to me in January 2006. I asked for permission to use it:
He headed the message 'Tithing is Bullshit"

In my constant search for truth and after watching the number of so called religious channels appearing on T.V., I'd like to put forward my own views.
"Will a man ROB God?" How many untold tens of thousands of men will give account one day for teaching this verse in Malachi 3:8 totally out of context for their own sordid gain. I couldn't count the times I have heard self-appointed ministers of the gospel berate their congregations and listeners for "robbing God" in tithes and offerings.
  On any given Sunday morning there will be numerous men-of-the-cloth who will be bellowing out over the air waves that people are being "cursed with a curse" because they have failed to pay God ten percent of their pay-cheques. And should such a gullible listener decide to repent and give God ten percent of his salary, just how would he do that? Just keep reading. These men of the cloth who often have unquenchable worldly desires of the flesh, will be sure to give you an address where you can send them (or, ah, rather God) your tithe. And do they have a right to quote these Scriptures in this manner? No they do not, and furthermore they themselves know better.

SOME SHOCKING TRUTHS ABOUT THE CHRISTIAN TITHING DOCTRINE.

- *Abraham never tithed on his own personal property or livestock.*
- *Jacob wouldn't tithe until God blessed him first.*
- *Only Levite priests could collect tithes, and there are no Levite priests today.*
- *Only food products from the land could be tithed.*
- *Money was never a commodity to be tithed.*
- *Christian converts were never asked to tithe anything to the Church.*
- *Tithing in the Church first appears centuries after completion of the Bible.*

I congratulate you on opening the eyes of those people still daft enough to part with their hard earned cash to these thieves who steal in the name of God. My only regret is that more and more people don't have the brains and intelligent capacity to see how much harm the Bible has done to the world.

Glenn: He sent me this message in response to reading the information on our web site www.anewbelief.com.

When I wrote to him asking for his permission to use this message, he sent me the following reply:

Dear Glenn,
Thanks for your message, but I'd prefer it if you didn't draw attention to me. I'm your average man, quite happy to make a comment, but then when it comes down to actually standing up for my views, I'm likely to shit my pants and run a mile. By all means, feel free to 'rewrite' what I have written and put me down as anonymous, but I have no wish for fame and fortune, so please don't include what I posted verbatim in your book with reference to my identity.

I'm your average 'maybe' man, which is probably why I'm drawn to your site.

I feel I need to find some answers, and that there has to be more to life than what we already experience. This empty feeling inside and never having fulfiled my own ambitions, has to mean something. I actually believe for once that within your site, there is an element of truth and logic to everything that's been written. On your forum, I get to say what I think, without the wrath of her indoors, who thinks that religion is a load of bullshit and that it's high time I just got on with life. Maybe you could write a book for men like me, who don't think they really have a future and how to handle a nagging woman. Many of my mates are like me. They don't feel there's any hope left in the world and too few opportunities to be a man.

Glenn: Naturally I've respected his wishes to remain anonymous.

What's interesting here is how religious orders are preying on their followers to create wealth under the misrepresented guise of God. Often this tithing is to support the church or the costs of the T.V. channel. But that's not helping the people who are really needy for the tithing.

One of the T.V. channels was literally begging for donations, otherwise they were going to have to shut down. It was a British religious channel. Now I have to tell you, that although I'm British, we must have some of the most boring preachers in the world. It's no wonder that people are turning their backs on British churches in droves. The majority of preachers would send hyper-active children to sleep. And yet they expect people to tithe and support their dreary, boring, de-motivational services, which are mostly given in cold, damp smelly old churches.

Tithing is a great idea. But not when the goods or money are taken from people falsely, in the name of profiteering religious organizations and ministries. It's time the 'churchies' woke up to this and discovered just what the churches don't want you to know about God, Jesus and the Bible.

In response to the message that was sent to me about tithing, the following message was sent by a Christian. Once again I've kept his identity anonymous. Here's what the Christian wrote. Now it's a bit long-winded, so I won't mind if you speed-read through it. Sadly, this guy seems to have been programmed by the Bible; and writes like he's writing one too. It's not my style of writing so I'll apologise in advance. It's the message I want to give at the end of it that, to me, is important. I've **bolded** some of the points you might want to opinionate about:

It is my hope and desire *that this brief introduction into the Christian principles of tithing will **stimulate your interest in***

studying and ultimately becoming obedient to the Word of God - the Bible!

I am not going to give you 1,001 reasons why you should tithe on your income. I am not going to try and "sell" you on tithing. Rather, *I am going to present the Word of God to you* and believe that *by the power of the Holy Spirit you will be obedient to God's commandment to tithe!*

The way in which you handle your finances will mark your spiritual commitment to God! It has often been said that more could be learned about a person's commitment to Christ by looking at his check-book rather than his prayer book. We are no farther along in our walk with God than the point to which we have learned to trust Him with our tithes and offerings.

There are so many books, tracts, tapes, and teachings today attempting to convince the Christian to tithe that it is amazing. Many of them are excellent, but many are nothing more than weak compromises trying to gloss over the issue.

For example, I visited a church where the pastor had written a tract entitled, "Moving Towards the Tithe." The tract encouraged people to move in a positive direction to give 10% to God. It later emphasized, however, that the believer need not concern himself with the consequences of not tithing, which was an obvious contradiction of the subject of his tract. My question is not whether or not you are moving towards the tithe, but rather, WHY AREN'T YOU TITHING?

I realize that many people do not tithe simply because they have not had the proper teachings about tithing. Then there are others who know they should, but wilfully don't. My main concern is with the latter group - **those who are wilfully rebellious and disobedient to God's commands. Jesus clearly taught us that if we love him we will keep his commandments. Clearly that includes tithing and giving!**

We have all seen the bumper stickers that say, "HONK IF YOU LOVE JESUS!" Recently, I saw another bumper sticker that said, "TITHE, IF YOU LOVE JESUS...ANYONE CAN HONK!"

PRINCIPLE OF DIVINE OWNERSHIP VERSUS THE PRINCIPLE OF DOMINION

Many Christians have not learned the concept of Divine Ownership or that of Dominion. As a result, they have a distorted view of the purpose of their finances. Here is an explanation of these two important principles.

THE PRINCIPLE OF DOMINION GENESIS 1:26

Then God said, "Let Us make man in Our image, according to Our likeness; let them have dominion over the fish of the sea, over the birds of the air, and over the cattle, over all the earth and over every creeping thing that creeps on the earth." (NKJ)

GENESIS 1:27

So God created man in His own image; in the image of God He created him; male and female He created them.

GENESIS 1:28

Then God blessed them, and God said to them, "Be fruitful and multiply; fill the earth and subdue it; have dominion over the fish of the sea, over the birds of the air, and over every living thing that moves on the earth." (NKJ)

The word dominion comes from the Hebrew word radah, meaning to rule over, to reign over that which is owned by God. Strong's Exhaustive Concordance radah, raw-daw'; a prim.root; to tread down, i.e. subjugate; spec. to crumble off:-(come to, make to) have dominion, prevail against, reign, (bear, make to) rule, (-r, over), take. In other words, God has given us the ability and the command to rule and reign over his property and to become faithful stewards.

The Law of Tithing

*God has given mankind the exclusive right or dominion to rule over His property and world. We have not only been given the right of dominion, but we are also "free moral agents," able to make our own decisions and to determine our own actions. Therefore, man can bless God with his actions or curse God with his actions. **Obedience blesses God, while disobedience is a reproach unto God. Tithing blesses, while not tithing is obviously a reproach.***

DIVINE OWNERSHIP

*If this principle could finally be understood in the hearts of all Christians, then the problems associated with giving and tithing would be over. Therefore, I will quote several scriptures to support this principle. Please take the time to read each scripture, in fact, **underline them in your own Bible for future references.***

GOD OWNS EVERYTHING! PSALMS 24:1
The earth is the Lord's, and all its fullness, the world and those who dwell therein. (NKJ)

PSALMS 50:10
For every beast of the forest is Mine, and the cattle on a thousand hills. (NKJ)

PSALMS 50:11
I know all the birds of the mountains, and the wild beasts of the field are Mine. (NKJ)

HAGGAI 2:8
`The silver is Mine, and the gold is Mine,' says the Lord of hosts. (NKJ)

EZEKIEL 18:4
"Behold, all souls are Mine; the soul of the father as well as the soul of the son is Mine; the soul who sins shall die. (NKJ)

ROMANS 14:8
For if we live, we live to the Lord; and if we die, we die to the Lord. Therefore, whether we live or die, we are the Lord's. (NKJ)

1 CORINTHIANS 6:20
For you were bought at a price; therefore glorify God in your body and in your spirit, which are God's. (NKJ)

1 CORINTHIANS 10:26
For "The earth is the Lord's, and all its fullness." (NKJ)

God owns everything and we are merely stewards over His possessions!

*Based upon the above scriptures and many, many others, it is clear that the entire earth, world, gold, silver, animals, and all people are God's! The principle of divine ownership teaches us that there is nothing that does not belong to God **Himself!** Whereas, the principle of dominion teaches us that mankind has been given stewardship over God's property.*

I believe that this is a very timely message and teaching for the Body of Christ today! Especially living in a world of intense greed, selfishness and hedonism.
I am reminded of the very famous quote from the late president John F. Kennedy, "Ask not what your country can do for you, but ask what you can do for your country."

*So many Christians today fail to realize that **God has asked and even commanded them to give and to tithe!** It is a very disappointing fact that 80% of the finances of any church is given by only 20% of the people. What can you do, what can I do for Christ's church? TITHE!!!!!*

Christian maturity is not based upon the concept of "God, what can you give me?" Rather, it is an attitude which expresses gratitude to God and a thank you, Lord, for what you have done for me, now what can I do for you in return? Mature Christians see the need and fill it. They see their responsibility and respond to it.

One of the greatest injustices that many pastors have done to the church is to insist that God demands one-tenth of our income and one-seventh of our week. The implications are that the other nine-tenths of our income and the other six days of the week are ours to do as we please. The real truth is that everything belongs to God! Not only the tithe, but everything else: 100% belongs to Him. **We are simply stewards being obedient to our Heavenly Master - Jesus Christ, our LORD and Saviour.** The tithe is simply the basic starting point in our Christian financial commitment.

TITHE:-

The definition of tithe is derived from the Hebrew word, asair, which means to give the tenth part of. Strong's Exhaustive Concordance

MA'ASER, MAH-AS-AYR'; OR MA'ASAR, MAH-AS-AR'; AND (IN PLUR.) FEM. MA'ASRAH, MAH-AS-RAW'; FROM 6240; A TENTH; ESPEC. A TITHE:-TENTH (PART), TITHE (-ING).

asar, aw-sar'; a prim. root (ident. with 6238); to accumulate; but used only as denom. from 6235; to tithe, i.e. take or give a tenth:- x surely, give (take) the tenth, (have, take) tithe (-ing, -s), x truly.

Let us look at several scriptures that relate to the tithe. Once again, **I challenge you to read and meditate upon each of the following scriptures.** Mark them in your Bible and use them for references. When you do so, tithing will be come a Rhema word to you from God.

MALACHI 3:8

"Will a man rob God? Yet you have robbed Me! But you say, `In what way have we robbed You?' In tithes and offerings." (NKJ)

MALACHI 3:9

You are cursed with a curse, for you have robbed Me, even this whole nation. MALACHI 3:10

Bring all the tithes into the storehouse , that there may be food in My house, and prove Me now in this ," says the Lord of hosts, "If I will not open for you the windows of heaven And pour out for you such blessing That there will not be room enough to receive it . (NKJ)

MALACHI 3:11

"And I will rebuke the devourer for your sakes, so that he will not destroy the fruit of your ground, nor shall the vine fail to bear fruit for you in the field," says the Lord of hosts;

MALACHI 3:12

And all nations will call you blessed, for you will be a delightful land," says the Lord of hosts. (NKJ)

Did you notice God's response and question to the people who did not tithe in this passage of scripture? He asked the rhetorical question, "Will a man rob God? I don't know about you, but if I were going to rob someone, the last person that I would want to rob is God! Yet, that is exactly what He said the people were doing. What a serious indictment!

How can you and I literally rob God? How can you take from the one who owns everything? Malachi 3:8 says, "... in tithes and offerings." God is specifically telling us that if we do not tithe our 10% unto Him, then as far as he is concerned we are robbers or thieves. Then He proceeds to explain that as a result of our disobedience we are under a curse!

SACRILEGE

ROMANS 2:22

Thou that sayest a man should not commit adultery, dost thou commit adultery? Thou that abhorrest idols, dost thou commit sacrilege? (KJV)

It is interesting that Paul refers to sacrilege in this passage of scripture. In fact, the word sacrilege only appears once in the entire Bible. The Greek word for sacrilege is hierosuleo, to rob a temple, to rob God, to commit sacrilege. Strong's Exhaustive Concordance

Those who have a true understanding of God's Kingdom must come to the conclusion that **the tithe is clearly His basic Kingdom tax; while the offering is the evidence of our love and gratitude for His care and mercy toward us.**

Paul asks several, very important questions in Romans 2:22. He states their position not to commit adultery and then asks "...dost thou commit adultery?" Then Paul goes on to state, "...thou that abhorrest idols," or, you who abhor, detest, and hate the false worship to idols, the giving and sacrifice to idols, "...dost thou commit sacrilege?"

Paul is basically saying, "Practice what you preach!" He tells the Roman Christians that it is unjust to condemn the heathens *for their worship and commitment (their service and sacrifices) to their false gods and idols, and then proclaim to serve the true God of the universe and rob from His temple or to commit sacrilege.*

What a challenge for the church! Shall we continue robbing God through sacrilege? Shall we continue to justify our non-tithing and non-giving, and then use the tithe for our own personal pleasures?

Malachi clearly teaches us that the absence of tithes and offerings results in God's curse. *I know there will be some who will ask the question,* ***"Why do I emphasize the negative of not tithing instead of the positive of tithing?" The answer is because almost every book you will read that has been written in the last 25 years emphasizes only the positive nature of God, while ignoring the judgement of God.*** *It is through obedience and love for God that we tithe. The blessings of tithing are the by-products.*

I think it is quite interesting to note in Malachi, Chapter 3, that the curses from not tithing relate directly back to man's first rebellion against God in the garden.

GENESIS 3:17
And unto Adam he said, Because thou hast hearkened unto the voice of thy wife, and hast eaten of the tree, of which I commanded thee, saying, Thou shalt not eat of it: cursed is the ground for thy sake; in sorrow shalt thou eat of it all the days of thy life; (KJV)

GENESIS 3:18
Thorns also and thistles shall it bring forth to thee; and thou shalt eat the herb of the field; (KJV)

GENESIS 3:19
In the sweat of thy face shalt thou eat bread, till thou return unto the ground; for out of it wast thou taken: for dust thou art, and unto dust shalt thou return. (KJV)

Failure to tithe aggravates and develops the curse that originally came to man in the garden. Whatever our profession, work, or call is, life becomes marked by increased frustration and trouble to the non-tither.

When rebellious man realizes his sin and seeks restoration with God through redemption and sanctification, God, in His mercy, provides a life of blessings. In fact, Deuteronomy 28 shows us that as we obey the Word of God, not only will l we be entitled to blessings, but they will overtake us!

Let us look at Malachi, Chapter 3, Verse 7:

MALACHI 3:7

Even from the days of your fathers ye are gone away from mine ordinances, and have not kept them. Return unto me, and I will return unto you, saith the Lord of hosts. But ye said, Wherein shall we return < B> ? (KJV)

MALACHI 3:8

Will a man rob God? Yet ye have robbed me. But ye say, Wherein have we robbed thee? In tithes and offerings. (KJV)

The premise of God's reproof in verses 8 - 12 was the fact that the people were amazed that God wanted to return to them. They hadn't even realized that He had left them and wanted to return! They asked God, " Wherein shall we return?" (v.7)

As far as these people were concerned, they were good people who loved God and assumed they were in fellowship with Him. The same is true today. We have thousands of Christians who assume their relationship with God is okay. They live their lives as if tithing were not important to their LORD.

Peter challenges the church in Acts 5:29

ACTS 5:29

Then Peter and the other apostles answered and said, We ought to obey God rather than men. (KJV)

CHRIST IS KING!!!

The Christian declaration that "CHRIST IS KING!" is one of absolute authority and power! When you accepted Christ as your Lord and Saviour you were placed within His Kingdom.

COLOSSIANS 1:13

Who hath delivered us from the power of darkness, and hath translated us into the kingdom of his dear Son: (KJV)

Every king has the power and the right of taxation; every king commands his kingdom. A king does not have to plead for support, he does not have to send out appeal letters. It is his right! The option to pay the tax does not come to the people for a vote! It is not a matter of their choice. It is their obligation to their king! Paul supports this position in Romans 13:7.

ROMANS 13:7

Render therefore to all their dues: tribute to whom tribute is due; custom to whom custom; fear to whom fear; honour to whom honour. (KJV)

If we are responsible to render our dues, tribute, custom, fear, and honour to earthly kings, how much more so of our Lord Jesus Christ! In the simplest terms, if we are members of Christ's Kingdom, then we must pay its taxes.

The Church must understand its responsibility to bring all the tithes into the storehouse. Much of the nonsense we have seen in recent years can be directly attributed to the lack of committed Christians who tithe. Is it any wonder why a recent poll in U.S.A. Today indicated that 40% of Americans believe that "very little Christian fund raising is either honest or ethical."

Recently, the church's image has been soiled by the constant appeal for money. Fund raising is filled with gimmicks, and many times outright lies! WHY? Because we have become a people who truly do not fear God! We do not tithe to our local churches. We do not support missions. Yet, we want and expect God to help us, heal us, protect us, etc.

HOW DO I DETERMINE THE AMOUNT I SHOULD TITHE?

The word tithe literally means 10 %. The amount we should tithe is 10 % of all our increase. This includes any and all increase in the value of the original capital investment. All capital gains from the sale of houses, real estate, stocks, bonds, machinery, etc. All increases based upon our wages or salaries, including fringe benefits: employer paid health insurance, dental insurance, life insurance, retirement contributions, etc.

LEVITICUS 27:30

And all the tithe of the land, whether of the seed of the land, or of the fruit of the tree, is the Lord's: it is holy unto the Lord. (KJV)

LEVITICUS 27:31

And if a man will at all redeem ought of his tithes, he shall add thereto the fifth part thereof. (KJV)

LEVITICUS 27:32

And concerning the tithe of the herd, or of the flock, even of whatsoever passeth under the rod, the tenth shall be holy unto the Lord. (KJV)

God has commanded us to tithe on all our increases. Whatever you receive, whether it be from gifts, earnings, inheritances, etc. are to be tithed.

Those who tithe usually have little difficulty tithing on their gross wages. However, many fail to take into account the sales and profits from houses, cars, boats, etc. Whenever we receive an increase above our original investment, we are to tithe!

Sometimes I am asked the question, "What happens if I lose money on an investment?" My response is always the same: if we have an increase, God expects a tithe!

WHERE ARE WE TO GIVE OUR TITHES?

One of the most frustrating and damaging teachings in the Body of Christ today is the concept that our tithes can go to any ministry we choose. *For example, it is common practice for radio and T.V. evangelists to ask for the people to send in a "portion" or "all" of their tithes to support their air time. Another false concept is that of sending our tithe to evangelistic ministries, orphanages, paying school tuitions, etc. While these are good and important, scripturally they are not to receive the tithe!* **The tithe is to go to your local church and nowhere else!**

I would like to point out that it is your option to send your offerings and special gifts to ministries that do, in fact, bless you. I personally send money to many ministries and am happy to do so. In fact, our church has often received special collect ions for other ministries.

MALACHI 3:10

Bring ye all the tithes into the storehouse , that there may be meat in mine house, and prove me now herewith, saith the Lord of hosts, if I will not open you the windows of heaven, and pour you out a blessing, that there shall not be room enough to receive it . (KJV)

Storehouse Concept

The concept of the storehouse in the Old Testament plays a very important part in our understanding of New Testament tithing. The people, being primarily agricultural, would bring their tithes of the land, cattle, grain, fruits, vegetables, etc. to the local Levites who were responsible for the ministry in their local community. The Levites had a storehouse in which the grain, meal, cattle, etc. would be stored for later consumption and use. Notice that God said we were to bring all the tithes into the storehouse, that there may be meat in mine house. His house was in reference to what we call today the local church. It was that place in which people would be able to receive their ministry and care.

Unfortunately, T.V. evangelists lead many people believe they are being ministered to, exclusively by them. In fact, if the T.V. evangelists would come in line with New Testament authority, they would be supported and sent out by the local church. **Many times I have received phone calls from people who have not been attending church services and I know are not tithing to a local church, only to hear, "Pastor will you please come over and pray for me? Will you visit my mother in the hospital? Will you marry us?" I have**

wanted to say, but I have not as of yet, "Why don't you call Bro. T.V. Evangelist, or such and such T.V. program to come and help you?" You see, it is the local church that is responsible for the daily ministry of the saints of God. It is the local shepherds who the Bible says are to lay down their lives for the sheep. It is the local church who must baptize, marry, counsel, and bury the individuals. Therefore, **God's plan is for the local church to receive the tithe for its services.**

Again, there is absolutely no scriptural support for the idea that the tithe is to go anywhere but to the local church.

I CORINTHIANS 16:1
Now concerning the collection for the saints, as I have given order to the churches of Galatia, even so do ye. (KJV)

I CORINTHIANS 16:2
Upon the first day of the week let every one of you lay by him in store, as God hath prospered him, that there be no gatherings when I come. (KJV)

Notice the concept of laying in store for the first day of the week, Sunday. Now I realize that this verse is referring to the offerings that were designated for the suffering saints in Jerusalem, but I wish to point out the principle of storehouse and weekly giving in the New Testament setting.

The sole and primary purpose of the tithe is to support those who are in the ministry and their families. The tithe, as we will see, is not to be used for paying church mortgages or electric bills, but is to go towards the support of the ministers on staff in a local church.

1 CORINTHIANS 9:14
Even so hath the Lord ordained that they which preach the gospel should live of the gospel. (KJV)

1 CORINTHIANS 9:14
In the same way, the Lord has commanded that those who preach the gospel should receive their living from the gospel. (NIV)

LUKE 10:7
And in the same house remain, eating and drinking such things as they give: for the labourer is worthy of his hire. Go not from house to house. (KJV)

1 TIMOTHY 5:17
Let the elders that rule well be counted worthy of double honour, especially they who labour in the word and doctrine. (KJV)

1 TIMOTHY 5:17

The elders who direct the affairs of the church well are worthy of double honour, especially those whose work is preaching and teaching. (NIV)

These, as well as other scriptures, show us that the ministers are not to live in hardship, just barely getting by. As ministers are faithful to the Lord and as their ministries grow so should their support financially.

NUMBERS 18:21 And, behold, I have given the children of Levi all the tenth in Israel for an inheritance, for their service which they serve, even the service of the tabernacle of the congregation. (KJV)

NUMBERS 18:24 But the tithes of the children of Israel, which they offer as an heave offering unto the Lord, I have given to the Levites to inherit: therefore I have said unto them, Among the children of Israel they shall have no inheritance. (KJV)

Verse 24 shows us that the Levites were to tithe, and that tithe was called the heave offering. The heave offering was used to support the priest that supported the Levites.

NEW TESTAMENT TITHING

Some critics of tithing try to maintain that tithing is an Old Testament law and not subject to New Testament obedience. However, Jesus Christ our Lord and Saviour maintains the principle of tithing in Matthew 23:23.

MATTHEW 23:23

Woe unto you, scribes and Pharisees, hypocrites! For ye pay tithe of mint and anise and cumin, and have omitted the weightier matters of the law, judgment, mercy, and faith: these ought ye to have done, and not t o leave the other undone. (KJV) (KJV)

Also see Luke 11:42

LUKE 11:42

But woe unto you, Pharisees! For ye tithe mint and rue and all manner of herbs, and pass over judgment and the love of God: these ought ye to have done, and not to leave the other undone. (KJV)

LUKE 11:42

"Woe to you Pharisees, because you give God a tenth of your mint, rue and all other kinds of garden herbs, but you neglect justice and the love of God. You should have practiced the latter without leaving the former undone. (NIV)

Clearly Jesus is telling the Pharisees and scribes that they were to tithe on their increases and possessions! The emphasis was not that they were not to tithe or that we are not to tithe, but that they should understand judgement, mercy, and faith. Whatever we do today is in vain if it is not done in faith and love. But, please do not overlook the fact Jesus expected them to continue tithing!

"Pastor, tithing is Old Testament and we are no longer under the law and I am not going to tithe!"

Tithing was not initially instituted in the Mosaic law. In fact, it was a Biblical principle instituted by God before the Law! Let us take a look at Abraham who tithed unto the priest Melchizedek.

GENESIS 14:18
And Melchizedek king of Salem brought forth bread and wine: and he was the priest of the most high God. (KJV)

GENESIS 14:19
And he blessed him, and said, Blessed be Abram of the most high God, possessor of heaven and earth: (KJV)

GENESIS 14:20
And blessed be the most high God, which hath delivered thine enemies into thy hand. And he gave him tithes of all. (KJV)

This passage of scripture clearly shows us the principle and the law of tithing hundreds of years before the Mosaic Law was given.

Another example of tithing before the Mosaic Law was Jacob in Genesis 28:20-22.

GENESIS 28:20
And Jacob vowed a vow, saying, If God will be with me, and will keep me in this way that I go, and will give me bread to eat, and raiment to put on, (KJV)

GENESIS 28:21
So that I come again to my father's house in peace; then shall the Lord be my God: (KJV)

GENESIS 28:22
And this stone, which I have set for a pillar, shall be God's house: and of all that thou shalt give me I will surely give the tenth unto thee. (KJV)

Jacob made a vow unto God to serve Him and to tithe on all that the Lord would give him. Let us look at the end result of Jacob's life as a result of his tithing unto the LORD.

GENESIS 33:11
Take, I pray thee, my blessing that is brought to thee; because God hath dealt graciously with me, and because I have enough. And he urged him, and he took it. (KJV)

I heard one man say, "I am not going to tithe. I live strictly by the New Testament and I don't believe tithing is New Testament!"

I then proceeded to shout, "Praise the Lord! Let us look at the New Testament!"

MARK 10:21

Then Jesus beholding him loved him, and said unto him, One thing thou lackest: go thy way, sell whatsoever thou hast, and give to the poor, and thou shalt have treasure in heaven: and come, take up the cross, and follow me. (KJV)

ACTS 2:44

And all that believed were together, and had all things common; (KJV)

ACTS 2:45

And sold their possessions and goods, and parted them to all men, as every man had need. (KJV)

ACTS 4:32

And the multitude of them that believed were of one heart and of one soul: neither said any of them that ought of the things which he possessed was his own; but they had all things common. (KJV)

ACTS 4:33

And with great power gave the apostles witness of the resurrection of the Lord Jesus: and great grace was upon them all. (KJV)

ACTS 4:34

Neither was there any among them that lacked: for as many as were possessors of lands or houses sold them, and brought the prices of the things that were sold, (KJV)

ACTS 4:35

And laid them down at the apostles' feet: and distribution was made unto every man according as he had need. (KJV)

ACTS 4:36

And Joses, who by the apostles was surnamed Barnabas, (which is, being interpreted, the son of consolation,) a Levite, and of the country of Cyprus, (KJV)

ACTS 4:37

Having land, sold it, and brought the money, and laid it at the apostles' feet. (KJV)

I then proceeded to tell the man that if he were strictly New Testament, he would have to sell all that he had and bring it into the church, to the apostles' feet. After reading these scriptures, I *was surprised at how quickly this man changed his theology regarding the law of the tithe.*

PROVERBS 3:9

Honour the Lord with thy substance, and with the first fruits of all thine increase: (KJV)

PROVERBS 3:10

So shall thy barns be filled with plenty, and thy presses shall burst out with new wine. (KJV)

Tithing is the means through which God is released to bless his people. Scripture after scripture shows us that it is God's desire for us to prosper and be in health. The Bible also tells us that whatever we give shall be given back to us good measure, pressed down, shaken together and running over. It teaches us that God will open up the windows of heaven and pour out blessings that our storehouses will not be able to contain.

The question is not whether you can afford to tithe, but rather, how in the world can you afford not to tithe?

Tithing is one of God's means of bringing us into maturity and prosperity.

Tithing honours the LORD!

Tithing demonstrates our faith in God's power to supply all our needs. We receive peace of mind knowing we are obeying God's Word.

Tithing is an act of our faith because it allows God to bless the remaining 90% of our income.

Tithing blesses the church by enabling it to carry out a greater ministry to the world.

Through our obedience to God in tithing, we become good examples of financial stewardship in God's Kingdom.

Please let me remind you that we are the stewards and not the owners of our possessions. GOD OWNS ALL!

TITHING IS NOT AN OPTION IT IS GOD'S COMMANDMENT!

You can tithe without loving God with all your heart, but you cannot love God with all your heart without tithing!

Additional Scriptures Relating to Tithing: The Law of Tithing

2 CHRONICLES 31:5

And as soon as the commandment came abroad, the children of Israel brought in abundance the first fruits of corn, wine, and oil, and honey, and of all the increase of the field; and the tithe of all <things> brought they in abundantly.

2 CHRONICLES 31:6
And <concerning> the children of Israel and Judah, that dwelt in
the cities of Judah, they also brought in the tithe of oxen and
sheep, and the tithe of holy things which were consecrated unto
the LORD their God, and laid it; them by heaps.

NEHEMIAH 10:38
And the priest the son of Aaron shall be with the Levites, when
the Levites take tithes: and the Levites shall bring up the tithe of
the tithes unto the house of our God, to the chambers, into the
treasure house.

NEHEMIAH 13:12
Then brought all Judah the tithe of the corn and the new wine
and the oil unto the treasuries.

MATTHEW 23:23
Woe unto you, scribes and Pharisees, hypocrites! For ye pay
tithe of mint and anise and cumin, and have omitted the
weightier <matters> of the law, judgment, mercy, and faith:
these ought ye to have done, and not to leave the other undone.

LUKE 11:42
But woe unto you, Pharisees! For ye tithe mint and rue and all
manner of herbs, and pass over judgment and the love of God:
these ought ye to have done, and not to leave the other undone.

LEVITICUS 27:30
And all the tithe of the land, <whether> of the seed of the land,
<or> of the fruit of the tree, <is> the LORD'S: <it is> holy unto the
LORD.

LEVITICUS 27:32
And concerning the tithe of the herd, or of the flock, <even> of
whatsoever passeth under the rod, the tenth shall be holy unto
the LORD.

NUMBERS 18:26
Thus speak unto the Levites, and say unto them, When ye take
of the children of Israel the tithes which I have given you from
them for your inheritance, then ye shall offer up an heave
offering of it for the LORD, <even> a tenth <part> of the tithe.

DEUTERONOMY 12:17
Thou mayest not eat within thy gates the tithe of thy corn or of
thy wine, or of thy oil, or the firstlings of thy herds or of thy
flock, nor any of thy vows which thou vowest, nor thy freewill
offerings, or heave offering of thine hand:

DEUTERONOMY 14:22
Thou shalt truly tithe all the increase of thy seed, that the field
bringeth forth year by year.

DEUTERONOMY 14:23
And thou shalt eat before the LORD thy God, in the place which he shall choose to place his name there, the tithe of thy corn, of thy wine, and of thine oil, and the firstlings of thy herds and of thy flocks; that thou mayest learn to fear the LORD thy God always.

DEUTERONOMY 14:28
At the end of three years thou shalt bring forth all the tithe of thine increase the same year, and shalt lay <it> up within thy gates:

NUMBERS 18:26
Thus speak unto the Levites, and say unto them, When ye take of the children of Israel the tithes which I have given you from them for your inheritance, then ye shall offer up an heave offering of it for the LORD, <even> a tenth <part> of the tithe.

NUMBERS 18:28
Thus ye also shall offer a heave offering unto the LORD of all your tithes, which ye receive of the children of Israel; and ye shall give thereof the LORD's heave offering to Aaron the priest.

DEUTERONOMY 12:6
And thither ye shall bring your burnt offerings, and your sacrifices, and your tithes, and heave offerings of your hand, and your vows, and your freewill offerings, and the firstlings of your herds and of your flocks:

DEUTERONOMY 12:11
Then there shall be a place which the LORD your God shall choose to cause his name to dwell there; thither shall ye bring all that I command you; your burnt offerings, and your sacrifices, your tithes, and the heave offering of y our hand, and all your choice vows which ye vow unto the LORD:

DEUTERONOMY 26:12
When thou hast made an end of tithing all the tithes of thine increase the third year, <which> <is> the year of tithing, and hast given <it> unto the Levite, the stranger, the fatherless, and the widow, that the y may eat within thy gates, and be filled;

2 CHRONICLES 31:12
And brought in the offerings and the tithes and the dedicated <things> faithfully: over which Cononiah the Levite <was> ruler, and Shimei his brother <was> the next.

NEHEMIAH 10:37
And <that> we should bring the first fruits of our dough, and our offerings, and the fruit of all manner of trees, of wine and of oil, unto the priests, to the chambers of the house of our God; and

the tithes of our ground unto the Levites, that the same Levites might have the tithes in all the cities of our tillage.
    NEHEMIAH 10:38
And the priest the son of Aaron shall be with the Levites, when the Levites take tithes: and the Levites shall bring up the tithe of the tithes unto the house of our God, to the chambers, into the treasure house.
    NEHEMIAH 12:44
And at that time there were some appointed over the chambers for the treasures, for the offerings, for the first fruits, and for the tithes, to gather into them out of the fields of the cities the portions of the law for the priests and Levites: for Judah rejoiced for the priests and for the Levites that waited.
    NEHEMIAH 13:5
And he had prepared for him a great chamber, where aforetime they laid the meat offerings, the frankincense, and the vessels, and the tithes of the corn, the new wine, and the oil, which was commanded <to be given> to the Levites, and the singers, and the porters; and the offerings of the priests.
    AMOS 4:4
Come to Beth-el, and transgress; at Gilgal multiply transgression; and bring your sacrifices every morning, <and> your tithes after three years:
    MALACHI 3:8
Will a man rob God? Yet ye have robbed me. But ye say, Wherein have we robbed thee? In tithes and offerings.
    MALACHI 3:10
Bring ye all the tithes into the storehouse, that there may be meat in mine house, and prove me now herewith, saith the LORD of hosts, if I will not open you the windows of heaven, and pour you out a blessing, that <there shall> not <be room> enough <to receive it>.
    LUKE 18:12
I fast twice in the week, I give tithes of all that I possess.
    HEBREWS 7:5
And verily they that are of the sons of Levi, who receive the office of the priesthood, have a commandment to take tithes of the people according to the law, that is, of their brethren, though they come out of the loins of Abraham:
    HEBREWS 7:6
But he whose descent is not counted from them received tithes of Abraham, and blessed him that had the promises.

HEBREWS 7:8

And here men that die receive tithes; but there he <receiveth them,> of whom it is witnessed that he liveth.

HEBREWS 7:9

And as I may so say, Levi also, who receiveth tithes, paid tithes in Abraham.

Glenn: At this point our Christian is on a roll and wants to bombard us with Prosperity Scriptures. I really found this hard work, so in the interests of keeping you interested; I've reduced the size of the font. You can still read it if you want to; and you'll also know which part to skip, if you want to.

Prosperity Scriptures

NUMBERS 23:19 God is not a man, that he should lie; neither the son of man, that he should repent: hath he said, and shall he not do it? Or hath he spoken, and shall he not make it good? (KJV)

JOSHUA 1:5 There shall not any man be able to stand before thee all the days of thy life: as I was with Moses, so I will be with thee: I will not fail thee, nor forsake thee. (KJV)

JOSHUA 1:6 Be strong and of a good courage: for unto this people shalt thou divide for an inheritance the land, which I sware unto their fathers to give them. (KJV)

JOSHUA 1:7 Only be thou strong and very courageous, that thou mayest observe to do according to all the law, which Moses my servant commanded thee: turn not from it to the right hand or to the left, that thou mayest prosper whithersoever thou goest. (K JV)

JOSHUA 1:8 This book of the law shall not depart out of thy mouth; but thou shalt meditate therein day and night, that thou mayest observe to do according to all that is written therein: for then thou shalt make thy way prosperous, and then thou shalt have good success. (KJV)

ISAIAH 40:8 The grass withereth, the flower fadeth: but the word of our God shall stand for ever. (KJV)

PSALMS 119:89 For ever, O Lord, thy word is settled in heaven. (KJV)

PSALMS 119:90 Thy faithfulness is unto all generations: thou hast established the earth, and it abideth. (KJV)

1 KINGS 8:56 Blessed be the Lord, that hath given rest unto his people Israel, according to all that he promised: there hath not failed one word of all his good promise, which he promised by the hand of Moses his servant. (KJV)< BR> 1 PETER 1:25 But the word of the Lord endureth for ever. And this is the word which by the gospel is preached unto you. (KJV)

LUKE 18:27 And he said, The things which are impossible with men are possible with God. (KJV)

MARK 10:27 And Jesus looking upon them saith, With men it is impossible, but not with God: for with God all things are possible. (KJV)

ROMANS 8:32 He that spared not his own Son, but delivered him up for us all, how shall he not with him also freely give us all things? (KJV)

PSALMS 35:27 Let them shout for joy, and be glad, that favour my righteous cause: yea, let them say continually, Let the Lord be magnified, which hath pleasure in the prosperity of his servant. (KJV)

3 JOHN 1:2 Beloved, I wish above all things that thou mayest prosper and be in health, even as thy soul prospereth. (KJV)

2 CORINTHIANS 8:9 For ye know the grace of our Lord Jesus Christ, that, though he was rich, yet for your sakes he became poor, that ye through his poverty might be rich. (KJV)

1 TIMOTHY 6:17 Charge them that are rich in this world, that they be not high minded, nor trust in uncertain riches, but in the living God, who giveth us richly all things to enjoy; (KJV)

PHILIPPIANS 4:19 But my God shall supply all your need according to his riches in glory by Christ Jesus. (KJV)

2 CHRONICLES 1:12 Wisdom and knowledge is granted unto thee; and I will give thee riches, and wealth, and honour, such as none of the kings have had that have been before thee, neither shall there any after thee have the like. (KJV)

2 CORINTHIANS 9:11 Being enriched in every thing to all bountifulness, which causeth through us thanksgiving to God. (KJV)

PROVERBS 10:22 The blessing of the Lord, it maketh rich, and he addeth no sorrow with it. (KJV)

1 CHRONICLES 29:12 Both riches and honour come of thee, and thou reignest over all; and in thine hand is power and might; and in thine hand it is to make great, and to give strength unto all. (KJV)

PROVERBS 22:4 By humility and the fear of the Lord are riches, and honour, and life. (KJV)

DEUTERONOMY 8:18 But thou shalt remember the Lord thy God: for it is he that giveth thee power to get wealth, that he may establish his covenant which he sware unto thy fathers, as it is this day. (KJV)

ISAIAH 48:17 Thus saith the Lord, thy Redeemer, the Holy One of Israel; I am the Lord thy God which teacheth thee to profit, which leadeth thee by the way that thou shouldest go. (KJV)

PSALMS 112:1 Praise ye the Lord. Blessed is the man that feareth the Lord, that delighteth greatly in his commandments. (KJV)

PSALMS 112:2 His seed shall be mighty upon earth: the generation of the upright shall be blessed. (KJV)

PSALMS 112:3 Wealth and riches shall be in his house: and his righteousness endureth for ever. (KJV)

ECCLESIASTES 5:19 Every man also to whom God hath given riches and wealth, and hath given him power to eat thereof, and to take his portion, and to rejoice in his labour; this is the gift of God. (KJV)

DEUTERONOMY 29:9 Keep therefore the words of this covenant, and do them, that ye may prosper in all that ye do. (KJV)

PROVERBS 28:25 He that is of a proud heart stirreth up strife: but he that putteth his trust in the Lord shall be made fat. (KJV)

2 CHRONICLES 26:5 And he sought God in the days of Zechariah, who had understanding in the visions of God: and as long as he sought the Lord, God made him to prosper. (KJV)

1 KINGS 2:2 I go the way of all the earth: be thou strong therefore, and shew thyself a man; (KJV)

1 KINGS 2:3 And keep the charge of the Lord thy God, to walk in his ways, to keep his statutes, and his commandments, and his judgments, and his testimonies, as it is written in the law of Moses, that thou mayest prosper in all t hat thou doest, and whithersoever thou turnest thyself: (KJV)

1 CHRONICLES 22:13 Then shalt thou prosper, if thou takest heed to fulfil the statutes and judgments which the Lord charged Moses with concerning Israel: be strong, and of good courage; dread not, nor be dismayed. (KJV)

PSALMS 1:3 And he shall be like a tree planted by the rivers of water, that bringeth forth his fruit in his season; his leaf also shall not wither; and whatsoever he doeth shall prosper. (KJV)

PSALMS 34:10 The young lions do lack, and suffer hunger: but they that seek the Lord shall not want any good thing. (KJV)

PSALMS 37:4 Delight thyself also in the Lord: and he shall give thee the desires of thine heart. (KJV)

JOB 36:11 If they obey and serve him, they shall spend their days in prosperity, and their years in pleasures. (KJV)

DEUTERONOMY 28:12 The Lord shall open unto thee his good treasure, the heaven to give the rain unto thy land in his season, and to bless all the work of thine hand: and thou shalt lend unto many nations, and thou shalt not borrow. (KJV)

PROVERBS 10:4 He becometh poor that dealeth with a slack hand: but the hand of the diligent maketh rich. (KJV)

2 CORINTHIANS 9:8 And God is able to make all grace abound toward you; that ye, always having all sufficiency in all things, may abound to every good work: (KJV)

PROVERBS 28:27 He that giveth unto the poor shall not lack: but he that hideth his eyes shall have many a curse. (KJV)

LUKE 6:38 Give, and it shall be given unto you; good measure, pressed down, and shaken together, and running over, shall men give into your bosom. For with the same measure that ye mete withal it shall be measured to you again. (KJV)

PROVERBS 19:17 He that hath pity upon the poor lendeth unto the Lord; and that which he hath given will he pay him again. (KJV)

PROVERBS 11:25 The liberal soul shall be made fat: and he that watereth shall be watered also himself. (KJV)

PROVERBS 21:13 Who so stoppeth his ears at the cry of the poor, he also shall cry himself, but shall not be heard. (KJV)

EPHESIANS 6:7 With good will doing service, as to the Lord, and not to men: (KJV)

EPHESIANS 6:8 Knowing that whatsoever good thing any man doeth, the same shall he receive of the Lord, whether he be bond or free. (KJV)

GALATIANS 4:7 Wherefore thou art no more a servant, but a son; and if a son, then an heir of God through Christ. (KJV)

GALATIANS 3:13 Christ hath redeemed us from the curse of the law, being made a curse for us: for it is written, Cursed is every one that hangeth on a tree: (KJV)

GALATIANS 3:14 That the blessing of Abraham might come on the Gentiles through Jesus Christ; that we might receive the promise of the Spirit through faith. (KJV)

GALATIANS 3:29 And if ye be Christ's, then are ye Abraham's seed, and heirs according to the promise. (KJV)

ROMANS 8:16 The Spirit itself beareth witness with our spirit, that we are the children of God: (KJV)

ROMANS 8:17 And if children, then heirs; heirs of God, and joint-heirs with Christ; if so be that we suffer with him, that we may be also glorified together. (KJV)

GALATIANS 3:26 For ye are all the children of God by faith in Christ Jesus. (KJV)

GALATIANS 3:29 And if ye be Christ's, then are ye Abraham's seed, and heirs according to the promise. (KJV)

2 CORINTHIANS 1:20 For all the promises of God in him are yea, and in him Amen, unto the glory of God by us. (KJV)

HEBREWS 6:12 That ye be not slothful, but followers of them who through faith and patience inherit the promises. (KJV)

MARK 10:29 And Jesus answered and said, Verily I say unto you, There is no man that hath left house, or brethren, or sisters, or father, or mother, or wife, or children, or lands, for my sake, and the gospel's, (KJV)

MARK 10:30 But he shall receive an hundredfold now in this time, houses, and brethren, and sisters, and mothers, and children, and lands, with persecutions; and in the world to come eternal life. (KJV)

PROVERBS 3:5 Trust in the Lord with all thine heart; and lean not unto thine own understanding. (KJV)

PROVERBS 3:6 In all thy ways acknowledge him, and he shall direct thy paths. (KJV)

PSALMS 37:5 Commit thy way unto the Lord; trust also in him; and he shall bring it to pass. (KJV)

MARK 9:23 Jesus said unto him, If thou canst believe, all things are possible to him that believeth. (KJV)

JOB 22:25 Yea, the Almighty shall be thy defence, and thou shalt have plenty of silver. (KJV)

1 TIMOTHY 2:5 For there is one God, and one mediator between God and men, the man Christ Jesus; (KJV)

PHILIPPIANS 4:13 I can do all things through Christ which strengtheneth me. (KJV)

1 CORINTHIANS 15:57 But thanks be to God, which giveth us the victory through our Lord Jesus Christ. (KJV)

PSALMS 68:19 Blessed be the Lord, who daily loadeth us with benefits, even the God of our salvation. Selah. (KJV)

ISAIAH 45:3 And I will give thee the treasures of darkness, and hidden riches of secret places, that thou mayest know that I, the Lord, which call thee by thy name, am the God of Israel. (KJV)

PROVERBS 21:17 He that loveth pleasure shall be a poor man: he that loveth wine and oil shall not be rich. (KJV)

JOSHUA 1:8 This book of the law shall not depart out of thy mouth; but thou shalt meditate therein day and night, that thou mayest observe to do according to all that is written therein: for then thou shalt make thy way prosperous, and then thou shalt have good success. (KJV)

MATTHEW 6:33 But seek ye first the kingdom of God, and his righteousness; and all these things shall be added unto you. (KJV)

MATTHEW 6:34 Take therefore no thought for the morrow: for the morrow shall take thought for the things of itself. Sufficient unto the day is the evil thereof. (KJV)

PROVERBS 3:9 Honour the Lord with thy substance, and with the first fruits of all thine increase: (KJV)

PROVERBS 3:10 So shall thy barns be filled with plenty, and thy presses shall burst out with new wine. (KJV)

MALACHI 3:10 Bring ye all the tithes into the storehouse, that there may be meat in mine house, and prove me now herewith, saith the Lord of hosts, if I will not open you the windows of heaven, and pour you out a blessing, that t here shall not be room enough to receive it . (KJV)

MATTHEW 7:11 If ye then, being evil, know how to give good gifts unto your children, how much more shall your Father which is in heaven give good things to them that ask him? (KJV)

PROVERBS 10:24 The fear of the wicked, it shall come upon him: but the desire of the righteous shall be granted. (KJV)

JOHN 10:10 The thief cometh not, but for to steal, and to kill, and to destroy: I am come that they might have life, and that they might have it more abundantly. (KJV)

1 JOHN 4:4 Ye are of God, little children, and have overcome them: because greater is he that is in you, than he that is in the world. (KJV)

MATTHEW 18:18 Verily I say unto you, Whatsoever ye shall bind on earth shall be bound in heaven: and whatsoever ye shall loose on earth shall be loosed in heaven. (KJV)

ROMANS 8:31 What shall we then say to these things? If God be for us, who can be against us? (KJV)

ROMANS 1:17 For therein is the righteousness of God revealed from faith to faith: as it is written, The just shall live by faith. (KJV)

2 CORINTHIANS 5:7 (For we walk by faith, not by sight.) (KJV)

HEBREWS 11:6 But without faith it is impossible to please him: for he that cometh to God must believe that he is, and that he is a rewarder of them that diligently seek him. (KJV)

JAMES 1:6 But let him ask in faith, nothing wavering. For he that wavereth is like a wave of the sea driven with the wind and tossed. (KJV)

JAMES 1:7 For let not that man think that he shall receive any thing of the Lord. (KJV)

MARK 11:23 For verily I say unto you, That whosoever shall say unto this mountain, Be thou removed, and be thou cast into the sea; and shall not doubt in his heart, but shall believe that those things which he saith shall come to pass; he shall have whatsoever he saith. (KJV)

MARK 11:24 Therefore I say unto you, What things soever ye desire, when ye pray, believe that ye receive them, and ye shall have them. (KJV)

MATTHEW 21:22 And all things, whatsoever ye shall ask in prayer, believing, ye shall receive. (KJV)

JOHN 16:23 And in that day ye shall ask me nothing. Verily, verily, I say unto you, whatsoever ye shall ask the Father in my name, he will give it you. (KJV)

JOHN 15:7 If ye abide in me, and my words abide in you, ye shall ask what ye will, and it shall be done unto you. (KJV)

MATTHEW 7:7 Ask, and it shall be given you; seek, and ye shall find; knock, and it shall be opened unto you: (KJV)

MATTHEW 7:8 For every one that asketh receiveth; and he that seeketh findeth; and to him that knocketh it shall be opened. (KJV)

JOHN 16:24 Hitherto have ye asked nothing in my name: ask, and ye shall receive, that your joy may be full. (KJV)

JOHN 14:13 And whatsoever ye shall ask in my name, that will I do, that the Father may be glorified in the Son. (KJV)

JOHN 14:14 If ye shall ask any thing in my name, I will do it. (KJV)

1 JOHN 5:14 And this is the confidence that we have in him, that, if we ask any thing according to his will, he heareth us: (KJV)

1 JOHN 5:15 And if we know that he hear us, whatsoever we ask, we know that we have the petitions that we desired of him. (KJV)

JOHN 11:22 But I know, that even now, whatsoever thou wilt ask of God, God will give it thee. (KJV)

1 JOHN 3:22 And whatsoever we ask, we receive of him, because we keep his commandments, and do those things that are pleasing in his sight. (KJV)

PSALMS 23:1 The Lord is my shepherd; I shall not want. (KJV)

EPHESIANS 3:20 Now unto him that is able to do exceeding abundantly above all that we ask or think, according to the power that worketh in us, (KJV)

EPHESIANS 3:21 Unto him be glory in the church by Christ Jesus throughout all ages, world without end. Amen. (KJV)

ROMANS 8:37 Nay, in all these things we are more than conquerors through him that loved us. (KJV)

ISAIAH 41:10 Fear thou not; for I am with thee: be not dismayed; for I am thy God: I will strengthen thee; yea, I will help thee; yea, I will uphold thee with the right hand of my righteousness. (KJV)

PSALMS 89:34 My covenant will I not break, nor alter the thing that is gone out of my lips. (KJV)

PSALMS 89:35 Once have I sworn by my holiness that I will not lie unto David. (KJV)

MARK 13:31 Heaven and earth shall pass away: but my words shall not pass away. (KJV)

HEBREWS 13:8 Jesus Christ the same yesterday, and to day, and for ever. (KJV)

Suggestions For Training Children To Tithe

Begin early to train your children the importance of tithing and giving. If your children are taught in their childhood the blessings of tithing they will have very little problems giving as an adult.

Teach them to set aside 20% of their allowance, gifts from parents, earnings to first of all, tithe and then give 10% to other special needs such as missions.

Teach your children that as their incomes increase so should their giving.

Developing Non-Cash Gifts

Throughout the year each department in the local church has special needs that require an expenditure from the general budget. Many of these expenditures may be gifting opportunities for the local church membership. This expands the budget base of the local church by allowing people to give non-cash gifts.

Examples of Non-Cash Gifts

Low Cost Gifts
1) Gallon of paint for a classroom
2) A square yard of carpeting for lounge or classroom
3) Cooking Utensils, Pots & Pans
4) Landscaping - shrubs, flowers, garden tools, fertilizers
5) Chalk boards for classrooms
6) Pulpit Bible or Pew Bibles
7) Hymnals
8) Choir robes
9) Guest Registrar
10) Prayer book
11) Library Books
12) Christian School Supplies
13) Sports Equipment for School
14) Sunday school equipment and supplies
15) Office supplies
16) Curtains for classrooms

Moderate Priced Gifts
1) Furniture such as a couch for waiting room or lounge
2) Carpet for a classroom
3) Scholarship tuition for children in Christian School or Day Care
4) Kitchen appliances
5) Pews
6) Cassette Tape Deck for Services
7) The cost of paving one parking space
8) Tires for the church van
9) Overhead Projector
10) Communion table
11) Communion Service Set
12) Slide Projector
13) Car Phone for Pastor
14) Office Equipment
15) Desks for the classrooms

Major Gifts
1) Bell tower
2) Church Van
3) Ramps for the disabled
4) Organ or piano

5) Salaries for new ministry personnel
6) Sponsorship of a radio program or T.V. program
7) Church remodelling

Creativity, imagination, time and money can develop a solid basis of Christian stewardship. ***Please do not abandon God and the Bible, for it is your manual to finding God.***

OK! There you go! If you managed to read all through that lot without giving up on this book, you did exceptionally well. I was a little worried about putting all this in the book, in case the rest of the book didn't get read.

Did he try to sell tithing to you? Yes he did.

Did he give you 1001 reasons as to why you should tithe? Well; not far off.

Is he cashing in on God? You're damn right he is.

Is God a HIM? No! God is light; the one conscious energy. Should we fear the judgement of God? No; but you might fear what happens in or after death, if you don't know. In this earth plane you have unconditional love from God; unless you harm a child. At this moment; the only consequence I understand from harming a child, is that you won't cross over.

Has God commanded us to tithe? No; we are asked to share and offer kindness to each other, since we are all connected. There are no hard and fast rules.

Should tithing only go to your local church? Hell no! Your conscience will decide where it should go. The churches are institutions which, in their opinion, are representing God. Yes they are; but they're not the 'only' institutions; and not the only way to connect to God.

"You cannot love God with all your love without tithing?" What a pious comment. Course you can!

"Please do not abandon God and the Bible, for it is your manual to finding God." If only we knew which parts of the Bible were an accurate representation of what was said and what really happened. As the angels have said: there is too much misrepresentation, embellishment and missing scripts to waste time trying to dissect the Bible for the truth. It was written for then; not now. There are many good parts; but it's not easy for people to dissect them from the stories. It's time to move on and learn how to get the word direct.

Talk about your typical Bible-basher? This Reverend is really on a mission. He probably rules his flock with fear. The sad thing is that he's been totally programmed by an out of date book and methodology. I'm reminded by three films that spring to mind: Pollyanna, Star Trek; The Motion Picture; and the third one you're going to have to bear with me. I've searched for the title, but with no success. The film was a science fiction movie about a group of people that either ended up on a different planet, or some time in the future on our planet. The planet was ruled by a 'Governor' called Manuel. It was a futuristic environment with strict laws, rules and procedures. The population adhered to all these laws and procedures to the letter. The people that had arrived in this time, or on this planet, were never allowed to meet Manuel, until the end of the film. They were taken to a large cavern with a huge computer and introduced to Manuel; who turned out to be a 'manual', for the computer, for the regeneration of the planet. A whole nation had been programmed by this 'manual'.

Our Bible-bashing Christian is one of around 2 billion people on this planet, who've been programmed in a similar way, by such as the Bible, Quran, Tanakh, Torah, Tao-Te Ching and Bhagavad Gita. He's been brainwashed that the word of the Bible is the absolute; sacrosanct, chipped in stone; never to be changed.

In Pollyanna, Carl Malden plays a Bible-bashing priest in a town called Harrington in the mid-west of the USA. The town is 'owned' by Polly Harrington who is very wealthy. She supports all the businesses, so no-one wants to cross her. She manipulates the preacher to keep unrest in the town. Under her direction, he preaches hell and damnation for anyone and everyone if they don't follow the words of the Bible. He rules the congregation with a rod of iron, and repeatedly puts 'the fear of God' in people. When there is adversity in the town, it's God's punishment for not being pure in heart. No-one looks forward to the Sunday sermon. Pollyanna, played by a young Hayley Mills, brings positivity into the town, by way of a game her father used to play with her called the 'glad game'. She encourages people to find the good in every adversity. She eventually shows the preacher a locket she wears, which her father inscribed with: *"When you look for the bad in mankind' you will surely find it." Abraham Lincoln.*

She explains that her father was a minister too, and that he'd found 800 glad sayings in the Bible. The preacher is devastated and falls to his knees as Pollyanna leaves. He realises he's sold his soul to Polly Harrington; goes home, reads the Bile through the day and night; and finds 826 glad sayings. The following morning he reads the first one in his sermon, against the direction of Polly Harrington; and tells the town it will take him in the region of 16 years of Sundays to read one every Sunday to them. He intends to leave them with happiness every week.

The Bible-bashing of our Christian above, is definitely not what God; light; the one conscious thought, wants of us; as you've already read in chapters before. Which brings me to the third film: Star Trek; The Motion Picture.

In this film, an alien force is heading towards our planet. It's already destroyed other alien (Klingon) spaceships. There seems no way of stopping this alien force. Finally at the end of the film, Captain Kirk; Spock, et al, are allowed to the core of the alien force, which is 16 kilometres from its outer perimeter. The alien is an artificial intelligence that answers to the name of Veejer. The crew discover that at the core of this intelligence is an old space shuttle. When they see the name plate, it reads Vger. On closer inspection, and a little cleaning up; it reads Voyager 6: a non-manned space exploration ship, sent out into the galaxy to seek information.

The reason I'm relaying this film to you, is that the end of the film gives the audience watching, a paradigm shift. We're looking for a similar paradigm shift. This movie is closer to being representative of the infinite intelligence of The Creator, than some old book, which was written 2000 years ago, meant for people in that time; and yet idolised by so many people today. In the film, the cast couldn't identify with the intelligent life-force; yet they could relate to a scientific, mechanical space-ship. Just like our logical, scientific colleagues can relate to facts and scientifically proven energy; but can't relate to conscious energy. Everything relates to light. Just think about it. All things vibrate at different speeds. At a certain speed, they produce light; as we know it.

When watching the film, what we initially thought was an alien menacing life-force, turned out to be an infant in its early stages of growth of intelligence.

God; light; the one conscious thought, is still developing. We; are part of that development. An experiment, to see how we develop, with a view to learning from the experience, to further the development of the infinite intelligence. Yet we've been a disappointment. Instead of progressing spiritually and physically; we've taken the physical, scientific route, and most of us have resigned and restricted our spiritual route to a 2000 year old story book.

Our Christian friend, who sent me the message on tithing means well. He put a tremendous amount of effort into producing that message; but at the end of the day, he's just another one of the flock who's cashing in on God; for all the wrong reasons.

We don't need churches to talk to The Maker. We don't need Sunday school and Bible classes to learn about an old, out of date, embellished and incomplete journal of religious stories. We can do our own form of 'giving.' Just give to the right needs. If we have more than the next person, giving can be very rewarding. The Law of the Universe dictates that if you give in abundance; good things will come back to you. Not necessarily from the same source that you give to. There are plenty of needy people to give directly to. There are plenty of organisations that you can give to; just check out where the money or goods goes, for peace of mind.

Our Christian friend, like so many other devout Christians keeps referring to God's commandments. Since being able to communicate with The Divine, I'd like you Christians to consider the following:

1. ***Thou shalt have no other gods before me.*** So stop with the Jesus thing. God is the 'I AM THAT I AM'; not Jesus.

2. ***Thou shalt not make unto thee any graven image, or any likeness of any thing that is in heaven above, or that is in the earth beneath, or that is in the water under the earth: Thou shalt not bow down thyself to them, nor serve them.*** Those graven images that you serve and bow down to, are Jesus being crucified; the cross, the Madonna and the Bible.

3. ***Thou shalt not take the name of the LORD thy God in vain; for the LORD will not hold him guiltless that taketh his name in vain.*** Here's an interesting one. Most people I ask interpret this as saying or writing things like "For Christ's sake, God knows! Jesus wept! God almighty! Oh my God!"; to name a few. Having listened to Archangel Metatron; my interpretation of this, is that when you 'have' learned to connect with God; if you let your ego get in

the way and portray that you are better than others, or infer you have power over others because of it; you'll be disconnected from being able to access God.

4. **Remember the Sabbath day, to keep it holy. Six days shalt thou labour, and do all thy work: But the seventh day *is* the Sabbath of the LORD thy God: *in it* thou shalt not do any work, thou, nor thy son, nor thy daughter, thy manservant, nor thy maidservant, nor thy cattle, nor thy stranger that *is* within thy gates.** As I understand it, the Sabbath is Saturday. Yet this has been changed by Christians to Sunday.

5. *Honour thy father and thy mother: that thy days may be long upon the land which the LORD thy God giveth thee.* It's hard for the child who suffered an abusive childhood to forgive their parents, however, we should still honour (respect) the fact that they gave you birth; and without that, you wouldn't be here. You don't have to like them; perhaps just respect them for bringing you into this world; for without them, you wouldn't be here.

6. *Thou shalt not kill.* I'm told that 'kill' should be interpreted as murder; otherwise we'd be in deep doodoo when it comes to feeding ourselves. As Christianity moved to the Americas and to the East, people were murdered in their thousands until their colleagues succumbed to the Christian belief.

7. *Thou shalt not commit adultery.* A simple matter of respect.

8. *Thou shalt not steal.* Yet what are many of the churches and ministries doing? They are taking money from people in the name of God. To me; that's stealing. Many of them are cashing in on God for their own benefit. You don't need elaborate churches to connect to God and fulfil the purpose of why we were put on this planet.

9. **Thou shalt not bear false witness against thy neighbour.** Mankind is your neighbour. Yet the different religions fight against each other for control. Women were excluded from being a part of the Catholic church and most other Christian churches. We exclude people for their different colour, creed (I had to look this one up. It's one of those words that

people use freely, yet many don't really know what it means. It means a system of beliefs.), language, shape, dress and habits. We judge our 'neighbour' through greed, avarice, envy and fear.

10. ***Thou shalt not covet thy neighbour's house, thou shalt not covet thy neighbour's wife, nor his manservant, nor his maidservant, nor his ox, nor his ass, nor any thing that is thy neighbour's.*** Here's another word I struggled with: Covet means to crave or long for. To be jealous of. Yet we've become a world of 'Keeping up with the Joneses'; craving for what other people have. The new car, mobile phone, conservatory, new front door, fashion; someone else's partner. We're back to ego again. The conscious growth of mankind's ego is diminishing spirituality.

I wonder just how many things on the Christian's tithing list was down to keeping up with the Jones'? Paint? Remodelling? A car phone for the Pastor? Carpet?

Cashing in on God???

43: Good news about the Bible

24th January 2006

Metatron: Greetings, it is wonderful that we have the chance to commune again; and I know that there are many questions that you have. To enable you to be able to move on, perhaps it would be more wise if we deal with some of these issues that you feel the need for further clarification.

Perhaps we should first address Glenn's concerns or quest of truth on Joshua. Joshua was killed in Judea. Because of his channelling ability, there were many jealousies by the religious leaders, so it was decided in the interests of keeping law and order; a drink served with snake venom would be a quick and efficient way of removing Joshua. His physical body was left in an unmarked cave.

It would perhaps help you more, if you can understand that at this time, someone who owned sacred texts of God's words held extreme powers. They used these words as weapons. Others feared that, if what they claimed was true, they would bring upon themselves the wrath of God. This is why you will find so many so called Gospels and Sacred Texts. Anyone and everyone who could write, would write to ensure that they and their families were protected. Fear is a very powerful commodity if you are the one who can instil fear into others. Remember, if you tell a lie long enough, people will believe it as the truth.

So many of you are searching to find what life is all about, yet very few of you have really taken the time to live life, discover who you are, and to take time out to experience everything around you without any habitual assumptions or beliefs. The word reality really doesn't mean anything. Only when you can free yourself from your opinions and look around you with fresh eyes will you be able to connect with your world, God; light; the one conscious energy.

We greatly felt Glenn's pain and surrounded him with love and light when Brett had decided to stay where he was born; and we know how much he struggles with our comments when he finds that they have taken a change in direction. However, it is equally important that it is just as frustrating for us, when a human being decides to disconnect from divine direction and utilise their ego, mind and wounded self, to guide them

223

differently. We now have to work to try and bring that human being back onto their spiritual pathway.

Brett is currently allowing his fears and false beliefs to overthrow his true connection with the higher source. It is within the very nature of human kind to blame others, spirits or God, when expectations aren't met. Yet, it is not 'us' that have disconnected from you, but you, who have disconnected yourself from us.

Watching human beings is similar to watching a game of snakes and ladders. Many times you all aspire and try to work through the challenges, but then when some of you meet with challenges, a good percentage of you will slide back down, to have to go through everything again. Others will determinedly stay connected and focused, and move through the obstacles that lay ahead.

You will find that many people will assume that from our teachings, we are in fact asking you to totally discard the Bible, the religious practices; but remember that there is duality in everything. There are both good and bad parts to your traditional religions. What we are asking of you, is to discard the bad, the negative points that tell you, you are all sinners and destined for hell, and to take the symbolic teachings of loving one another and working towards peace and harmony. For some humans, the religious rituals help them to feel at peace, protected and safe.

Your religious holidays that ensure you all come together, similar to other traditional nostalgic events, again bring a reminder to humankind to think of others. You can still continue to honour these spiritual times as these are things that will help you evolve and move forward in your spiritual growth.

What we ask you to discard are the teachings that bring about religious, colour or sexual discrimination. Teachings that ensure you have little self-belief, and that you must pay for your sins and be lead by someone who claims they have an authority on who will and won't enter heaven.

We are asking you to become aware of your spirituality; the extremely unique person that you are, and the ability you have to help those around you. For when you help others, you also help yourself. We are asking you all to be open-minded and use your actual experiences of life, to help you understand your connection with others, the universe, God; light and the one conscious mind.

 www.anewbelief.com

You are not English. You are not American. You are not Arabic. You are not Russian. You are not Chinese. You are all human beings who share this planet. When you can grasp this, then you will discover the meaning of life. Remember you are not separate; you are all one.

You don't need to understand life, to enjoy it. Human beings will often tell stories to help others make sense of what they wish to convey. It doesn't necessarily mean that they tell the truth. So by being aware of this, you will find it easier to combine ideas, share your awareness and spiritual intuitions to find some form of agreement. Many humans are so inspired by their own stories, they eventually become the absolute truth, so we would leave you with this thought upon which to ponder.

Beware of concepts (Something formed in the mind by combining all parts and features to conceive something.), for concepts have the ability to disconnect you from the divine. When you next open your mouth to speak, are you speaking of concepts and theories gained from others, or from your own spiritual awareness and experiences? For when you speak from concepts, the end result will always be a battle of opinions.

Light and love.

Metatron

44: The tester unwittingly validates Jesus' death

8th February 2006

Our good friend Chris called in to see us. He's decided to have a go at meditation. This is the man that Metatron refers to as our 'tester'. He wanted to show us a ring he wished to use, to gaze into the imperfections in the stone, to allow him to 'lose' himself in meditation. Chris is a seeker of truth. It would be wrong to call him a 'Born-again-Christian'; although he is a Christian.

He's been banned from almost every church he's attended for any length of time, because he challenges the clergy for not following the word of God. He's happy to criticise church service on a Sunday, when he feels it should be Saturday; and as a seeker of truth he is willing to challenge the meaning of the phrases in some of the Bible. Chris will go to extraordinary lengths to seek the truth, the meaning and purpose of life.

As we talked in the kitchen, I asked him if he knew why Jesus was called Jesus Christ. He mentioned the Christ consciousness. I asked him which one he was referring to. He was referring to Jesus. He said that Jesus was the son of God, so was given the name Christ.

I reminded him that Metatron had told us we are all the children of God; so if that was the case, we should all be called Christ. The Christ consciousness is God. Jesus is a false idol. Metatron has taught us that no one person should be regarded any better than another; and that Jesus was, like Jill, an exceptional channeller, who was communicating the word of God.

I went on to say that it's interesting that all the great channellers; prophets, such as Abraham, Moses, Enoch, Jesus and Mohammed; are all dead. Their 'words' are believed by billions of people; and there is no way we can challenge them personally; yet Jill is channelling the word of God; and will not be believed by most people. The media will see us as sensationalists, heretics or crackpots; because it helps them sell copy.

When I referred to Moses, I reiterated that Metatron had told us that the stories about Moses were myths, in that, for example, there was no parting of the sea.

Chris went on to say that when Moses came from the mountain with the commandments, to give them to his people, they shunned him. So he held up a cross with a poisonous snake on it. This was his sign from God. The people were surrounded by poisonous snakes. Whilst he held the snake in the air, the snakes stayed at bay from his people, but when he lowered the snake to the ground, the snakes came forward, bit and killed some of the people. He raised the snake and the snakes would back off. This was God's way of showing the people his potential wrath if they didn't have some order in their life.

Chris went on to explain that this 'miracle' was validated by Jesus, many years later, who told the story of Moses with the snakes and the snake on the cross, and that Jesus foretold he would meet his death in the same way. Chris was trying to validate the story not being a myth.

At this point, I burst into laughter. You see, Chris had a mind set that Jesus was referring to his death on the cross. Yet several days earlier, as you'll have already read, I transcribed the channelling from Metatron; that Jesus had been killed by the poison from snake venom put in his drink; and he was discarded in an unmarked cave.

I explained my mirth to Chris, and his mind went on overdrive. He wanted so much to disprove this thought process. At one point he referred back to the snake held by Moses and said he held it up on a stake. I reminded him that earlier he'd said Moses held the snake up on a cross. Chris explained that his sub-conscious had slipped back to stake, because there was much theory that Jesus would have been crucified on a stake, not a cross. Later he referred to the snake on a pole. Again I burst into laughter and reminded him of what he'd just said.

"Cross, stake, pole; what does it matter. It could have been a length of rope. It was symbolic," said Chris in frustration, "Just like when Moses led his people through the parted sea to the promised land; and God had them walking around in circles for 40 years, because he'd performed another miracle, by tapping a large rock with the branch of a tree, to expose water; when there was none to be found elsewhere. Instead of saying it was God who provided the water; Moses claimed it to be his own miracle."

By this point, Jill and I were having a good laugh. I explained to Chris that he'd just given a wonderful example of how the Bible is so easily embellished, glorified, mis-interpreted and mis-translated. Chris had gone from cross, to stake, to pole to 'Indian Rope Trick' with a snake, in a matter of minutes. What is likely to happen to the recording of events over days, months and years?

I then pointed out that God had disconnected with Moses because ego had got in the way; and that Metatron had already recorded with us that if ego gets in the way of anyone who channels the word of God, they are disconnected from channelling the word of God.

Do we believe in coincidences? Or are all things meant to be. A few days ago we wrote about Jesus being poisoned by the venom of a snake in his drink. Then along comes our tester who tells us that Jesus foretold of his death as the result of a snake. Chris thought it was crucifixion as the result of the cross; stake; pole; when it could just as easily be a reference to death by snake poisoning.

This is the point where Chris got really frustrated, and wished for some evidence from Metatron, so he could believe. I explained that there has never been any evidence such as miracles. Then I said to Chris; if in the near future, there are terrorist bombings in Los Angeles, New York and Atlanta in the USA; as had been predicted earlier by spirit; would he believe then? At that he said he'd have to.

I explained to him that wasn't the way. The way is to connect with God; light; the one conscious thought; through meditation. Since we've been told that we all have the ability and we just have to raise our vibration level; then the only absolute way to discover the reality of what has been channelled to us, is to be able to connect ourselves.

Chris, being of a logical mindset, finds it extremely difficult to meditate. He's programmed his mind that he can't sit with a blank mind; even though we've explained that most people have that same problem initially; and that with perseverance, anyone can bring back their spirituality.

Chris left us saying that he would have a go. We explained to Chris that we weren't laughing 'at' him earlier; but laughing at the situation and the 'coincidences'.

45: We are not alone

8th February 2006; evening

Jill and I were sat finishing our dinner. Jill told me that Azrael was 'hovering' around. I asked Jill to describe Azrael to me. She said he looked like an old, wizened man. He was wearing a plain browny-grey robe with a hood. He had little hair; just a band at the back of his head. I asked why the simple look. Azrael explained there was no need for pomp and ceremony; but he did wear white when he was receiving people to the other side. I asked him if he'd wear gold for me when 'I' cross over. Jill laughed and explained that she'd seen him make a gesture of a flamboyant, extroverted gay person saying, "It's not my colour," as he place a hand across his chest. We both fell about laughing. It's great that these entities can share our humour with us.

He explained that his form of an old, wizened man was welcomed as the friendliest image to someone crossing over.

I asked if he had ever been physical on our planet. He told us that he was one of the founders of the light; one conscious thought; and had never been a part of the physical world, on our world, or any other.

I asked what it was that I'd seen when I was meditating. I explained the face with the black and white mottled face, no hair; and the big black shiny eyes. I explained that it was none threatening.

Azrael explained that they were the Greys. Mankind has already had experience with them. They mean us no harm. They come to learn from us. They are a much more advanced species, who went through similar mistakes to Mankind, and destroyed their own world. Now they are looking to learn from our mistakes; and successes too. Azrael said we know of them in 'Area 51' in the USA. He said I was not to be afraid of them and that I would encounter two other species soon in my meditation; the Sirians and the Assirians. Now I don't know whether I've spelt this the right way, so I've just spelt it phonetically.

Time will tell.

46: Metatron: Black holes in the universes

16th February 2006

Black holes are Toroidal Fields. This is the beginning of all things created of which there are two polarities. For example: planet earth you have the North Pole and the South Pole. If you look at the way an apple or orange is formed you will see the two polarities and how the sphere shape takes place.

The human is very much limited by having only six senses (Sight, hearing, touch, taste, smell, intuition.). You do not have the ability to 'see' all matter, hence the reason why you perceive space. The black holes that you see in space are Toroidal Fields which enable you to pass through different dimensions. These are not holes, but tunnels of energy swirling in a vortex. They are also blue, not black.

Although I have spoken to you of this many times, once you understand duality, and that everything must balance equally, then you can truly grasp the understanding required to help you connect with all things.

We will discuss this in more detail later, for I know you have many things distracting you at this time from really taking on board the messages given. I know that you have many questions and we could spend an eternity answering everything that mankind would really like to know. However, we ask that you put your energies into the task ahead; of helping us to communicate to others the importance of balancing their physical lives with their spiritual lives. One without the other creates chaos and much discord.

Many children are being brought into this world originally very spiritual; and then over a period of time, their light and connection to God, is being killed; by over-stimulation, toxins and teachings that disconnect them from God; light; the one conscious energy.

I will ensure that everything you need is given in the correct way. Mankind must learn the art of existence, to experience the moment. Your term 'curiosity killed the cat'; is so much more profound than you can realise. For mankind's curiosity to learn how to create a universe and control it, will be its downfall; unless new harmony and balance can be realised, through accepting differences in humans; but at the same time, understanding that these differences also are one and the same. It is just the way you perceive things that creates the differences.

We shall leave it there for now, and perhaps reconvene when your energies are a little more relaxed and receptive to the quantum physics that you struggle with. I have given you the tools to help you understand this process more easily. Your application to such matters would help us.

As always we surround you with love and light.

Blessed be. Metatron.

47: Metatron: In the beginning, there was... NO word.

16th February 2006

Metatron: Greetings! It is lovely that we have another chance to commune. I know that you're feeling quite despondent at the moment, but be aware that this is a passing phase in your life that is bringing you closer to realising your dreams.

I feel it's important that we look to what we wish to achieve by our communications with yourself. As you are already aware there has been a tremendous shift in the energies that surround your planet. We are greatly concerned with the imbalance of energies. Many souls are brought into the world to learn spiritual growth. But we ask: how can this be achieved when the children of the future are being blocked from learning to be spiritual; and have faith in themselves; and have the ability to connect with God; light; the one conscious energy?

Our only aim with you is to bring about a new belief to enable everyone to acquire the wisdom that will enable them to cleanse the soul and connect with God; light; the one conscious energy. Never be discouraged by the adversities you experience, for when your heart is open to the spiritual transformation, God; light; the one conscious energy can give you, it is never experienced alone and without help.

To connect with God; light; the one conscious energy, all that is required is for you to open your heart and trust in God; light; the one conscious energy. And have an open and receptive mind to the lessons that God; light; the one conscious energy chooses to reveal to you.

When you connect with God; light; the one conscious energy on a daily basis, you will discover the spiritual wisdom and positive energy that can exist in your every day life.

(Jill: I asked Metatron, about what Chris, our Tester, had said regarding God's judgement, rewards and punishments and if there were any judgements passed.)

Many of your punishments and rewards are self-created. Mankind seems to relish the idea, that as a separate individual they can decide who should merit a reward or punishment. Very few realise that in reality, when they punish someone they punish themselves. When they reward someone, they reward others. Those who choose to turn away from divine inspiration and spiritual guidance, will create their own punishment, for they will not be able to ascend when the time comes. It is not God that will punish them. They will have punished themselves for choosing to turn away from the light. Just as they will reward themselves by connecting with God and being embraced into the light, if they open their hearts and minds to being all one; and accepting the divine light that lies in all people.

What is of the utmost importance now, however, is that the children being born in the world today cannot find something they have no knowledge of. Hence the reason for our communication with yourself and Glenn.

We wish you to share the spiritual messages we bring to you, so that you can connect with as many people as possible and enable them to achieve their purpose in life, which should be allowing God into their hearts and minds; to be joyful, embrace and rejoice in the divine flow that is in each and everyone of you.

When you truly love yourself and respect your fellow beings, then you give praise to God. When you can recognise that there is no discrimination, it really doesn't matter what name you call out in your prayers. Be it Adonai, Allah, Elohim, Hashem, Mohammed, God, Buddha, Shadai Eheyeh, Yahweh or Yehwah; the one conscious energy is all combined.

You all have lessons to learn and lessons to teach each other. Your intolerances of each other are God's way of showing you that you have still not learnt your lessons. Everyone needs help. Seeing yourself separate and different from others creates weakness. Togetherness brings great strength.

If we look at your personal circumstances: feeling down is your own spiritual divinity telling you that you have lost your connection with God, so you have no personal direction. Remember, others do not control your destiny. You do. By learning to reconnect with your divinity, understanding and learning the difference between right and wrong, then; your life will bring happiness and fulfilment.

Disturbed by Glenn...

16 February 2006

Jill: I asked Metatron about the Bible statement: **"In the beginning there was the Word."**

Metatron: The Word:–

In the beginning, there was no word. There was, to be more accurate, the thought. Before word can exist there has to be thought. A word is an utterance that you use to communicate with one another. Sound has no physical form, and it is pure energy vibrating at a particular resonance. It was God's thought that created the universe you live in. It is the energy put into creation that symbolised the breath of life. For it was this vortex of energy, as we have just spoken about, that brought everything into being. The planets in your universe existed long before mankind.

Remember that we have shown you that it is the symbolic meaning of some of the teachings within your holy scriptures; and not the literal words of mankind that you must take notice off. Mankind wastes so much energy disputing the rights and wrongs of another man's word.

The beginning is not of your time. Yes it is important from the view point that this explains how your existence comes into being; but now you are created, you should expend your energies on helping others to understand, communicate and share experiences with one another.

Remember; being spiritual is having an open heart, and a positive and open mind to life's lessons. So many of you yearn for change in your world, yet very few actually go beyond the thought and put into action what needs to be started to bring about a change in the world you live in.

Instead of looking and learning that what your forefathers did before you, has only created more misery; mankind continues to argue about who is right and wrong. It is not about deciding who is right and wrong. It's about finding a solution that both can mutually benefit from and work from that view point; to then develop a more balanced approach to each other.

To help you further, you have to understand that mankind, at the beginning of time, was an intuitive spiritual being that did not possess the reasoning and psychological understanding you are blessed with.

It was God's thought that created your universe. Thought became form. From form came utterances, which eventually became words. Remember that Jesus the Saviour is a man-made idol. Words have created the notoriety of Jesus through stories. Stories are brought about to convey a message that most people can relate to.

We understand that you struggle with this, but try to imagine a time when the population of your planet was small. People lived in villages. And to them, the village was the whole of their universe. Nothing existed beyond their experiences. So travellers, who brought news, were often believed; and over a period time, the stories passed from generation to generation were expanded upon; until the original story got lost in the passing of time.

Today you have the ability, through your own creations, to communicate and experience everything at the same time, so that you all, more or less, experience the same thing, at the same time. You have the technology to take a snapshot of time through your creation of the camera. You have the ability to capture sound. However, unless you have the knowledge of how to use the technology, then you will not be able to access that information and the information is useless.

So imagine for one moment that humankind no longer existed and eventually another form of intelligent life form was created. Upon finding objects that belonged to humankind, all they can do is try to assume what existed and how life may have been. Stories would be created and these stories would be handed down through the generations, and perhaps used to teach others about this strange life form that existed many years ago.

From these teachings a new belief and structure for life begins to take form. Remember it is physically impossible for you to recite word for word, the message you hear. Each and every one of you spiritually interprets the message being conveyed. It's not about the words. It's about how you communicate the feelings, pictures and emotions that ensures whether or not your message can be fully understood by everyone to mean the same thing.

Blessed be, Metatron.

48: What next?

I started this book writing about the way that religion is cashing in on God. So let's just consider that again. Is it wrong for people to be exploiting the meek, the people with low-self-esteem; people who want to repent, people who want to give to God, people who are searching for the truth? Well the argument 'for' religion is that if it makes people feel good, then it must be OK; so let it be. The argument against is that most of these people are being misled. Do we ever find out if the 'donations' given, make the people feel better? Do we ever get to know where the money goes from the charities? Are people better off in blissful ignorance?

When people take a spiritual pathway, they are often seeking the truth. The difference in what Jill and I are doing, as opposed to religious orders and the other ministries, as that we are giving people the truth.

There have been prophets for thousands of years. Sadly, mankind seems to have adopted an attitude towards prophets: sole acceptance if they are dead and we have their written testimony that's difficult to disprove, because it was written so long ago. It seems we're prepared to be programmed by religious orders that a prophet, who lived a few thousand years ago, who tells people that he spoke to God, is sacrosanct; chipped in stone. Why? Because there's no one around who can tell us it was any different.

These prophets never spoke to God. Their head would have caved in trying to access the energy. This is why Metatron is the sole link to God for human kind. He has the ability to scale that energy down and become the voice of God; light; the one conscious energy.

Today there are prophets around the world talking to Metatron; the one direct link to God; light; the one conscious energy; yet they are ridiculed by the masses. Why? Because people don't believe that someone could be a prophet today, unless it's the long-awaited second coming of Jesus. Well; they've got a long wait. Meanwhile, Jill and I are on a journey, to show people how to connect with God; light; the one conscious energy; to experience the wonders of the creative universal life force.

Our journey will take us in front of people to spread the word of this new belief. We'll help people to raise their self-esteem to give them a new hope. We'll teach them that there is no need for the upkeep of elaborate churches to be at peace with God. Hopefully at some point, the churches may be used as educational establishments to show people how to develop and connect to God; light; the one conscious energy.

Ministries and religious orders are cashing in on God for the wrong reasons. Religion has become a placebo (Something taken in place of the 'real' thing.) for people who need 'something' to give them faith and a substitute for the meaning of life.

It's time to cast off the archaic shackles of the 'old ways'.

Christianity and Islam have a 'hold' on human kind. The cross is used to manipulate the masses through guilt, and ensure they know their place and keep them down. Questioning this faith is tantamount to being stoned; persecuted and resigned to hell and damnation.

Just remember: hell is what we make it. It's the result of our negative thoughts and actions. War is hell. Nuclear explosion is hell. Poverty is hell. Biological warfare is hell. Exclusion is hell. And hell; who wants 'any' of it?

As our prophet Jill has communicated to us: there was no water turned into wine. There was no walking on water. No crucifixion. No flogging. Yet 2 billion people have been programmed to believe that Jesus' atonement was sacrificing his body for mankind; for the power and control of religion, to keep the people down and make them feel they should suffer too.

Let me ask you this. Where were all the women prophets? It's a fact that there are more women in the world that 'tune-in' to spirit than there are men. Having studied gender difference, I firmly believe that women have more of an innate ability to tune in to spirit than men, due to their brain composition which allows them to process logic and emotion at the same time. Add to this that women are up to 5 times more emotional than men and you have a recipe for receptive channelling.

The logical mind wants to dismiss the spiritual, whereas the emotional mind is more accepting. Since the vast majority of men can only use each side of their brain one at a time; the logical left side of the brain dismisses the spiritual thought process. As my good friend John said to me yesterday, when discussing this journey, "I'm logical. Give me some proof and I'll look at it."

Men generally have to re-programme their brain to accept. This is part of the process of what I'm going through right now.

One of the reasons I was chosen for this journey is because of my high level of emotional intelligence. I've had to learn it. It's almost a 'given' for women. So if women are more susceptible to channelling naturally, why don't we read of the women prophets? I guess you know the answer to that already if you've been paying attention to the rest of this book. They were seen as a threat. Religious orders suppressed them out of fear. It's taken thousands of years for women to realise their true potential as natural leaders in the world. They are the natural people-people; natural educators. Men and woman have distinct differences which makes each better at different things. There are many things that men and women are equally capable of doing. We should respect the differences; of which there are too many for this book, however there is enough publication available about those differences and equality.

Woman is on the rise. Even in the Middle East there is now a crusade starting by women, to discard the veil and rise to the surface in the workplace and market place. It's probably the last frontier for women; but the movement has started. It will be many years before we witness the change. Just like it will be many years before we witness the change from religious order and control, to the acceptance of the new belief in God; light; the one conscious energy.

Mankind has to learn to embrace spirituality with science before we can advance much further. The technology is within us. We just have to reinvent ourselves and learn how to tap into it.

The movement has started. God; light; the one conscious energy has had enough of the way that mankind has ignored the spirit and focussed on science, greed, avarice and ego. Free will is mankind's current protection, so the process has to be steered in the right direction. That steering has just had a radical change. Mankind will be hearing from more and more prophets, with spiritual and scientific knowledge that the sceptics won't be able to refute.

To reiterate: The allegorical myths in the Bible have, over time, become one the most profound novels of all time. So much so, that it now deceives people into believing the accounts are actual historical events. Few people lack the ability to really decipher for themselves, what is truth, and what is fiction. They possess lamentable ignorance, and use the written word as a weapon for 'covering' themselves.

Because it was written so long ago, people feel comfortable with it, because it's not easily contested; and whilst they feel comfortable with it, they don't feel a need to change. They don't want to come outside their self-concept bubble; their comfort zone. For if they do, it will cause them anxiety. Most people are resistant to change.

Most religious people are even more resistant to change; which leads me now to some of the reasons why I know Jill and I been chosen for this.

Let's reflect upon the composition of the 12 elements of mankind: physical body, etheric body, astral body, ego, soul, spirit, earth, fire, water, air, consciousness and self-development. The last nine are what I'm actively involved with. I teach about control of ego when educating people about emotional intelligence. I'm married to a prophet who has the highest vibrational level mankind can achieve to access the universal life force energy; and I'm now being taught how to access that same energy.

Earth, fire, water and air is the representation of our behaviour. I'm a professional behavioural analyst. I teach and coach people how to understand their own behaviour; to understand and recognise other different behaviours; so they can adapt to people for better understanding, increased levels of communication and greater appreciation of one another. I teach people 'emotional intelligence'.

People have varying degrees of earth, fire, water and air.

The earth element is similar to the compliant and conscientious behaviour of people: accurate, precise, cool, calculating, logical, concise; data and information overload, detail; afraid of not being able to follow the rules and live up to their own high standards they set for themselves. They can appear cold and emotionless. This compliant behaviour is a large proportion of religious following. They tend to do as they're told. We need this behaviour for accuracy, procedure and constraints.

The water element is similar to the steady behaviour of people: unassuming, reliable, security-sensitive, amiable, non-confrontational, sweet, relaxed, resistant to change, passive, patient, possessive, predictable and stable. They conceal their emotions and have a tendency to agree for the sake of agreeing, just to keep the status quo. We need this behaviour for pace and consistency. This is another large proportion of religious following.

These are the two behavioural traits that you will find most of in religious circles. These are the people that need most help with self-esteem and acceptance of change. These are the people that I'll spend most of my time helping.

The fire element is similar to the dominant behaviour of people: direct, demanding, domineering, dogmatic, aggressive, ambitious, competitive, determined; and have huge egos. They get angry very quickly and like to take control of people. They are natural leaders, but don't always make the best leaders. We need this behaviour to handle challenges and problems.

The air element is similar to the influential behaviour of people: inspiring, interesting, impressive, impressionable, persuasive, enthusiastic, optimistic, charming and talkative. They tend to look at everything from the positive point of view; can talk too much and can be seen as shallow by others. We need this behaviour to handle people and contacts.

I also teach people N.L.P.: Neuro Linguistic Programming; which encompasses understanding of the relationship between the conscious and sub-conscious mind. How we create our sub-conscious programmes such as walking, balance, swimming, riding a bicycle and driving a car.

This brings us into the 12th element of mankind's composition: self-development. Here I teach people how to use this NLP technique to create new programmes such as receptiveness to change, better communication skills, negotiation skills, assertiveness, confidence and a positive mental attitude. In fact, anyway you want to personally improve and anything you want to be through using goal-setting techniques to achieve the self-development you want.

I'm a past non-believer who's had a lot of pain in my life and Jill and I are marketers, which enables us to reach the world. I'm a writer, who writes in layman's terms, so it's easy for people to read. I've achieved the ability to be a motivational speaker. This means I can teach, with skill and conviction, about the nine elements of what God; light; the one conscious energy, ordained for mankind. I can teach about how to connect with God; light; the one conscious energy. I can share the wonders of the universal life-force energy, with mankind. I can be a part of the start of the movement.

Jill is spiritual. She's a great counsellor and also a great public speaker and teacher. So after repeating, "Why me? Why me?" for long enough, I now understand why Metatron chose Jill and I for our unique combination.

Following the archaic, embellished words of the Bible has created a world that has suffered a thousand years of misery in their own negativity; their own living hell and damnation. The vast majority of mankind are no nearer reaching the kingdom they refer to as heaven than they were 4000 years ago. How many more thousands of years do you all wish to be in misery for? Mankind has taken the gift of duality and taken the scientific, technical, logical route; which has moved mankind further away from self-fulfilment.

The weak will continue to cling onto traditionalist religion for as long as they can, because they feel safer in their comfort zone. There's also another major element to take into consideration here. Fear! People are frightened of the unknown. If people can't see and know what's ahead, they're afraid of the consequences or outcome.

What if they tried this new belief; learnt to meditate and connect with God; and failed? What then? Failure for most people is not an option. Take the least route of resistance. Stick to what you know. Better the devil you know, than the devil you don't. Put you hands over your ears so you can't hear; so you won't be susceptible to evil thoughts.

What if?

The writing is on the wall. Traditional religion is doomed. No longer can we hang on to a medieval world that no longer exists. It's a new dawn. It's a new day. It's time for a new belief. You are about to be awakened to the reality of who you truly are. Your continued belief in the status quo is what draws misery and suffering. The power you give to your religious leaders are the ones who perpetuate division amongst you all, thus leading to violence, hatred, discrimination, abuse and suffering.

It's time for you to awaken to the fact that you are all one and the same, so you can happily share the food and possessions you have; choose love, forgiveness and peace to create and define for you the world that God; light; the one conscious energy; actually had originally intended.

It's time for you to understand that, even without trust in the Bible; the message is still the same: a belief in God; light; love; the one conscious energy.

But this belief needs to be with loving actions and liberation, not guilt, blame and brutality. We're talking about a new dawn; a new day; a new belief; needs of people today, not of thousands of years ago.

Transform your thinking. Understand yourself, your life and what life is all about. Question which is the truth.

Scientists are already being stopped in their tracks, having to accept that there is a force 'out there' that they can't explain. A force that defies all logic and all current laws of science. Until you embrace your duality and connect once again with your spiritual side; the barriers will remain. No amount of logic, calculation or invention will explain this force that eludes scientists. It has to come from within. You need to stop thinking about mankind being a dispensable commodity, and start accepting we are all connected and have access to that force. Take a leaf from the book of Star Wars: May the force be with you. The 'force' in that series of films is closer to reality than people will presently accept.

Remember, God; light; the one conscious energy, cannot be comprehended by mankind, but it 'can' be connected; through your words, deeds, thoughts and beliefs.

It's time for you to learn about the universal life force grid that keeps everything unified; and how to utilise this energy to manifest for yourselves, total healing, acceptance of each other and harmonisation.

Wake up and smell the roses. It's time to stop putting money into the banks of those that want you to continue to live in fear of the wrath of God; want to take money for atonement; want you to 'gift' money for an archaic book of prophecies with embellishment which was written thousands of years ago, for people in those times; want you to give for the sake of Jesus; want you to subscribe to the teachings of the Bible; want you to pay to listen to someone giving their own interpretation of the Bible... Stop!; and listen to the word of God; light; the one conscious mind in the 21st century.

For those of you who've been totally brainwashed by your religion and the Bible, consider this. Why would you believe the words of a book containing stories that are thousands of years old, that you believe contain the words from God; yet you are sceptical about hearing from God today?

Well let me give you some ideas. The word of God in the Bible is fixed. It's chipped in stone. Never to be changed. This means it's controllable. There are finite words which can be dealt with. It's also written in the past, so most of the words don't apply to us today. This means you can learn from it, but there's no 'direct' effect; only indirect. You're left with your own way of connecting with God: prayer. When you pray, if your prayers aren't answered, you can blame God. It's not your fault is it? You prayed. Nothing happened. Not your fault. You did what you could. God wasn't listening. But hey! God 'was' listening. And you probably got an answer. It may not be the answer you wanted, but then you wouldn't know would you? Because you can't hear it. It may be the message was, "Help you WHAT?"

People are often very generalist when they pray. You make the angels laugh. How do I know? Because they tell me, through Jill.

How about the many people out there who pray to God asking 'him' to help them win the lottery. Well if some of them could hear, they'd hear a voice saying, "Help us out here. At least go and buy a ticket." Some people just don't know how to help themselves.

God, light; the one conscious energy, won't help you if you're not prepared to meet half way and help yourself. Some of you need to get off your backside and take some action.

What if now, someone gives you the opportunity to connect with God; light; the one conscious energy; but you're told that many of the things that you believe to be the truth, are not; and that you need to dismiss centuries of tradition. That the symbolic cross is a false idol, which has no real Godly meaning because Jesus wasn't crucified?

Now hang on a minute, if we were to accept that Jesus wasn't crucified; that would make a mockery of Christian religion. That would be scary for you. So who 'did' say that Jesus was crucified? Well it's written in the Bible, from accounts thousands of years ago. So what is the difference between the word of God; light; the one conscious energy, and the word of God thousands of years ago? Well the Bible's safe. There's no-one alive to challenge, ridicule and tear their testimony apart. You don't want to hear the truth. It hurts sometimes. It removes the stability of the rock on which you stand. It may lead to failure.

You fear change. You fear failure. You fear the unknown. Better to stick with what you know. For you; it will take a long time, and maybe not in your lifetime. You'll no doubt continue to support the people who are cashing in on God for the wrong reasons.

For the rest of you who've seen even the slightest of re-kindling of the fire of your duality; spread the word. There's much more to come.

I've talked about the fact that many people who are trying to connect with God are low on self-esteem. Metatron wants us to help people raise their self esteem and their self-worth. Part of that journey includes gaining assertiveness and confidence. Do 'you' have the confidence to consider and embrace this new belief against traditional religious beliefs?

Children are being programmed away from spiritualism...

22nd February 2006:

One of Jill's customers (Who happens to be the 19 year old daughter of one of Jill's friends); brought along two of her girl friends for a psychic reading. They were aged 19 and 20. They had been impressed by the feedback given on Jill's reading.

I asked them what percentage of the children in their last years at school, were religious and believed in God. They all confirmed that they were atheists and that there weren't many at school that weren't. This further confirmed to me, that even though there's a swing from religion to spiritualism; the connection is still missing for many people, to God; light; the one conscious energy.

Let me leave you with a little story about 'confidence':

A seven year old girl is at school and they have been asked to draw anything they want. As the teacher is walking around the children, she innocently bends down over the little girl and asks her what she's drawing.

Little girl: I'm drawing God Miss.

Teacher (Smiling with amusement.): Oh poppet; you can't draw God. Nobody knows what he looks like.

The little girl displayed a concerned look on her face, as she fixed her eyes on her drawing. She then drew a deep breath; put a big beam on her face, continued drawing and said, "They will in a minute!"

Sometimes we need to look at the world through the eyes of a child. Unless we start now, with the education process of duality, love, spiritualism, self-esteem, harmony, better communication and what God is; that young child will probably be programmed the same way as most children today; and never experience her true destiny.

It's a new dawn; it's a new day; it's a new belief.

Book Glenn Harrison for your next conference / event speaker.

Glenn is available to speak for associations, ministries, churches and societies.

Glenn is an international motivational speaker, who will travel anywhere in the world.

He speaks on spiritual subjects such as:

How to connect to God.
To change your life; you have to change yourself.
From atheist to believer.
The leader within.
Just who do you think you are anyway?
Moving from 'being' to 'doing'.
Living from the heart, not the head.
Bridging the gap from here to there.

Contact: **glenn@anewbelief.com**